Politics, Markets, and Congressional Policy Choices

Politics, Markets, and Congressional Policy Choices

Peter M. VanDoren

Ann Arbor

THE UNIVERSITY OF MICHIGAN PRESS

Published in the United States of America by
The University of Michigan Press
Manufactured in the United States of America

1994   1993   1992   1991   4   3   2   1

Distributed in the United Kingdom and Europe by
Manchester University Press, Oxford Road,
Manchester M13 9PL, UK

Library of Congress Cataloging-in-Publication Data

VanDoren, Peter M.
    Politics, markets, and congressional policy choices/ Peter M.
VanDoren.
        p.   cm.
    Includes bibliographical references and index.
    ISBN 0-472-10238-9 (alk. paper)
    1. Energy policy—United States. 2. United States. Congress.
I. Title.
HD9502.U52V37   1991
333.79'0973—dc20   91-19317
                                                          CIP

British Library Cataloguing in Publication Data

VanDoren, Peter M.
    Politics, markets and congressional policy choices.
    1. United States. Markets (Economics). Policies of
    government
    I. Title
    338.973

    ISBN 0-472-10238-9

Acknowledgments

I would like to thank the individuals and institutions that have assisted me during the ten years I have spent on this research effort. Steven Rosenstone believed in and nurtured this project from its inception. On those frequent occasions when I doubted my sanity for embarking on this enterprise, Steven always urged me to continue. My other teachers—Gary Brewer, Ted Marmor, and David Mayhew—provided much help and criticism along the way and allowed me to pursue my own research interests despite their doubts.

I survived seven years in New Haven because of the camaraderie and intellectual stimulation of my friends. Special thanks to Jason Cheever, who edited the manuscript and provided programming assistance for the empirical work. Mark Hansen, Laurie Rhodebeck, and Dawn Rossit read drafts of the manuscript and provided empirical assistance. Debbie Buchanan helped gather the cases during the early stages of the project. Roy Behr, Ed Lazarus, Sandy Nuhn, Gerry Rosenberg, and Janet Stearns provided both intellectual stimulation and friendship, even though they were disturbed that I was a closet economist.

My Princeton colleagues Doug Arnold and George Downs read the manuscript and improved the precision of my writing immeasurably. Rebecca Blank provided superb econometric advice and moral support. Scott Michael, Nancy Selbst, and Marc Treviño provided excellent research assistance.

Dean Donald Stokes of the Woodrow Wilson School was generous in his financial support, research assistance, and intellectual support throughout the long gestation period of this project.

I especially want to thank those individuals who made my sabbatical year in Pittsburgh so enjoyable and productive. Ray Ernest provided expertise on natural gas matters, as well as an introduction to the cultural opportunities in Pittsburgh. Elaine Weissberg raised by spirits whenever I felt lonely in a strange city. I also would like to thank the political economy program at Carnegie-Mellon University for funding my year in Pittsburgh. Alberto Alesina, Dennis Epple, John Londregan, Alan Meltzer, Keith Poole, Tom Romer, and Howard Rosenthal have created an environment in which truly interdisciplinary political economy research can flourish.

This manuscript could not have been completed without the expert secretarial and word-processing assistance I received at both Carnegie-Mellon and Princeton. Gail Knowland and Marlane Fedorowich at Carnegie-Mellon and Jayne Bialkowski, Ellen Kemp, and Gail Martinetti at Princeton deserve many thanks for their efforts. The editorial staff at the University of Michigan Press, under the direction of Christina L. Milton, also deserve praise for their excellent grammatical and stylistic advice.

Finally, the physical education facilities and programs at Yale, Princeton, and the Racquet Club at Pittsburgh deserve some recognition because without hockey, squash, and softball I never would have completed this book.

Contents

Tables

Figures

Part 1
Improving Market Performance

CHAPTER 1

The Political Management of Markets

The U.S. national anthem tells us that America is the land of the free. Although it may be the land of free speech and religious freedom, it most certainly is not the land of free markets. Economic transactions, to be sure, are essentially conducted through markets. But a more accurate description of America, at least in terms of its economic landscape, would be the land of the managed because Congress continually manages and alters the characteristics of a wide variety of market relationships. Farmers, for example, are thought to be too important to have their fate determined by market prices and have been subsidized since the 1930s. Home ownership also occupies a privileged place in American mythology, and Congress has enacted numerous tax provisions that treat homes more favorably than other forms of wealth. In the same vein, the tax code treats life insurance savings more favorably than stocks and bonds.

Congress has exhibited similar interventionist behavior toward energy markets, the policy area discussed in detail in this book. In response to the petroleum "shortages" experienced during the early 1920s, Congress enacted various tax privileges to spur exploration. By 1935, the glut was so large that Congress approved a state-regulated price-support system, which did not disappear until 1973. Congress also has sheltered nuclear power from true market forces by providing liability insurance and by not including the cost of capital or inventories in its charges for nuclear fuel.

My purpose here is not to numb you with examples but to convince you that Congress micromanages the details of market relationships. Once Congress is seen as a key player in the design of market relationships, four general questions become important. First, what role should Congress play in the design of market relationships? If we were to design an ideal market society, what role would we want legislators to perform? Under what conditions would we want Congress to alter markets to create results that were different from the outcomes of private market behavior? Second, what policies has Congress actually enacted to alter relations in markets? Do the policies the legislature enacts differ from those that would improve market performance? Third, if policies enacted by Congress do not improve market performance, what theories might account for the discrepancy between what Congress does and what it ought to do? How could these theories be tested empirically? Finally, if scholars can determine which market altering (microeconomic) policies Congress should pass, track which policies it does pass, and successfully account for the discrepancy between the two, what can be done to align Congress's performance more closely with its goals?

In this book, I attempt to respond to both the normative and explanatory questions in general and then apply these principles to energy markets. In the conventional sense, the book is neither about Congress nor about energy policy. Rather, it examines generic issues in the relationship between politics and markets, which I illustrate with energy examples. If I examined transportation, housing, or banking markets, the specific reasons for the existence of market failures, the selection of cases, and the effects of various factors on policy outcomes probably would differ from those offered in the energy context (chaps. 3, 4, 7, and 8, respectively), but the general discussions about the proper relationship between politics and markets, theories of congressional behavior, research design issues, and possible institutional reforms (chaps. 2, 5, 6, and 9, respectively) apply to all markets affected by congressional policy choices.

I open the book with an examination of general principles guiding the relationship between politics and markets. Politics can improve market outcomes only if market failures exist. Market failures exist if economic transactions that could increase some people's welfare without decreasing others' have not occurred, or if economic transactions decreasing some people's welfare have taken place without their consent. If market failures exist, Congress can use combinations of taxes, subsidies, and changes in property rights to improve market performance.

Congress also may choose to redistribute income and wealth, as well as correct market failures. Economic analysis has nothing to say about how much redistribution should occur, but it has plenty to say about how it should occur. In particular, redistributive policies should not directly alter the supply of or demand for any particular commodity (although any redistribution will alter the demand for all commodities in general). Attempts to redistribute income through the direct alteration of the prices or characteristics of particular markets have four important negative side effects:

- Redistribution through microeconomic techniques always requires more resources per recipient dollar than more direct policies because of deadweight loss.
- Indirect redistribution occurs only if firm and labor entry into the sector receiving the subsidies is restricted, and even then the redistribution occurs only once.
- Price supports and controls, entry barriers, and other similar micro-

economic policies, if they redistribute at all, often redistribute income from poorer to richer people, which usually is contrary to the stated congressional purpose.

• When microeconomic policies are utilized to achieve distributional objectives, price signals become distorted, and consumer and firm behavior evolves to undermine the viability of the policy scheme.

Oil price controls, for example, actually transferred resources to those already well off and sent price signals to consumers and producers that exacerbated energy-market problems.

Noneconomists object for several reasons to the division of labor between politics and markets as envisioned by economists. First, some political scientists argue that economists' advocacy of unanimous consent as a social decision rule places too much emphasis on arbitrarily determined status-quo property rights. Political scientists favor the use of majority rule to determine social choices that involve gains and losses and do not believe that the provision of compensation can transform potential Pareto improvements into social decisions that actually improve everyone's welfare as often as economists do. Second, some believe that sector-specific policies that alter prices or quantities directly (and are adamantly opposed by economists) allow Congress to redistribute income to some extent, whereas the direct lump-sum transfers favored by economists would result in extensive voter opposition. Finally, some scholars argue that the provision of public goods and the correction of negative externalities through techniques favored by economists do not provide certain symbolic products, including altruism and a concern for the motives of those who create negative externalities.

As I demonstrate in chapter 2, the first argument has more merit than the latter two, although Congress may not be able to design policy systems that compensate successfully without fatal side effects. I conclude, however, that Congress generally should follow the advice of microeconomists.

Chapters 3 and 4 examine the economic characteristics of energy markets in light of the general principles described in chapter 2 and compare the policies Congress has enacted to alter energy markets with ideal policies. Energy markets have very few genuine market-failure characteristics. Most energy-market conflicts and political demands arise from income- and wealth-distribution disputes rather than from market failures. Congress, however, typically confuses market failure with equity sources of political demands and, as a consequence, enacts legislation that alters the characteristics of particular markets even though more general tax and transfer schemes would be more appropriate. Inappropriate microeconomic policies create incentives for the affected market to evolve in ways that create additional policy problems and political demands.

What accounts for congressional energy-policy decisions? Chapter 5 discusses what a general theory of congressional decisions would have to accomplish and then examines the hypotheses that political scientists have proposed to explain congressional policy choices. Attention is given to both agenda formation (the sources of energy-policy proposals), and legislative action (congressional decisions regarding actual legislative proposals), but more can be gained, I argue, by focusing on legislative action. The literature on the U.S. Congress suggests that legislators' own preferences and the positions of constituents, interest groups, bureaucrats, the president, and congressional colleagues all directly affect policy decisions. In addition, all of these actors attempt to influence one another and thus also have indirect effects on outcomes. The economic context, the use of political resources, the distribution of costs and benefits, and strategic considerations enter the picture as well.

Which alternative theories have more explanatory power? Many political scientists have proposed hypotheses that they believe explain why legislation gets passed, but (as I discuss in chap. 6) the evidence they employ leaves readers uncertain about the accuracy of their conclusions. The literature contains numerous and often conflicting explanations of legislative enactment. To sort out the confusion, I describe an ideal empirical research design and show how the failure of previous policy studies to follow the ideal has severe explanatory consequences. To determine the validity of possible explanations, an empirical study should accomplish the following tasks:

- Specify the events to be explained (the dependent variable).
- Decide which alternative theories are to be tested, taking care to distinguish aggregate- from individual-level phenomena.
- Define the unit of analysis.
- Choose the population of cases and gather an appropriately drawn sample.
- Gather data that satisfactorily represent the theories.
- Establish the marginal effect of various factors, controlling for alternative theories.

Although the merits of this research design are well recognized, policy analysts generally have not conducted their inquiries in this manner, much to the detriment of the field. There is a good reason, of course: Applying this framework to the causes underlying policy enactment requires the resolution of some rather messy details.

Chapters 7 and 8 illustrate how one would resolve those messy details and determine the relative effect of different factors on policy outcomes in the context of atomic-energy and coal markets. As in the normative chapters of the book, if my generic empirical design were implemented in market contexts other than nuclear power and coal, the specific results might well differ, but the general simultaneous-equation framework would remain the same.

The multivariate results support all of the theories presented in chapter 5. Some interest groups have a large effect on outcomes; others do not. The president has an effect, but only in certain contexts. And economic conditions alter outcomes independent of interest-group, administrative, and congressional preferences. Some readers may be apprehensive about the complexity of the analysis, but multivariate methodology gives a more realistic, though admittedly less dramatic, view of causation than the case-study method that dominates existing policy studies.

In particular, my results shed some light on the role that legislators' own policy preferences play in decision making (Bauer, Pool, and Dexter 1963; Kalt 1981; Wildavsky and Tenenbaum 1981). I do not directly model members' preferences, but my results do clarify which interest groups heavily influence decision making and which do not. Members have discretion with respect to the demands of those groups with little influence and thus can implement other views, including their own. I cannot ascertain the relative importance of members' own views relative to all other policy preferences, but I do identify those situations in which members have the opportunity to implement their own views.

To demonstrate the dramatic effects that interest groups have on policy outcomes and to illustrate how multivariate inferences are superior to case-study inferences, I use the empirical model estimated in chapter 8 to simulate the policy-making process for two hypothetical surface-mining cases and to understand the outcomes of an actual case described by Ackerman and Hassler (1981).

Chapter 9 speculates about possible remedies for the congressional tendency to enact legislation with perverse microeconomic consequences. In particular, I examine the role that political parties, public interest groups, better policy-analytic information, and the courts can play in producing more efficient policies.

Although I would encourage all those readers who have gotten this far to read the entire book, I recognize that the disparate interests and training of political scientists will make certain chapters more interesting to some than others. Congressional scholars should find chapters 4, 5, 8, and 9 to be of interest. Policy analysts and those readers with an interest in applied economic analysis should read chapters 2, 3, 4, 8, and 9. And political methodologists should pay particular attention to chapters 5, 6, 7, and 8.

CHAPTER 2

General Normative Theory

The central problems in political economy are the aggregation of individual preferences into social decisions and the design of institutions that implement the aggregation rules. Economists favor the use of the unanimous consent rule to aggregate preferences and believe that unfettered markets adequately implement unanimous consent in most situations. When markets do not implement unanimous consent successfully (market failures), economists believe that collective action (public policies), such as the provision of public goods, can improve citizens' welfare above the level achieved through market activity. Economists recognize that equity claims, such as the distribution of property rights and income, present problems that are not easily handled within the unanimous consent framework (the amount redistributed under unanimous consent will be too small) but, nevertheless, argue that allocational efficiency should guide decision making even when the choice is among redistributive policy options. For example, economists argue that equity claims are best remedied through general taxation policies and not through programs that alter the supply of or demand for particular commodities, such as rent control or price supports.

Noneconomists criticize these claims on several grounds. First, some political scientists argue that unanimous consent places too much emphasis on arbitrarily determined status-quo property rights. Political scientists believe that majority rule should be used to determine social choices that involve gains and losses, whereas economists often believe that compensation can transform potential Pareto improvements into social decisions that actually improve everyone's welfare. Second, some political scientists also believe that inefficient modifications of particular markets (policies adamantly opposed by economists) allow Congress to redistribute income to some extent, whereas the direct redistributive policies favored by economists would result in extensive voter opposition. Finally, some scholars argue that the enactment of incentive-based policies will undermine the essential role that altruism plays in the provision of public goods and prevent inquiry into the motives of those who create negative externalities.

In this chapter I normatively evaluate unanimous consent and majority rule as social choice rules, the ability of markets to implement the unanimous consent rule, and the ability of Congress to remedy both equity problems and market failures.

What Should Congress Do about Allocation?

Economic transactions can be divided into three mutually exclusive categories: (1) those transactions that make everyone better off or make at least some better off and no one worse off; (2) those that make some people better off and others worse off; and (3) those that make all involved worse off. What decision rules should apply to each type of transaction? Which real-world institutions effectively implement those decision rules?

Allocational Choices and Decision Rules

Historically, philosophers and political economists have devoted their attention to transactions that create both gains and losses because everyone favors those transactions in the first category—those that make at least some better off and no one worse off—and opposes those transactions that hurt everyone. However, transactions of the second sort—mixed gains and losses—are a source of contention. Scholars have offered various versions of utilitarianism as decision rules for choices involving both gains and losses.

Strict utilitarians (following Bentham) suggest that we assess the gains and losses across individuals, weight them according to some criterion, and approve those transactions with net benefits. The actual outcomes of such a process, of course, hinge on the weighting scheme and on how one assesses costs and benefits. In certain situations, strict utilitarianism can sanction social decisions that are reprehensible to nonutilitarians. Hence, philosophers have searched for alternatives (Miller and Williams 1982; Sen and Williams 1982).

Modified utilitarians (followers of Pareto) rule out interpersonal comparisons of gains and losses and require unanimous consent for transactions to occur (Buchanan and Tullock 1962). On the positive side, this change prevents the sacrifice of individuals. As a direct consequence, however, the status quo becomes the privileged position because any individual can veto a transaction, a likely occurrence for those choices in which some individuals suffer losses. In addition, logical problems arise if unanimous consent cannot be obtained either to transact or to remain at the status quo (Rae 1975).

The new welfare economics offers a promising compromise to the alternatives proposed by Bentham and Pareto. Scitovsky (1941) and Little (1957) argue that compensation schemes should be used to gain the consent of those who lose—in effect transforming transactions involving gains and losses into transactions having only gains by using a weighting scheme the losers themselves provide.

Political scientists trained in social choice argue that majority rule should be used to aggregate preferences into choices in those situations in which both gains and losses are involved (Rae 1969; Taylor 1969; Mueller 1989). Majority rule optimizes the average person's benefits as long as the incidence of gains and losses in these decisions is symmetrically distributed across individuals and individuals care no more about their losses than their gains. In addition, majority rule increases the likelihood that social decisions actually will occur, as compared to compensation schemes, in which individuals easily can veto transactions or extract a large amount of money for their consent to social choices that reduce their welfare.[1] Under majority rule, however, the losers are forced to accept social decisions without compensation.

The fairness of majority rule depends on whether the members of winning coalitions vary across decisions. If those who lose under majority rule lose repeatedly, then gains and losses do not balance across time and lack of compensation may become a severe problem depending on how often and how much citizens lose.

Majority Rule with Compensation Categories
The choice, then, between majority rule and Little's (1957) version of the new welfare economics involves determining whether changes in the status quo that negatively affect someone's welfare should be purchased through compensation or simply enacted by majority rule. One possible alternative is to categorize changes in the status quo as compensable or noncompensable and allow majority rule to enact changes only in noncompensable situations. In compensable situations, losers would give their consent to changes in return for cash.

Compensable losses might include those created by transactions that are analogous to takings in land-use law, in which governments may take land but also must compensate the owner. For example, the siting of roads, prisons, and hazardous-waste facilities often creates negative externalities for surrounding residents, who purchased their homes with a different collective ambience in mind. Compensation could accompany the construction of such facilities.

Noncompensable changes would include those windfall losses created by the proper treatment of public goods and market failures—in other words,

---

1. In this discussion, when I refer to the likelihood of reaching a decision under majority rule, I am ignoring all the findings of positive political theory that document majority rule's difficulties in aggregating voters' preferences among more than two choices into decisions in the absence of single-peaked preferences.

those losses arising in situations in which citizens should have foreseen the need for reform. For example, if Congress enacted policies only when genuine market failures existed, then citizens never would have had the privileges created by milk-marketing restrictions or airline and trucking regulation. The removal, therefore, of the privileges created by policy errors could be declared noncompensable.

In practice, the distinction breaks down between losses created by privilege eradication (noncompensable) and those created by normal alteration of the status quo (compensable). Public policies that create privilege (augment the income of a particular sector) initially increase the value of existing assets, but as new entrepreneurs seeking excess profits enter the industry, the asset values return to their pre-privilege levels. Even if entry does not dissipate the excess profits entirely, only those entrepreneurs who owned assets prior to the policy change would receive windfall wealth gains. Those who buy assets after the policy change pay for the increased income through higher asset prices and, consequently, do not receive excess profits.

The reverse occurs when a policy change removes or alters a policy privilege. Returns are lowered to below normal levels initially, but disinvestment and unemployment occur to restore the equilibrium. If the industry is competitive, then only those who go bankrupt lose wealth. If the industry is not competitive (entry and exit are difficult), two results occur. Those firms that were in business prior to the enactment of the privilege and remain in business simply lose the windfall gains they received. Firms that enter the industry after the enactment of the policy privilege and remain in business after its removal lose real wealth because they never received windfalls when they entered the industry (Tullock 1980; Dorfman 1981).

The enactment of policy privileges creates wealth windfalls only if entry is restricted and only for existing owners. The repeal of policy privileges creates compensable losses in competitive situations for those firms that become bankrupt (and those employees who lose their jobs) and in oligopolistic situations for those newcomers who paid for the policy privileges and then suffer real wealth losses. Thus, a classification scheme that sorts economic transactions involving gains and losses into compensable and noncompensable categories based on the origins of those benefits that were lost would require an extensive tracking system to monitor entry and exit from industries and the timing and price of asset sales.

Compensation Useful Even If Imperfect
Even if an accounting system to track gains and losses could not be developed, some compensation, even if imperfectly distributed, would be better than none at all for two reasons. First, regimes that frequently rearrange property rights through majority rule without compensation run the risk of

undermining the stability of property rights and lowering total investment because of uncertainty among investors about wealth losses. Second, the provision of compensation improves the likelihood of enacting social decisions that promote allocational efficiency—decisions that would otherwise be blocked through political action.

Recent changes in the income tax law illustrate both propositions. Because tax reform has occurred so frequently in recent years (1978, 1981, 1982, 1984, and 1986), each time creating windfall income and wealth changes, many political actors have supported a tax-reform moratorium to create stability in the rules of the game (Shanahan 1986). The 1986 reform, for example, also contained 686 transition rules that protected many citizens and firms from one-time losses of wealth. These rules were criticized by the press and some members of Congress, such as Howard Metzenbaum, as favors to the rich; but, in fact, the transition rules did address the wealth-loss concerns of firms and individuals and thus facilitated the passage of reform. To be sure, the transition rules did not really provide full or equitable compensation because the privileges were not given to all firms, but the tax-reform experience illustrates that explicit attention to wealth losses resulting from policy changes can facilitate the passage of reforms that enhance allocational efficiency.

Obstacles to Compensation: Preference Revelation and Moral Hazard

The main obstacles to the widespread use of compensation schemes are the identification of those persons to be compensated and the determination of their level of compensation. With private goods, these two issues are resolved through property rights, which define the persons to be compensated (the owners of resources), and through competition among owners, which determines the level of compensation (the price). Public policy changes, however, are public rather than private goods. Consumption of the change cannot be restricted to those who are compensated, and consumption of the new policy is nonrivalrous.

In the case of public goods, the identification of both winners and losers and their appropriate payments (tax or compensation) involves preference-revelation problems. Citizens have no incentive to reveal either their true willingness to pay for public goods or their need for compensation. They will underreport the former and overreport the latter.

Economists have developed schemes that create incentives for individuals to reveal the true marginal benefit (or cost) of a public good to themselves, but these schemes require individuals to take the time to ascertain their actual benefit or loss (Clarke 1971; Groves and Loeb 1975; Tideman and Tullock 1976; Groves and Ledyard 1977a, 1977b; Mueller 1989, chap. 8). In particular, these schemes present people with an exogenous amount of the good and ask them separately what they would pay (or require in compensation) to expand its supply by some small amount. If those preferences were revealed, adding everyone's result together would create the aggregate marginal benefit and cost curves and identify which people to tax, which to compensate, and to what extent.[2]

Some economists believe that compensation would not enhance efficiency even if accounting systems were developed to determine how policy decisions affect asset values and even if other preference-revelation problems were solved (Baumol 1986, chap. 5). In particular, Baumol believes that compensation both discourages externality victims from protecting themselves and encourages nonvictims to become victims. For example, Baumol believes that once citizens suspect that a policy change will occur, they will buy the relevant assets or seek employment in the affected industries in order to receive compensation when the wealth loss occurs.

I believe that moral hazard of this sort could be minimized through the asset-monitoring system just discussed and through enactment of retroactive legislation. Congress already manages the wealth effects created by policy changes by making provisions retroactive to the time when they were first discussed. For example, the repeal of the investment tax credit in the Tax Reform Act of 1986 was made retroactive to January 1, 1986, even though the act was actually enacted in August, 1986, to avoid a last-minute surge in equipment purchases.

If the meaning of compensation is expanded to include schemes that legislatively create a limited but nonzero amount of property rights for harms (such as SO_2 emission rights), allocate them equally among individuals, and require those who commit harms to buy the rights to do so (compensation), then Baumol's position is even less tenable for two reasons. First, surely victims' consent ought to be an input in the production process. At competitive equilibrium, the price of consent (compensation) would equal the cost of the least expensive preventative measures that victims could practice to keep their welfare constant. If they choose to accept compensation but not practice preventative measures, allocational efficiency would not be reduced because it is their consent that would be purchased rather than their preventative behavior per se. Second, Baumol also assumes that the victims' behavioral choices include only prevention and inaction. The absence of compensation, however, induces citizens to use political activity to block externalities. Political activity, of course, consumes resources and must be considered in any claims about the optimality of compensation schemes.

---

2. Most economists treat these preference-revelation mechanisms as theoretical curiosities rather than practical plans. An exception is Kunreuther et al. 1987.

Obstacles to Compensation: Windfall Gains

An additional obstacle to compensation is the need for symmetry in the treatment of windfall gains and losses created by policy activity. If compensation is provided to those who lose from policy changes, then they need not expend resources fighting them. The benefits from reduced political activity will not be fully realized, however, if we do not tax the windfall gains that result from policy changes, because interest groups will have a great incentive to secure government benefits that cannot be taken without compensation. To enhance allocational efficiency and distributional equity, the same preference-revelation devices used to determine compensation also must be used to extract taxes from those who benefit from public action.

Congress, then, can provide compensation to those who lose and tax those who gain because of changes in microeconomic public policies, or it can enact such changes through majority rule without compensation. At equilibrium, both policies would have the same distributional effects because if compensation were never offered (and windfall-gain taxes were never extracted), all asset prices would reflect uncertainty about whether majority-rule political activity would create losses or gains (Posner 1980). The expected value of profits for any given investment would be identical under both regimes.

Allocational efficiency, however, probably would differ under the two schemes. Total investment and income would be higher under a compensation system if owners knew that (1) wealth losses created by majority-rule political activity would be compensated, (2) the actual transaction costs involved in determining the scope and level of compensation would not be prohibitive, (3) the compensation schemes would not create moral hazard as discussed by Baumol, and (4) windfall gains would be taxed. If compensation were not provided, total investment probably would be lower and resources would be devoted to blocking legislative decisions that promote efficiency but create wealth losses. On balance, then, unanimous consent (compensation) is preferable to majority rule if the costs of implementation do not exceed the benefits.

Institutional Implementation of the Pareto Rule

The second important allocational issue is whether real-world institutions can successfully implement the agreed-upon decision rules. Pareto's contribution to economics was the proof that, under certain plausible assumptions, markets are a sufficient condition for the implementation of the unanimous consent rule (Pareto-approved transactions).[3] While markets certainly are not neces-

---

3. Formally, under certain assumptions markets satisfy the duality conditions and are sufficient for the existence of Pareto optimality—the state of affairs in which all economic

sary to implement the Pareto rule, they are the preferred method because they minimize information and decision-making costs.[4]

Under many circumstances, however, market institutions are not sufficient for the implementation of the Pareto rule. Sometimes transactions that make some citizens better off and none worse off (positive externalities) do not take place, while at other times transactions that make some citizens worse off (negative externalities) do take place.

Positive externalities often are referred to as public goods. Private uncoordinated behavior will supply these goods in less than optimal amounts because consumption cannot be restricted easily to those who pay and because one person's consumption does not detract from others' consumption. Knowledge, defense, and local streets are examples of commodities that are provided suboptimally by private markets.

Negative externalities occur when markets for harms do not exist or are underdeveloped. Bad outcomes are oversupplied in these situations because the commodity in question does not have to be purchased. Noise, air and water pollution, congestion, and land-use conflicts are examples of negative externalities that exist because property rights do not adequately protect third parties from losses in welfare.[5] What institutions can overcome market failure and successfully implement the Pareto rule?

Economists and Market Failures
Positive externalities can be remedied through governmental provision of public goods. Public goods are provided optimally when the sum of the marginal benefits equals the marginal costs of producing the goods (Samuelson 1954).[6] The optimality conditions, however, say nothing about how taxes should be apportioned among those individuals paying the costs. Economists often recommend that each individual's tax share equal his or her marginal benefits (Lindahl pricing) because such a tax scheme would elicit unanimous consent as long as preferences were sincerely revealed.

Hines (1988), however, argues that Lindahl pricing does not capture an essential feature of Pareto optimality in competitive private markets. In private markets, consumers can purchase as much of a commodity as they wish

---

transactions that increase participants' welfare have taken place and transactions that decrease nonparticipants' welfare have not occurred. The failure of markets to satisfy these conditions constitutes market failure (Duffie and Sonnenschein 1989).

4. Robert Paul Wolf (1970), for example, has proposed the use of interactive cable television to allow citizens to register their consent to various social choices.

5. See Kneese and Schultze 1975 or Schultze 1977 for the standard argument.

6. For discussion of schemes that implement Samuelson's theory, see also Clarke 1971; Groves and Loeb 1975; Tideman and Tullock 1976; Groves and Ledyard 1977a, 1977b; and Mueller 1989.

at the market price. Moreover, consumers unanimously prefer a price at which all their differing quantity demands can be satisfied. With public goods, however, consumers must jointly consume the same quantity even though individuals have different demands, and under Lindahl pricing, consumers with the largest demand for public goods are charged the most even though they are only able to consume quantities much smaller than they would prefer. Hines proposes that instead of being charged high taxes, those consumers of public goods who are quantity constrained should be compensated if public-goods provision schemes are to be benefit neutral.

In practice, of course, Congress uses majority rule to make separate revenue and expenditure decisions. Many analysts have concluded that current procedures result in overexpenditure on essentially private goods that interest groups secure from Congress and in underexpenditure on genuine public goods (Mueller 1989, chaps. 13, 14).

The resolution of negative market failures involves two separable problems—the public-goods character of negotiation services and the allocation of initial property rights that define the default if negotiations are unsuccessful. Coase (1960) has shown that the resolution of negative externalities does not always require public action. In the absence of transaction costs, private behavior itself will "correct" negative externalities because negotiation assistance is not required. In other words, one of the parties will pay the other to change his or her behavior. The resulting equilibrium will be efficient, but the distribution of income (and, in some circumstances, the actual amount of nasty behavior that occurs) will depend on the assignment of status-quo property rights. For example, if firms must bribe residents before initiating the production of negative environmental effects, the ambient amount of pollution may be lower and the income transfer certainly will be higher than if citizens must bribe firms to reduce negative environmental effects.

Most real-world externalities, however, involve gains and losses for groups of people and not for individuals such as the farmer and rancher used in Coase's analysis. In group situations, externalities will not be resolved optimally because the benefits of the bargain cannot be restricted to those who contribute to the negotiations and subsequent income transfer. Externality negotiations are a public good from the perspective of individual members of the group. In these situations, collective action by government can improve citizens' welfare. For example, the legislature could provide bargaining, negotiation, and preference-revelation services to facilitate consumers' bargaining abilities when they negotiate with a firm, airport, or any other organized entity.

If the distribution of property rights that define the default if Coasian negotiations fail affects the specifics of the actual externality resolution, how should Congress allocate these rights? The distribution of property rights for

SO_2 emissions, airport noise, or the use of imported oil is a pure political problem. As long as the rights are dispersed sufficiently to allow a robust competitive market to develop, economic efficiency is not served better by one distribution than by another. I personally favor an equal distribution unless an unequal distribution would aid equality, but other distributions are defensible.

Lawyers and Market Failures

The noneconomic regulatory approach for managing externalities and providing public goods differs from the economic prescription in several important ways. First, the regulatory approach has no particular procedures to establish what amount of a public good should be provided. For example, environmentalists, who typically are strong advocates of the use of bureaucratic standards to create a clean environment, often argue that the standard for ambient air quality should embody the preferences of those individuals who favor the cleanest air. Other environmentalists, however, simply calculate the desirable level of clean air indirectly by computing the maximum level attainable through technically feasible pollution-reduction efforts. Numerous environmental laws, for example, require firms to install equipment that reduces emissions as much as is technically feasible (Ackerman and Hassler 1981). Whatever ambient air quality results from this reduction effort is the collective choice.

The second difference between the economic and regulatory approaches is the latter's insistence that public-goods obligations be identical across individuals, regardless of relative costs or differences in tastes. From this perspective, contributions to public goods are analogous to contributions to national military service. Just as no one should be able to evade his or her draft responsibilities in exchange for money (i.e., the initial obligations are identical and can't be traded), no one should contribute unequally to other public goods such as environmental quality.

Third, when negative externalities are rectified through the command-and-control approach, only harms exceeding the standard are subject to fines and penalties. Firms may emit substances into the environment in amounts less than the standard without charge. Under economists' schemes, all emission rights must be purchased, although the government may give away the initial property rights in some circumstances to serve a distributional objective.

Finally, proponents of the regulatory approach believe that economic methods cannot supply certain essential components of a good society. Kelman (1981) argues that the application of economics to the supply of clean air and other market failures

- does not stigmatize those who violate the rules of a public-goods provision scheme;
- prevents society from examining the motives of those who don't comply with the rules of a public-goods provision scheme; and
- reduces the value of public goods compared to provision motivated by altruism.

Does the regulatory (command-and-control) approach supply these extra outputs, as Kelman asserts? Is the economic approach incapable of supplying them? If the regulatory approach actually supplies the extra outputs, are they worth the costs that economists describe?

The Outputs of Regulatory Solutions to Market Failures

Kelman correctly asserts that an *ideal* regulatory system would castigate and stigmatize those who violate social rules and would send signals to the rest of us to internalize norms and abide by the law because we should, not because our interests are served. In practice, however, the regulation of behavior through legal procedures deviates from the ideal, and, as a result, the symbols that Kelman values are not produced. Legal procedures are extremely expensive, and collectively we seem unwilling to expend the resources necessary to operate an effective legal system. The actual behavior of many court systems resembles the market that supporters of the legal approach so deplore. Those who break the rules of the game and get caught often plea-bargain, and then pay a charge for their bad behavior.

The production of stigma by regulatory procedures is probably less closely related to the use of judicial procedures per se than to the percentage of the population that engages in the behavior, the severity of punishment, and the degree of public exposure. Automobile moving violations probably endanger more lives, and arguably deserve as much or more stigma, than heroin operations run by the Mafia, but legal procedures really do not stigmatize those who commit moving violations because so many people commit them and the punishment is not severe. Similarly, laws against marijuana use do not create stigma because so many people behave illegally. Legal procedures create stigma if and only if other social norms condemn and limit the incidence of the behavior.

If we examine laws regulating corporate behavior, stigmatization seems even less likely. The Energy Policy and Conservation Act of 1975, for example, established fuel-economy standards for automobiles and fines for those manufacturers whose sales-weighted fuel consumption exceeded the standards. Subsequent gasoline price reductions increased the demand for large cars, and Ford and General Motors did not comply with the 27.5 miles-per-gallon standard. The Reagan administration chose to delay enforcement and save each company $500 million to $700 million. If GM and Ford paid the fines, would they be stigmatized? How would we know?

The second virtue of traditional legal-regulatory approaches, in the view of their supporters, is that they allow motives to be taken into account. Not all people who shoot others are convicted of murder because the law requires that consideration be given to intent and not simply to the fact that someone has killed another. Kelman correctly asserts that the economic approach to pollution abatement is concerned with results—ambient air quality, for example—and their costs, and not just with the reasons firms pollute, but in my view the regulatory approach is also not concerned primarily with motives. Motives play a role in the adjudication of violations of the command-and-control system, but not in the functioning of the system itself. Traditional regulatory techniques directly prescribe behavior, while economic techniques prescribe property rights and prices, but motives play no role in either system until someone violates the rules. Then, and only then, do motives play a role, and, as I explain in the next section, motives *can* play a role in the adjudication of violations under either system.

The final and most difficult claim to assess is whether the standards-and-fines approach, through its emphasis on equal contribution to a public good (or prevention of a public bad), effectively promotes norms that discourage free-rider behavior. When floods, fires, and similar disasters strike small towns, citizens simply pitch in and repair the damage. They don't free ride. But how much should the small-town analogy govern national public-goods policies?

Because small towns are small by definition and often homogenous through self-selection and exclusion, equal contribution to public goods occurs voluntarily and with few costs. As people grow in number and diverge in beliefs and circumstances, however, identical behavior creates costs for those individuals who disagree. As groups grow in size and become more heterogeneous, should people be allowed to trade what were previously equal public-goods obligations? If they are allowed to do so, will they retain enough shared norms to maintain a civil society?

Kelman answers both questions negatively. I share Kelman's concerns but believe that national public goods realistically cannot be provided in the same manner as small towns rebuild barns. Second, and more important, the regulatory system does not create the emotional bonds and internalized norms that Kelman so values. In fact, many argue that the extensive use of legal methods to resolve disputes in the United States has eliminated the role of trust in professional and managerial relationships (Vogel 1983).

The Outputs of Market Solutions to Market Failures

Regardless of whether regulatory solutions to market failures produce valued symbolic outputs, if the solutions favored by economists also can provide stigma, motive examination, and emotional bonds, then the hard trade-offs involved in choosing between the two approaches disappear. Both proponents and opponents of market solutions to policy problems often forget that market systems require enforcement, and therefore require legal methods, to the same extent that a command-and-control regulatory system does. Firms that discharge pollutants in excess of the air rights they have purchased are similar in these respects to firms that violate standards under a regulatory approach. In both cases, violations must be detected and legal methods must be used to determine guilt and punishment. Thus, stigma and motive examination easily can be a part of the economic approach because enforcement through legal methods is integral to the system.

The one attribute of a command-and-control approach that cannot be replicated by a market solution is the equality of contributions to a collective good. Since the structural heart of the market approach is the ability to trade (and therefore to allow contributions to vary), whatever outputs are created by equal contributions cannot be supplied by market methods. As argued in the previous section, however, I do not believe that nonmarket regulatory methods actually produce the shared norms and community that proponents cite; hence, the apparent loss is not a real one.

Are Symbols Worth the Cost?

Assume for a moment that the arguments concerning the important benefits that flow from nonmarket regulatory methods are correct. The implementation of these methods still might not be a sound social policy because they impose costs. The first cost is the deadweight loss that arises because firms can't contribute differentially to collective goods. Under existing air-quality policy, for example, costs and benefits are not equated across pollutants or across different point sources for the same pollutant. While precise estimates of the welfare loss are unknown, Crandall (1983, 64) has demonstrated that incorrect pollution fees (marginal costs lower or higher than marginal benefits) create smaller efficiency losses than incorrect pollution standards as long as threshold health effects of the pollutant are minimal (the marginal benefit curve is relatively flat).

Standards are optimal only for those externalities for which errors in the amount of discharge reduction would create enormous costs. If the tax on nerve gas, for example, were incorrectly set and a bit too much were released, the nearby population would die, creating a large welfare loss. The industrial pollution debate, however, is about particulates, hydrocarbons, sulfates, and nitrogen oxides (the bulk of industrial and auto pollutants) that do not have pronounced threshold effects, and not about nerve gases.

Another cost of standards is the tendency for Congress and the bureaucracy to design and implement standards that create additional wealth windfalls for existing firms beyond those already created by the lack of payments for discharges that are less than the standards set by Congress and EPA. Jackson and Leone (1981), for example, argue that implementation of water pollution regulation in the paper industry created quasi-rents for existing firms and delayed entry of new firms. Pashigian (1984) concludes that a main effect of environmental laws has been to sharply reduce the growth of small firms and increase the size of the optimal plant. Crandall (1983, chap. 7) argues that the new source performance standards are an attempt by northern legislators to slow the growth of new industry in the South and West. The redistribution of wealth from taxpayers to firms created in the existing system by the lack of payment for discharges less than the standard and the use of differential standards for existing firms does not seem defensible on distributional grounds. Certainly most environmentalists would be appalled when informed that the policies they treasure transfer wealth to the "bad guys."

What Should Congress Do about Distribution?

Normal market operations have negative consequences for distributional objectives because the market's most salient feature is instability. Consumer preferences and firm production strategies change constantly in a process that Schumpeter (1950) described as creative destruction. Dynamic markets allow innovation to occur, but excessive short-term incomes and profits (rents) and general income instability are direct consequences.[7]

Both individuals and firms like the consumption advantages that flow from market organization but dislike the unstable incomes and profits that inevitably result. While our nation's ideology glorifies the market and the minimal state, many individuals and firms attempt to exempt their incomes from market consequences. We desire flexible markets for the commodities we consume but not for the commodities we produce.

These dissatisfactions about market outcomes often result in political struggle. The state is an appeals court for those who feel that markets have deleterious distributional consequences. Under certain circumstances, of course, individual behavior in market settings does not result in optimal

---

7. For example, the Michigan Panel Study on Income Dynamics has determined that only 48.5 percent of those individuals whose family incomes were in the top fifth of the income distribution in 1971 were still in the top fifth in 1978 (Lilla 1984, 70).

consumer welfare. As just discussed, in these instances of market failure, Congress can alter property rights and prices to improve the situation of some with no negative consequences for others except transitional wealth losses.

In many circumstances, however, dissatisfaction with market outcomes does not arise from market failure but stems from the income instability, income inequality, and short-term excess profits that are an inherent by-product of consumer and firm flexibility. These problems can be remedied only by breaking the link between market outcomes and the distribution of income. The redistributive methods available to governments have varying consequences for consumer and firm behavior, but they all improve the condition of some people at the expense of others and thus differ from market-failure corrections.

The possible decision rules that can be used to resolve distributional issues and the considerations that affect rule selection are similar to those discussed in the allocation section.[8] Benthamite utilitarianism sanctions redistribution of income as long as the marginal utility of money to the donor is less than that experienced by the recipient. In practice, such calculations are extremely fact-dependent and prone to mischief: Some dislike utilitarianism because it sanctions income equality; others dislike utilitarianism because the benefits and costs can be arranged to sacrifice individuals.

The use of unanimous consent (the Pareto rule) as a decision rule would not appear to be very useful at first glance; however, income distribution is a collective good, and people might be willing to pay some amount toward income stability and fairness as long as others also contributed. As with other public goods, the state could tax people what they promised to pay toward redistribution. The amount that would result from such a procedure, however, might not be very large.

Majority rule optimizes a citizen's utility from decisions that involve gains and losses if the individual and his or her descendents find themselves normally distributed across the income distribution over time.

Because economists doubt whether the practical problems of implementing unanimous consent (preference revelation and compensation) can be solved, majority rule is the most viable scheme for placing limits on general inequality, compensating those who suffer income decline, and redistributing some portion of the excess profits that arise from short-term shocks. But the greater the similarity between majority-rule taxation and what people would pay under a unanimous-consent redistributive scheme, the greater the support for redistribution.

---

8. Compensation is not an option because you gain nothing if you transfer money and then compensate those you took it from.

Implementation of Majority Rule

Congress should ameliorate equity problems through the use of tax measures that cause the fewest possible allocational distortions. Although it is not clear how much redistribution citizens favor, they should agree that Congress ought to redistribute income directly through transfers rather than through alteration of the prices or characteristics of particular markets. As stated in Chapter 1, there are four important reasons why this is so:[9]

- Redistribution through microeconomic techniques always requires more resources per recipient dollar than more direct policies because of deadweight loss.
- Indirect redistribution occurs only if firm and labor entry into the sector receiving the subsidies is restricted, and even then the redistribution occurs only once.
- Price supports and controls, entry barriers, and other similar microeconomic policies, if they redistribute at all, often redistribute income from poorer to richer people, which usually is contrary to the stated congressional purpose.
- When microeconomic policies are utilized to achieve distributional objectives, price signals become distorted and consumer and firm behavior evolves to undermine the viability of the policy scheme.

Energy policies illustrate all four problems. Kalt (1981, 187) estimates that oil price controls prevented crude-oil producers from receiving $50 billion in economic rents as of early 1980. Approximately $32 billion was redistributed to refiners and $12 billion to consumers. Five to six billion dollars became deadweight loss, that is, oil sales that didn't take place because of distorted prices. If direct transfers had been used to help poor consumers instead of price controls, at least $5 billion extra would have been available to aid low-income citizens.

Second, microeconomic policies do not redistribute income at all if new firms enter the sector receiving the subsidies. The tax provisions affecting oil companies provide an illustration. Since the 1930s, liberals have railed against the depletion allowance and the intangible drilling-cost allowance—two features of the corporate income tax that allegedly create excess profits for oil-well owners. After these tax provisions became law, the rate of return on petroleum wells did indeed rise above the market rate of return. Those

---

9. When I refer to the superiority of direct transfers, I am referring only to the form of taxation and not the form in which the transfer is distributed. As Thurow (1976) has shown, the superiority of cash over in-kind transfers is much more problematic than scholars usually believe.

excess profits, however, spurred entry into the petroleum business to the point where the rate of return dropped to the market level for both new and existing firms. To the extent returns did not fall to the market level because of various entry barriers, the higher than normal cash flow created by the tax provisions was capitalized into the price of petroleum assets. Existing owners and their employees received windfall gains, but all subsequent owners paid a higher price for the assets, reducing their rate of return to the market level.

The third problem with indirect price-and-quantity regulatory attempts to augment incomes (when they actually do redistribute) is their pronounced tendency to aid those individuals who don't require help. When prices for energy are kept below market levels, the benefits flow mainly to upper-income people because energy use rises with income. In addition, the owners of assets involved in production processes that utilize the price-controlled item as an input can reap large windfalls. As stated earlier, Kalt (1981, 187) notes that the bulk of crude-oil rents was not redistributed to consumers but rather to refiners that imported high-cost oil and received entitlement checks. If prices for steel, autos, and other commodities are held above market levels, high-wage workers and the owners of assets are beneficiaries. Rarely are indirect strategies utilized to raise the incomes of K Mart employees.

Finally, redistribution by indirect means creates allocational distortions that alter consumer and firm behavior to the point where new policy problems are created and governmental intervention in the economy is discredited. Petroleum policies again illustrate this pattern.

Since the 1930s, attempts to augment the incomes of petroleum producers through tax privileges and price stabilization measures generally have induced more investment, more petroleum production, and further downward pressure on incomes. By 1966, wells in Texas were producing only at 34 percent of capacity in order to preserve prices at the levels desired by producers (McDonald 1971, 189). These restrictions on Texas's production, however, caused entrepreneurs to produce oil elsewhere and create an imported-oil problem.

Efforts to protect consumer incomes also have induced counterproductive behavior. Domestic petroleum price controls, used during the years 1973–79 to protect consumer incomes, created unequal profits for refiners. To equalize the profits of refiners that had differential access to price-controlled oil, the Department of Energy developed an oil-entitlement program that gave money to those refiners that imported more than average amounts of crude oil. Refiners responded, of course, by importing oil and placing pressure on the world market exactly at the time when our stated policy was energy independence (Kalt 1981).

Elected officials use sector-specific microeconomic policies to redistribute income because most Americans assign special moral status to incomes earned through labor-market activity. Legislators *do not* get elected on the basis of campaign slogans stating that federal spending could be greatly reduced if only we paid people to live in rural states instead of calling them farmers and paying them to grow commodities for which there is no demand. Politicians *do* get elected by promising to save farmers, save industries, and save communities. Economic analysts cannot argue that such slogans are wrong, but only that we pay an extremely high price to shroud our redistributive efforts with political symbols. If the public were fully informed of the arguments against any microeconomic redistributive efforts, perhaps citizens would favor more direct redistribution and oppose such steep prices for symbols.[10]

Conclusion

Social choices involve questions either of allocational efficiency or of distributional equity. Conflicts about allocational choices involve two issues—how should preferences among these choices be aggregated, and which real-world institutions effectively implement the aggregation rules. Preferences about allocation can be aggregated through either majority rule or unanimous consent. Majority rule imposes losses on individuals but allows arbitrary status-quo property rights to be altered more easily. Unanimous consent protects individual welfare but sanctifies the status quo. Unanimous consent is preferable to majority rule because total economic activity will be higher if investors know that majority rule will not create wealth losses without compensation. However, if individuals frequently become pivotal under unanimous consent schemes and extort others or if the costs of actually obtaining consent exceed the benefits, then simple majority rule without compensation is preferable.

Market failures arise when actual market institutions fail to perfectly implement the unanimous consent (Pareto) rule. Some transactions that would increase all citizens' welfare (positive externalities) fail to occur, and other transactions that reduce some citizens' welfare (negative externalities) do occur. Economists tell us that a legislature can rectify positive externalities through the use of various blind-bidding procedures to provide optimal amounts of public goods. To remedy negative externalities, a legislature must overcome the public-goods character of negotiations and allocate initial property rights in the commodity that is overconsumed. In my view, such property rights should be assigned equally unless an unequal distribution would result in advantages to those with little wealth and income, although other distributions are also defensible. After property rights are distributed, the legislature

---

10. If citizens continued to favor the use of microeconomic policies to redistribute income even after they were fully informed of the consequences, then economists could not argue against the practice. They could only note the price paid for such tastes.

should provide services to reduce the transaction costs inherent in negotiations by groups about externalities.

Congress, however, rarely enacts domestic microeconomic policy prescriptions without substantially altering the characteristics preferred by economists. Those who defend elected officials' alterations offer three justifications. First, economic policy changes create wealth losses and gains that are neither compensated nor taxed. Second, the use of microeconomic techniques to redistribute income allows political institutions to quietly ameliorate the negative distributive consequences of markets without directly repudiating the generally held belief that the market distribution of income is fair (Hochschild 1981). Finally, rectifying market failures with command-and-control techniques, as opposed to market methods, produces some valuable symbolic and emotional outputs.

Of the three classes of argument, only the first, in my judgment, provides a sound basis for modification of economists' recommendations by political institutions. Because all policies that alter prices or property rights create wealth losses for some parties, political institutions legitimately can alter the distributional consequences of policies that promote allocational efficiency in an effort to compensate those who suffer wealth losses and tax those who receive wealth gains, although, as Baumol (1986) demonstrates, such compensation schemes may produce more problems than benefits.

Equity disputes arise because income instability and short-term rents are inherent by-products of consumer choice and firm innovation in markets. As with allocational disputes, preferences about equity can be aggregated through either majority rule or unanimous consent, although the redistribution achieved through unanimous consent probably will not reduce inequality very much. Of greater importance than the decision rule are the techniques used by the legislature to redistribute. The legislature should redistribute income and wealth directly, rather than through the alteration of the characteristics of particular markets. Deadweight loss, unintended benefits for the affluent, the capitalization of privileges in asset markets, and perverse allocational distortions all detract from the benefits of indirect microeconomic redistribution.

CHAPTER 3

Petroleum Markets and Policies

Energy markets have numerous characteristics that generate consumer and producer dissatisfaction. Some are genuine market failures, but many are simply struggles over the appropriate distribution of excess profits (economic rents) and over market dominance (income security).

Public policies can improve market outcomes that consumers and firms dislike without creating perverse behaviors as a side effect only if Congress adopts general taxation policies in the case of equity concerns and market-specific price and property-rights policies in the case of market failures. The energy policies that Congress has adopted have generally not reflected an adequate understanding of the differences between the equity and market-failure sources of political demands. Even when the enacted policies were reasonably sound responses to market difficulties, Congress often has not altered these policies fast enough when energy markets changed. As a consequence, periodic crises have erupted that largely are rational responses by consumers and firms to previously enacted policies that are no longer appropriate. Congressional decisions on energy policy proposals usually reflect a poor ability to use public policy to improve the allocational and equity characteristics of market outcomes.

Chapter 3 offers evidence from the petroleum context to support these arguments, while chapter 4 examines coal, natural gas, and nuclear power policies.

The Origins of Petroleum-Market Problems:
Market Failures

The characteristics of petroleum ensure that both its consumers and producers often will be dissatisfied with market outcomes.[1] Genuine market failures include the failure of surface property rights to coincide with reservoir boundaries, oil pipelines' economies of scale, and consumer dependence on the smooth functioning of futures markets.

---

1. Petroleum markets are the starting point of my analysis of energy markets because other fuels are substitutes. As long as petroleum supplies are plentiful and inexpensive, little concern is exhibited about other fuels.

Early in this century, courts applied rules developed for the extraction of solid minerals to disputes involving the production of oil (McDonald 1971, 31). Surface owners had rights to the oil below their property. The lack of congruence between surface property rights and actual petroleum reservoir boundaries created a severe market failure called the problem of capture, because each owner produced rapidly to ensure that others did not drain the oil first, even though that reduced total reservoir output.[2] Capture problems have been a cause of political struggle whenever new petroleum discoveries have been made in areas not under the control of major multinational companies. The most famous incidents occurred in Oklahoma and Texas between 1926 and 1932.

Oil pipelines possess scale economies.[3] The per-barrel transportation cost is less for one forty-eight-inch pipeline than for sixteen twelve-inch pipelines, even though they contain similar volumes. In addition, pipelines are much cheaper than rail transportation. As a result, the owner of an unregulated pipeline network will receive monopoly rents from the economies of scale and inframarginal rents based on the market clearing price set by railroad tank-car transportation. These rents were the basis for the Standard Oil empire created by John D. Rockefeller. Excess profits from both pipeline ownership and vertical integration have been a source of political dispute ever since. Whenever independent (not vertically integrated) producers, refiners, or marketers experience economic difficulty during price troughs, they usually argue that the economic power and excess profits of the vertically integrated companies (majors) are the cause of their distress (see table 3.2).[4]

The final genuine market-failure characteristic of the petroleum market is its dependence on people's expectations about the future. Entrepreneurs' decisions about exploration for new reserves and production of existing reserves depend on their beliefs about both absolute future prices and their growth rate.[5] Consumers' and marketers' general inventory behavior, always extremely dependent on expectations, is more volatile with respect to oil (Verleger 1982). Petroleum's low elasticity means that severe shortages may appear quite suddenly as a result of changes in inventories even though the actual reduction in world supplies is minuscule. Both of the "oil shortages" that

---

2. For a concise explanation of the engineering and economic characteristics of oil production, see McDonald 1971, chaps. 2, 4–6.

3. For information on oil pipelines, see Cookenboo 1955; Johnson 1967; Mitchell 1979; and Hansen 1983.

4. John Blair's *Control of Oil* (1976) is the most recent leading work to make this claim. See also U.S. Congress, Senate, *The International Petroleum Cartel: Report to the Committee on Small Business,* 82d Cong., 2d sess., 1952.

5. See McDonald 1971, chap. 5, for the standard explanation. At equilibrium, the net price of petroleum reserves must rise at a rate equal to the real rate of interest.

occurred during 1973 and 1979 were really the product of rapid changes in inventory behavior exacerbated by perverse pricing policies (Verleger 1982).

In response to these three problems, Congress could enact policies that improve petroleum-market performance. In the capture situation, the legislature could create new pumping-rate property rights. In order to pump crude, Congress could specify that one would have to own land and pumping-rate rights. These rights would ensure that the aggregate pumping rate did not exceed the technological optimum no matter how many landowners existed. Natural monopolies, such as pipelines, set prices above marginal cost. Social welfare would be improved if the state taxed firms' excess profits and then bribed them to increase output and lower prices. Markets with few participants, such as long-term futures markets, are public goods and will work better if the legislature subsidizes them. Public subsidy of long-term petroleum storage is our best policy against future oil shocks.

The Origins of Petroleum Market Problems: Equity Disputes

Other characteristics of petroleum markets give rise to equity concerns. The extremely low short-run price elasticity of demand and supply creates extremely rapid changes in the incomes of consumers and producers. The fungibility of oil creates additional difficulties for producers in preserving their incomes because brand-name loyalty cannot be generated easily. Finally, the extreme variance in actual production costs across supply sources creates excess profits for the low-cost producers and voter demands for action.[6]

Low short-run elasticity, ubiquitous use, and few short-run substitutes together mean that petroleum-market aggregate behavior responds poorly to price changes.[7] The inability of petroleum markets to respond quickly to supply and demand changes has resulted in a boom and bust cycle. Table 3–1 lists the peaks and troughs of the cycle over roughly a 116-year period, along with the real prices at each stage of the cycle in 1967 dollars. Figure 3–1 graphically displays the same data. During both troughs and peaks, petroleum political struggles erupt. Producers resist allocation by price during the trough periods (and consumers resist during the peaks) in order to preserve their incomes.

Fungibility means that producers will have difficulty creating brand loyalty.[8] Coca-Cola can charge much more than store-brand soft drinks because consumers do not consider the latter to be an exact substitute for the former.

---

6. Adelman (1972, 76) reports a seventeen-fold difference between the long-run U.S. supply cost of $1.22 per barrel and the Iraqi cost of $.07 per barrel.

7. Verleger (1982, 126) reports that the published nongovernmental estimates range from $-.08$ to $-.22$. Petroleum demand drops from 8 to 22 percent for a 100 percent increase in price.

8. See McLean 1954, 101–5; and Blair 1976, 235–46.

TABLE 3-1.   U.S. Petroleum Price Cycles, 1873-1989

Dates			Average Domestic Wellhead Prices			Percentage Change in Price	Duration in Years
Trough	Peak	Trough	Trough	Peak	Trough	Trough to Peak	Trough to Trough
—	1876	1892	—	9.88	2.50	295.2	16
1892	1900	1910	2.50	5.67	2.40	126.8	18
1910	1920	1931	2.40	5.97	1.83	148.8	21
1931	1937	1946	1.83	3.23	2.61	76.5	15
1946	1957	1972	2.61	3.81	2.62	46.0	26
1972	1981	1988	2.62	12.14	3.72	363.4	16

Note: I wish to credit Edward Morse, managing director of Petroleum Finance Co., for the ideas in this table. The data before 1975 are from the U.S. Bureau of Mines' *Minerals Yearbook* series. A portion of the 1934 Statistical Appendix (pp. 210–11) was used for the years 1892–1933. For the years 1934–75, every fourth *Minerals Yearbook* was used to obtain the previous four years. The 1976 figure is from the American Petroleum Institute's *Basic Petroleum Data Book*, vol. 7, no. 1, sec. VI, table 1. The 1977–84 data are from the U.S. Department of Energy, Energy Information Administration, *Annual Energy Review*, 1985, 131. The 1985–89 data are from the U.S. Department of Energy, Energy Information Administration, *Monthly Energy Review*, Jan., 1990, 91, The implicit GNP deflator for 1892–1933 is from Kuznets, as set forth in Friedman and Schwartz 1963, 122–25. It has been rescaled from a base year of 1929 to 1967 by multiplying by 0.4225. The 1934–81 values are from the *National Income and Product Accounts of the United States*. The figures for 1982–89 are from the *Economic Report of the President, 1990*, table C-3, 298. The data from *NIPA* and the Census Bureau's *Statistical Abstract* were in 1982 dollars and were converted to 1967 dollars by dividing by 0.359. There is a slight gap when the deflator shifts from Kuznets's to NIPa's. The year 1933 was chosen to minimize this gap when the two were equated. For 1933, the two deflators vary by only 0.2.

Different brands of petroleum, however, are perceived to be equivalent. Consequently, consumers will desert an existing supplier of petroleum if cheaper sources become available. Such behavior is not a market failure; nevertheless, during troughs in the petroleum price cycle, producers clamor for a variety of measures to restrict consumer choice. In the early 1930s, early 1970s, and mid-1980s, firms called for restrictions on imports, on the major oil companies, or on both (Nash 1968; Blair 1976; Diamond 1984; Hershey 1985).

Petroleum-market events also become political issues because supply sources are nonrenewable and have production costs that vary by large amounts. The true marginal replacement cost of a nonrenewable resource, somewhere between the current market price and the price of renewable substitutes, depends on the rate at which we discount the welfare of future generations. This cost will not be determined by market outcomes; it can only be set by public policy.[9] In addition, the allocation of excess profits created by

---

9. For discussions of the true replacement cost of oil, see Lovins 1977, 68–72; and Stobaugh and Yergin 1979, 46–55.

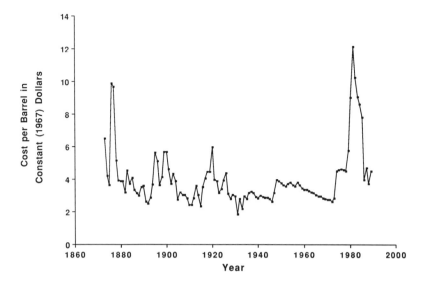

Fig. 3-1. U.S. petroleum price cycles, 1873–1989

the difference between the market-clearing or true replacement price and actual current production costs is a pure distributional problem.[10] Consumers who purchase oil at thirty dollars per barrel react angrily to the fact that some producers have actual production costs of only ten cents per barrel. And established producers do not enjoy new oil entrepreneurs whittling away at their above normal returns. The fact that thirty dollars per barrel actually may be equal to or below true replacement cost is politically immaterial. Both consumer and producer groups seek redress from Congress even though their grievances have no strictly economic basis.

The Congressional Response to Petroleum-Market Problems

Congress historically has responded to the equity problems that dominate petroleum politics by enacting policies that alter specific characteristics of oil markets, rather than more general redistributive policies possessing fewer

---

10. High energy prices have an allocative purpose: to make consumers aware of the true replacement costs of the resources they use. Microeconomics, however, has nothing to say about who should receive the excess profits (rents) that result from high opportunity costs but low actual production costs. The rents can be taken away from the energy producers and redistributed without altering anyone's behavior.

allocational distortions.[11] These microeconomic policies then create incentives that induce new market behavior that threatens the income of some other segment of the industry. The cycle repeats with another round of political demands. Congress typically responds to the negative effects of its decisions, not by repealing previous policies and passing more effective measures, but by enacting new legislation without repealing the old.

Begin by considering the policy responses to the petroleum price cycle experienced during the second and third decades of this century. At the price peak in 1920, many commentators believed that we were exhausting our oil supply. Conservation became the popular buzzword, and Congress constantly was confronted by requests to augment existing supplies and restrict demand. During the next decade, the situation was reversed completely. Prices were low and dropping. Orderly competition and price supports were the popular policy proposals. Congress, however, did not respond to the events of the 1930s by repealing the supply-enhancement policies enacted during the 1920s. Instead, Congress left them intact and enacted a price-support system. Similar cycles occurred again in the 1950s and 1970s. In each case, Congress enacted policies that "overreacted" to each peak and trough and failed to quickly repeal them when petroleum prices resumed their predictable cyclical pattern.

Oil Policy in the 1930s

Fears over declining oil reserves led Congress to enact a 27.5 percent depletion allowance in 1926.[12] This provision allowed oil companies to deduct 27.5 percent of gross revenues in their calculation of net income for tax purposes. Although a tax deduction is not the most efficient or equitable method for creating incentives, it is a legitimate response to a shortage. The depletion allowance, combined with an intangible-drilling-expense provision, resulted in deductions that, in many cases, exceeded drilling costs and in a rate of return far above most alternative investments.[13] These conditions, of course, induced additional exploration activity, particularly in locations that major companies previously thought were unlikely to have oil. The explora-

---

11. This history of petroleum policy draws on Pettingill 1936; Williamson 1936; Watkins 1937; McLean 1954; Lovejoy and Hoffman 1967; Nash 1968; Shaffer 1968; Odell 1970; Blair 1976; and Schneider 1983.

12. Since 1918, oil companies have been allowed to deduct a percentage of the discovery value of wells. The difficulties in bureaucratically setting an appropriate percentage for each firm, combined with a general perception of a shortage, led Congress to establish the 27.5 percent level.

13. The intangible-drilling-expense provision, in existence since 1916, allowed most of the expenses of drilling a well to be deducted in one year instead of being amortized over the life of the well.

tion activity resulted in the discovery of two extremely large reservoirs that were inexpensive to develop—the Seminole field in Oklahoma (1926) and the East Texas field (1931). Downward pressure on crude-oil prices created by the increased supply was exacerbated by the problem of capture and the economic orientation of the wildcatters who owned the wells in the new fields. As would be expected, these producers did not worry about the optimal economic depletion of a reservoir or the effect that their production would have on the world petroleum market.

From 1927 until 1932, different sectors of the oil industry proposed a variety of measures to deal with the related problems of capture and decreasing prices. The views of oil companies toward these policy proposals varied according to their perceptions of which alternatives would stabilize petroleum markets in their interests. Initially, the major oil companies supported federal-industry planning similar to that used during World War I.[14] The war experience left many corporate leaders favorably disposed toward corporate-managed capitalism under the protection of the state. In addition, in 1928, the leaders of Exxon, British Petroleum, and Royal Dutch Shell agreed not to compete for an increased market share through price competition in various parts of the world (Blair 1976, 54–56). The U.S. glut threatened the stability of their arrangement. Presidents Coolidge and Hoover, however, were reluctant to cooperate because of their strongly laissez-faire orientation.

The urgency of the oil-surplus situation caused the majors to shift their focus to the state level. They sought and received a statewide prorationing order from the Texas Railroad Commission in 1930. Prorationing was a program of production cutback orders, called allowables, that equilibrated supply with demand at the prices major oil refineries paid for crude. The wildcatters in East Texas ignored the order, and in *Macmillan v. Texas Railroad Commission* (1931), the district court ruled the order illegal. Governor Sterling, a former executive of Humble Oil, sought legislative approval for market-demand prorationing, but the legislature adamantly refused to approve anything that appeared to fix prices or restrict the right of Texas residents to earn a living from their land.

In 1932, the majors again demanded that the Texas legislature do something about overproduction. The legislature refused, and the major refiners promptly announced that the price they paid for crude oil would drop from

---

14. Henry Doherty led a one-man movement for mandatory unitization from 1923 on as a solution to the overproduction problem. Under unitization, the multiple surface owners of an oil reservoir relinquish their right to make decisions regarding production to an actor concerned with the optimal depletion of a reservoir as a whole, in return for a share of the profits equal to their share of the reservoir's surface area. The major oil companies (see table 3–2) resisted until 1929, when the American Petroleum Institute went on record as favoring production quotas. No organization ever favored mandatory unitization (Blair 1976, 155–59; McDonald 1971, 35).

over one dollar to ten cents a barrel. The legislature responded with the creation of new powers for the Texas Railroad Commission. Under the banner of conservation, the commission could now perform two functions: (1) limit total Texas production to market demand at the price the oil refineries offered, and (2) allocate that total among well owners in an attempt, although poorly designed, to deal with the capture problem.

So-called independent oil companies, those involved exclusively in U.S. domestic production, were not very successful with their legislative agenda. They lobbied for import quotas to restrict competition from oil produced abroad by the major multinationals; pipeline divestiture to redistribute rents and reduce the power of the vertically integrated companies; and federal allocation of market shares, not merely the federal sanction of industry agreements that the majors preferred. There were some sympathetic ears in Congress, but no legislation was enacted.[15]

New Deal Oil Policy
Unlike Coolidge and Hoover, Franklin Roosevelt was favorably disposed toward the unfinished "progressive" agenda. The National Industrial Recovery Act of 1933 (NIRA),[16] which passed with overwhelming support from large oil companies, substituted producer bargaining for price competition in the allocation of market shares to firms. The oil industry was the first to adopt a fair trade code under the act in 1934.

When the Supreme Court ruled the NIRA unconstitutional in 1934, the majors once again turned their attention to Washington. They favored a federal system of marketing controls, but Interior Secretary Harold Ickes, in a speech before the American Petroleum Institute in November, 1934, argued that the petroleum industry should be subject to regulations similar to those governing the public-utility industry (Nash 1968, 148).[17] The majors were not pleased

---

15. Proposals to impose a duty of one to two dollars a barrel on imported oil were offered in 1929, 1930, and 1931, but to no avail. Section 601(c)(4) of the Revenue Act of 1932 (PL72–154) placed a tariff of twenty cents on each barrel. Bills to prevent major refiners from owning pipelines were introduced into numerous congresses from 1931 on. None ever left committee. Hearings were held on Representative Marland's (D–Okla.) bill to impose federal regulation of petroleum prices and production (U.S. Congress, House, *Conservation of Petroleum: Hearing before the Committee on Ways and Means*, 73d Cong., 1st sess., 1933). These efforts were sidetracked by the National Industrial Recovery Act (PL73–67) and by Secretary of the Interior Harold Ickes's increasingly strident anti-corporate statements.

16. PL73–67

17. Sun and Texas Oil did not favor federal controls. See U.S. Congress, Senate, *The Federal Petroleum Act: Hearing before the Committee on Mines and Mining*, 73d Cong., 2d sess., 1934; U.S. Congress, House, *Oil and Oil Pipelines: Hearing before the Committee on Interstate and Foreign Commerce*, 73d Cong., 2d sess., 1934, 63.

with his remarks. Their support for federal regulation quickly vanished; instead, they supported the Connally Hot Oil Act,[18] which gave federal sanction to the state prorationing programs.

Because the depletion allowance remained intact and no direct restrictions were placed on well-drilling, investment in oil production continued as producers scrambled to capture the rents that resulted from the elaborate price-support system. Prorationing created price stability, a legitimate policy objective. Yet stabilizing production through direct restrictions on well-output did not really correct the capture problem; it merely shifted the competitive scramble from oil production to securing well-ownership and bureaucratic exemption from the allowables.[19] In addition, by holding prices above the marginal cost of the easily produced oil, prorationing created rents that actually encouraged more oil investment, which, in turn, required more prorationing.

Although prices were above the marginal production cost of flush production, they were still below long-run replacement costs. How can prices be both too low and too high at the same time? The contradiction arises from the failure to distinguish pricing from excess-profit issues. As I stated earlier, nonrenewable resources should be priced at levels that allow costs to be met, that deplete the resource over some fair time period, and that give consumers a realistic sense of the long-run sustainable price on which they should base their consumption decisions. No one knows what the long run is, but prices during the years 1930–70 induced consumers to adopt consumption patterns that were not sustainable. Steadily higher prices during this period would have made it less likely for consumers to have adopted the consumption patterns that were so rudely altered by 1973–79 events. Higher prices, of course, would have created even higher rents, but they could have been taxed to bring the rate of return to a level that would not have induced excess investment.

Postwar Oil Policy

The failure of Congress to deal effectively with the central issues of petroleum markets during the 1930s—capture and long-term replacement cost—encouraged petroleum-market behavior that undermined the false stability created by prorationing. The dramatic rise in oil imports after World War II, a

---

18. PL74–14

19. Wild price swings resulting from inelastic demand behavior will result in a less than optimal amount of capital investment. Public insurance against price instability would correct the market failure. McDonald (1971, 161) reports that in 1963, for example, 43 percent of Texas's production came from exempt wells.

TABLE 3–2. Typology of Major Oil Companies

United States		International	
Top Eight	Lesser Majors	Seven Sisters	Independents
Exxon	Getty	Exxon	Continental
Mobil	Phillips	Mobil	Amerada Hess
So Cal	Signal	So Cal	Marathon
Standard (Indiana)	Union	Texaco	Occidental
Texaco	Continental	Gulf	
Gulf	Sun	Shell	
Shell	Amerada Hess	BP	
Arco	Cities Service		
	Marathon		

Source: Blair 1976, xi.

rational response to the prorationing program, distressed domestic producers and led to another round of policy-making.

By the end of World War II, independent oil entrepreneurs such as Occidental and Amerada Hess, seeking to avoid domestic prorationing and to take advantage of the favorable U.S. treatment of taxes paid to foreign governments, began to invest abroad in countries (such as Libya) previously ignored by the so-called seven sisters. (See table 3–2.) These new international independents, nonparticipants in the oligopolistic bargaining arrangements that had governed the world oil market since 1928, proceeded to import low-cost oil into the United States and capture the rents created by the prorationing program. Domestic producers, particularly small- and medium-sized independents, became quite alarmed at the allowable cutbacks they suffered to equilibrate supply and demand under pressure from the imports. Table 3–3 lists crude-oil prices in Texas and the production restrictions that were necessary to maintain these prices in the twenty years after World War II.

In 1954, after a nine-year lobbying effort, Congress adopted a clause in the Reciprocal Trade Act Amendments of 1955[20] that authorized the president to limit imports of a commodity if he concluded such imports were detrimental to national security. In 1959, after a voluntary import-restriction program failed, President Eisenhower invoked the clause and implemented a mandatory oil-import quota program. The quotas subsidized small and inland refiners and protected existing sellers of refined products from the importation of products refined abroad.

The new international independents, now effectively shut out of the U.S. market, flooded Europe with oil. From 1960 to 1970, the increased use of oil

20. PL84–86

TABLE 3–3. Crude-Oil Prices and Production as a Percentage of Capacity in Texas, Annual Averages, 1948–66

Year	Crude-Oil Price (dollars per barrel)	Production/Capacity (percentage)
1948	2.61	100
1949	2.59	65
1950	2.59	63
1951	2.58	76
1952	2.58	71
1953	2.73	65
1954	2.84	53
1955	2.84	53
1956	2.83	52
1957	3.11	47
1958	3.06	33
1959	2.98	34
1960	2.96	28
1961	2.97	28
1962	2.99	27
1963	2.97	28
1964	2.96	28
1965	2.96	29
1966	2.97	34

Source: McDonald 1971, 189.

was dramatic. In West Germany, for example, oil use rose from 0.63 million barrels per day to 2.43 million barrels per day between 1960 and 1970, an increase of almost 400 percent. During the same period, U.S. usage increased only 50 percent.[21] Price cutting was extensive as the new oil fought its way into the world market. From 1957 until 1970, the world price of oil declined, in nominal terms, from $2.10 a barrel to $1.20 a barrel (Blair 1976, 213). The seven sisters, seeking to preserve their market share and profit margins, unilaterally lowered their royalty payments to Middle East countries. OPEC was formed as the result of such royalty reductions, and greater militancy ensued with successive cuts.

The Energy Crisis

As the preceding historical overview illustrates, the so-called energy crisis (the twin oil shocks of 1973 and 1979) was nothing more than a predictable

---

21. U.S. Department of Energy, Energy Information Administration, *Annual Report to Congress, 1981*, vol. 2:83.

upswing in the twenty-year petroleum price cycle exacerbated by perverse incentives—incentives created by inappropriate policies. My argument, in brief, is twofold. First, controls on oil imported into the United States, enacted in 1959, lowered the price of oil elsewhere in the world and increased consumption, particularly in Europe. Europe's newly found addiction to oil, and the concomitant decline in U.S. domestic supplies caused by import controls, resulted in more rigid petroleum demand during the 1970s price upswing than in previous cycles and fewer non-OPEC sources to meet the demand. Second, price controls, initiated by the Nixon administration, also made the price upswing in the 1973–81 period much more severe than in previous cycles because of the differential impact of price controls on large and small oil companies.

In the early 1970s, the oil industry exhibited all the characteristics of an industry on the skids. The elaborate production and marketing control mechanisms from the 1930s—developed by the majors to prevent low-cost producers from using price competition to enter the market—had collapsed. The price of oil had dropped almost to depression levels. Domestic profits were flat or falling after 1967 (Blair 1976, 241). The ingenious concession and foreign-tax-credit system that laundered foreign aid to the Arabs via the oil companies was in severe jeopardy because the Arabs demanded working control of their oil. At the same time, oil-import quotas and strong economic growth had exhausted the U.S. oil surplus. Domestic production reached a peak by 1970. Even though U.S. prices had been kept well above world competitive levels, petroleum demand was growing rapidly (4.5 percent per year), just at a time when the huge easy-to-produce pools discovered in the 1930s were producing at maximum rates.

OPEC members realized that they had become the only supplier of oil that had the ability to increase production when the pipeline connecting the Middle East with the Mediterranean broke in 1970.[22] OPEC, however, did not have the characteristics normally found in producers that expand production of a nonrenewable resource to meet growing demand. Instead of having the world's highest marginal costs, as one would normally expect, it had the lowest—approximately ten cents a barrel (Blair 1976, 47). All the substitutes for Middle East oil had marginal costs that were considerably higher. Consequently, OPEC was in a position to price its oil at the marginal cost of new supplies elsewhere in the world and capture huge rents as a result.

---

22. Muammar Qaddafi sensed his oil was both high quality (light and low in sulphur) and strategically located (on the Mediterranean) because of the pipeline break. He demanded forty cents more per barrel. The majors refused, but Occidental, totally dependent on Libyan crude oil, agreed because the majors would not guarantee to supply it with crude oil. Other Middle Eastern producers quickly noticed that the new price did not result in dramatic shifts in consumer behavior or in the emergence of new supplies (Blair 1976, chap. 9).

From 1973 to 1981, the defining characteristic of the world petroleum market was that OPEC had become the marginal supplier to the world and yet had actual production costs much below other petroleum and unconventional substitutes. Members of Congress, of course, wanted to prevent redistribution of U.S. consumer income to both domestic and foreign oil producers. Once again, however, congressional discussion confused equity and market-failure issues. As a result, the enacted policies actually exacerbated problems in petroleum markets.

Numerous proposals were offered in the 1973–74 period to deal with the exhaustion of non-OPEC low-cost supplies of oil:

1. Break up OPEC and the major oil companies. (Proponents reasoned that the price increases were the result of artificial restraint of supplies, did not reflect the marginal costs of new supply, and had no economic legitimacy.)
2. Allow domestic oil and gas prices to reach world levels to encourage consumers and entrepreneurs to search for alternatives; address equity problems through the tax code; and deal with the Middle East–dependence problem through a contingency tariff and public storage.
3. End the tax privileges enjoyed by oil and gas producers.
4. Place price controls on domestically produced oil and natural gas to make prices match production costs and to prevent excess profits.
5. Develop alternatives to imported petroleum through federal research and development and through subsidization of alternatives; reduce demand for conventional fuels through legal regulation.
6. Remove constraints on the use of alternative supplies.

As explained earlier, the allocation of rent is a legitimate political function. However, the methods used by Congress to control rents—price controls and petroleum allocation (proposal 4), subsidization of new supply technologies (proposal 5), and reduced concern for the environmental hazards posed by coal and nuclear power (proposal 6)—created incentives to import oil, caused mild world market shortfalls to have massive effects on domestic consumers (Verleger 1982), resulted in a deadweight loss to the economy of $5 billion per year (Kalt 1981, 187–88), and encouraged the development of high- rather than low-cost substitutes for imported oil.[23]

In the United States, the effects of a tighter world oil market were aggra-

---

23. Congress did enact two effective policies during the 1973–79 period. Public Law 94–12 (1975) repealed the depletion allowance for integrated petroleum companies and for those producers with an output of more than 2,000 barrels a year. The Energy Policy and Conservation Act of 1975 (PL94–163) created the strategic petroleum reserve, an intelligent remedy for the failure of private inventories.

vated by the price controls President Nixon had placed on the economy.[24] Petroleum prices were given special attention in the price-control program because they were rising rapidly. The major effect of these special petroleum rules was to prevent importers from recovering the rising costs of imports. The majors responded by cutting their imports. The consequences of this import reduction were felt largely by independent refiners and retailers, who, at that time, obtained 40 percent of their crude-oil supplies from major oil companies rather than independent producers (Blair 1976, 248). The contracts governing these sales contained force-majeure clauses that allowed the majors to end sales to the independents because of circumstances beyond their control. The loss of imports thus resulted in independent gas stations suffering large cutbacks, while the majors' own retail outlets received adequate supplies. These events easily aroused the strong antagonisms held by independents and consumers toward the major oil companies.

Congress responded to the price increases and independent-station shortages, not with the repeal of the price controls that caused the condition, but with the passage of the Emergency Petroleum Allocation Act (EPAA)[25] in September, 1973. The EPAA froze the price of *old* domestic oil, that volume of oil produced from wells during May, 1972, at $5.25 per barrel. *New* oil (that volume produced from old wells in excess of 1972 levels), imports, and newly discovered domestic oil were decontrolled. In addition, shortages, when they existed, were to be shared equally by all retailers.

Verleger (1982) has argued convincingly that the net effect of the EPAA was to create the very shortages it was supposed to ameliorate. By attempting to insulate the U.S. market from the world marginal price for oil as set in the Rotterdam spot market, the EPAA actually created incentives to hoard just at those times when inventories should have been released on the market— during the disruptions of 1973 and 1979.[26] Verleger's policy proposal, a stiff and predictably declining tax on crude oil implemented whenever supplies are

---

24. The wage and price controls during this era consisted of four phases. During the first phase (from August to November, 1971), all wages and prices were frozen, and petroleum importers were not allowed to pass on rising crude-oil import prices if the crude oil was transformed, which, of course, it had to be if it was to be of any use. During phase II (from November, 1971, to January, 1973), the prices charged by large oil companies were effectively frozen. Phase III (from January to August, 1973) applied controls only to large oil companies. Small oil companies bid up the cost of imports on the spot market, and the majors reduced their imports (Kalt 1981, 11–13). Phase IV (from August to November, 1973) regulations created the categories of old and new oil and controlled the price of the former. These regulations became the heart of the Emergency Petroleum Allocation Act (PL93–159).

25. PL93–159

26. Hoarding resulted because long-term contract prices did not rise to meet spot prices. Those with access to crude oil through long-term contracts faced strong incentives to accumulate as much oil below spot prices as they could.

disrupted, would create the opposite incentives because oil inventory owners would reap wealth windfalls by releasing oil on the market exactly when consumer fears should be calmed.

In addition, the two-tiered price system created rents for those refiners with greater than average access to old oil. Under the crude-oil entitlements program, the refiners that used more than the national average of price-controlled old oil paid these rents to refiners that used less than the national average of old oil (and more than the national average of imported oil). This transfer program subsidized crude-oil imports. Once again, a policy exacerbated the condition it was enacted to resolve (Kalt 1981, 50–58).

The second component of the congressional response to the energy crisis was to subsidize alternatives to oil and relax regulation of externalities created by energy supplies. Both of these policies entailed greater social costs than demand-reduction strategies (Stobaugh and Yergin 1979, chap. 6); indeed, Congress consistently prefers concrete commodity-creation strategies over more diffuse make-markets-work-better solutions.[27] Congress did enact provisions to reduce the demand for oil and increase the use of substitutes in the face of price signals that encouraged the opposite, but it subsequently retreated from coal conversion and appliance and home efficiency standards and is currently under pressure to do the same for auto efficiency standards.[28]

In 1975, the price-control/entitlements policies enacted in 1973 were scheduled to expire. Congress responded with the Energy Policy and Conservation Act (EPCA).[29] This law placed previously uncontrolled new oil under

---

27. The Trans-Alaska Pipeline Act of 1973 (PL93–153), the Energy Supply and Environmental Coordination Act of 1974 (PL93–319), and the 1975 reauthorization of the Price-Anderson Nuclear Insurance and Indemnification Act (PL94–197) were designed to minimize the regulation of externalities created by alternatives to oil. The following legislation was designed to subsidize and thereby augment alternative energy supplies: the Solar Heating and Cooling Demonstration Act of 1974 (PL93–409); the Geothermal Energy Research, Development, and Demonstration Act of 1974 (PL93–410); the Solar Energy Research, Development, and Demonstration Act of 1974 (PL93–473); the Nonnuclear Energy Research and Development Act of 1974 (PL93–533); the Electric and Hybrid Vehicle Research, Development, and Demonstration Act of 1976 (PL94–413); and the Energy Security Act of 1980 (PL96–294).

28. The legal-orders policies affect auto and appliance efficiency (Energy Policy and Conservation Act of 1975, PL94–163), home efficiency standards (Energy Conservation and Production Act of 1976, PL94–385), and coal conversion (Energy Supply and Environmental Coordination Act of 1974, PL93–319). The appliance standards were not to become effective until the mid-1980s under PL95–619, one of the Carter energy bills passed in 1978. The National Appliance Energy Conservation Act of 1987 (PL100–12) set up specific appliance standards that would require modest improvements (from 15 to 25 percent) but gave manufacturers five years to comply. The coal-conversion and home efficiency standards were diluted in Title X of the Omnibus Reconciliation Act of 1981 (PL97–35), and the provisions mandating coal conversion in new power plants were repealed in May, 1987, by PL100–42.

29. PL94–163.

price controls, increasing the incentives to import and decreasing consumer incentives to shift from oil to other energy sources, particularly demand-reducing conservation investments.

Carter's Energy Plan

President Carter, like Presidents Nixon and Ford before him, proposed a series of economically sound initiatives in 1977. The major thrust of these proposals was to raise energy prices to better reflect replacement costs, as well as redistribute the resulting rents to low-income persons to ameliorate the resulting equity problems. Congress balked, however, once again finding it easier to use subsidies and regulations to alter corporate behavior, rather than prices to alter consumer behavior.[30]

In a startling reversal of past sentiment, Congress allowed the price controls to expire in 1980 and placed a windfall-profits tax on oil price rises.[31] Although the expiration of the price-control entitlement system was a positive development, the windfall-profits tax actually may exacerbate future petroleum supply disruptions. If another disruption occurs, the tax could widen the difference between the price received by owners of oil in the U.S. and the Rotterdam spot price and cause diversion away from the U.S. market.

Conclusion

Economic disputes involve questions of either allocational efficiency or distributional equity. Though the language of market failure is used frequently by participants in petroleum-policy disputes, most struggles involve conflicts over the proper distribution of excess profits and the fate of those actors whose incomes fall or become unstable. The actual occurrence of market failures where Congress can improve petroleum-market performance is quite rare. Although pipeline scale economies, the problem of capture, and poorly functioning futures markets occasionally present Congress with opportunities to

---

30. Five laws were passed. Public Law 95–617 urged utilities to study alternative rate structures that penalized energy use during periods of peak demand, as well as heavy electricity use. Public Law 95–618 created tax credits for home and business conservation investments, established a schedule of taxes and fines for excessive gasoline use, and called for the establishment of energy-use standards for common household appliances. Public Law 95–619 subsidized conservation by low-income persons and local institutions such as schools and hospitals. Public Law 95–620 continued coal conversion, and PL95–621 initiated gradual decontrol of new natural gas.

31. PL96–223. The program taxes 70 percent of the increase in oil prices above the May, 1979, new-oil price level plus inflation. Marginal oil has a lower tax rate (30 percent) and a higher ceiling price (May, 1979, level plus two dollars). The Economic Recovery Act of 1981 (PL97–34) reduced the tax rate on marginal oil from 30 to 15 percent over the 1982–86 period and exempted small oil producers.

improve market outcomes, most petroleum-policy disputes involve equity concerns such as short-term excess profits and declining or volatile incomes.

Congress typically has responded to petroleum-market problems with inappropriate legislation. Firms, in turn, have responded to the perverse incentives created by Congress with behavior that causes additional problems and another round of policy-making.

In the 1930s, the problems of capture and rapid depletion of flush reservoirs were legitimate market failures. But the enactment of prorationing, combined with the failure to repeal the depletion and intangible-drilling-expense tax incentives, did not solve the problem and, in fact, created additional difficulties. Oil imports were a direct result of producer attempts to capture the rents created by the tax and prorationing system. Domestic producers objected to their income declines, and Congress allowed the president to enact a system of oil-import controls. The resulting world competition led to Middle East royalty cuts and OPEC militancy. The failure to separate questions about the proper long-term replacement price of oil from income-distribution questions after the 1973 panic in petroleum spot prices resulted in the enactment of policies that caused petroleum-market operations to deteriorate and actually made the income distribution less equal. Today, the expiration of the oil price, import-control, and tax-depletion policies has given oil markets a freedom they have not enjoyed since the 1920s, and consumers are much better off. However, the fundamental problem of charging consumers the replacement cost of oil imports has not been addressed, and the windfall-profits tax ensures that future oil-market shocks will cause major economic disruptions.

CHAPTER 4

Coal, Natural Gas, and Nuclear Power Markets and Policies

The Origins of Coal-Market Problems

Historically, coal producers have disliked markets because their incomes have been volatile and declining. Instability exists because entry into coal production is relatively easy. Small nonunion drift mines, found in Kentucky, Tennessee, and West Virginia (Moyer 1964, 109), and western surface mines make it difficult for the higher-cost underground unionized mines found in Pennsylvania, Ohio, Illinois, and Indiana to stabilize their market share.[1] The struggle is very similar to that between traditional petroleum producers, importers, and flush producers.[2] The drift and surface mines, historically, put intense downward pressure on coal prices, which, in turn, results in wage pressure since labor costs constitute over 66 percent of variable costs (Johnson 1979, 156). Additional distress is caused by competition with residual fuel oil, natural gas, and nuclear power in the boiler-fuel market. Overall demand for coal has dropped significantly during the postwar period.[3]

The income uncertainty of coal producers has manifested itself in terms of political disputes over wages, worker health and safety, and environmental protection. Political intervention, therefore, can be marketed and conducted in language that emphasizes market failure, lends legitimacy to public action, and disguises the producer-income origins of the dissatisfaction. To be sure, environmental protection and, to a lesser degree, worker safety potentially raise market-failure issues, and miners' incomes present legitimate questions about distributive justice; but the intensity and prolonged nature of these coal

---

1. Drift mines are cut into hillsides. They require less capital than traditional underground mines.

2. Flush producers extract oil from large reservoirs that are driven by natural gas or water pressure and, consequently, have low marginal production costs.

3. In 1945, 578 million tons of soft coal were mined; by 1961, however, production was only 403 million tons. U.S. Department of Energy, Energy Information Administration, *Annual Report to Congress, 1981*, vol. 2:125; U.S. Department of Interior and Insular Affairs, Bureau of Mines, *Minerals Yearbook, 1946*, 269.

conflicts stem from their origins in producer attempts to stabilize their incomes through acceptable channels.[4]

Coal-Market Problems: The Congressional Response

From the 1930s to the present, coal disputes have been struggles between traditional Appalachian (northern) underground mines, which are unionized, and their cheaper market substitutes: southern-drift and surface-mined coal, residual fuel oil, natural gas, and nuclear power.[5] The central question in these disputes has been whether public policy would severely constrain features of the substitutes that make them cheaper and/or subsidize aspects of underground mining that make its coal more expensive. The demands of coal groups in this respect have been similar to those made by petroleum interests; until recently, however, Congress largely ignored industry and union pleas for action.

Guffey Coal Act

Coal policy during the 1930s has remarkable parallels with petroleum policy. Efforts on the part of coal companies to substitute producer bargaining for price competition failed until the enactment of the National Industrial Recovery Act under the Roosevelt administration. After the Supreme Court ruled the NIRA unconstitutional, industry leaders and politicians from coal states immediately set out to enact a substitute. The Guffey Coal Act[6] was enacted in August, 1935, with the support of northern coal operators and the United Mine Workers (UMW). The law created twenty-three coal districts whose producers would establish minimum prices and labor rules. Producer votes in each district were weighted according to each firms' coal output. Consequently, large union mines could set the terms of competition for all mines. Nonunion mines resisted passage of this explicit attempt to eliminate price and wage competition, but to no avail.[7] This division between small nonunion (southern and western) mines and large northern union mines still continues (Ackerman and Hassler 1981).

---

4. Wages and worker safety normally would not be market-failure issues as long as miners have a variety of wage and safety packages to choose from; but the rural setting of coal firms restricts the options realistically available to workers and gives coal owners an unusual ability to affect the terms of political and economic life. See Gaventa 1980 and Viscusi 1983.

5. This section draws on Baker 1941; Moyer 1964; and Johnson 1979.

6. PL74–402.

7. Representative Hobbs (D–Ala.) offered a motion to strike the minimum price and wage provisions but was unsuccessful. U.S. Congress, *Congressional Record,* 1935, vol. 79:13550.

In May, 1936, the Supreme Court ruled the Guffey Act unconstitutional because of its labor provisions. The following year, a second Guffey Act passed without explicit labor provisions. The result was unchanged, however, because setting minimum prices eliminates price competition and removes the need for, though does not directly eliminate, wage competition. The law was renewed in 1941 and allowed to expire during World War II, when wage and price controls existed. Efforts to revive the policy after the war were unsuccessful. The large demand created by the war obscured the fact that the Guffey Act, like any price-based attempt to preserve incomes, created rents for low-cost producers, induced further investment, and created the need for output controls to prevent the excess capacity from reducing prices.

After the war, the temporary nature of the coal boom became apparent, and a variety of direct and indirect policies were introduced to stem the decline. Coal, unlike oil, enjoyed only a modest depletion allowance (5 percent). Attempts to raise it close to the 27.5 percent petroleum level failed, although in 1952 it was finally raised to 10 percent.[8] All further attempts to raise the rate were unsuccessful. Other direct efforts to raise the demand for coal, such as subsidizing synthetic fuel research and railroad transportation of coal exports, all failed to become law. In addition, attempts to regulate the use or terminate the subsidization of competitive products, such as nuclear power and residual fuel oil, also met with little success. Conventional wisdom holds that existing industries can successfully use the political system to delay declines that the market would impose.[9] The coal industry is a striking exception to this generalization.

Mechanization, Mine Safety, and Black Lung

After World War II, northern union mines ended direct attempts to regulate the price and wage behavior of their competitors. The locus of struggle shifted to mechanization and mine safety and later to black lung. Ironically, the story begins with union efforts to secure a better living for miners.

Mechanization
John L. Lewis, president of the UMW from 1920 to 1960, concluded that only increased worker productivity achieved through mechanization could ensure miner prosperity. Wage increases not matched by productivity gains would simply price coal out of the very competitive energy market. The problem, of course, was that increased productivity in a declining or stagnant market, such as the post–World War II coal market, would result in decreased employment.

---

8. Revenue Act of 1951 (PL82–183, sec. 319).
9. See Stigler 1971; Posner 1974; Thurow 1980; and Reich 1982, 1983.

Lewis agreed to accept the workforce reduction in return for mine operator recognition and acceptance of the UMW.[10] The results of mechanization were dramatic. From 1945 to 1969, underground productivity rose from 5.78 to 15.61 tons per man-day, average real earnings rose from $149 to $170 per week (in 1969 dollars), and average underground employment fell from 290,000 to 99,269.[11]

Union acceptance and management of mine mechanization, however, had side effects that worsened relations between the modern and marginal segments of the industry. Those miners who lost their jobs did not migrate. Instead, they opened drift mines.[12] Those miners who remained employed were exposed to increasing levels of fine dust created by the machines. The operators of union mines and their workers resisted these effects through political action: first, under the banner of worker safety and, later, black lung.

Mine Safety

Large coal mine disasters led the northern operators and the UMW to lobby for safety legislation. President Truman, using authority granted by the War Powers Act, nationalized the nation's mines to end a strike in spring, 1946. The UMW subsequently signed a contract with the Secretary of the Interior adopting the UMW safety code and giving the miners the right to strike if they felt that an imminent danger of explosion existed. In March, 1947, an explosion in Centralia, Illinois, killed 111 people. The UMW called for permanent use of the safety code, even after the mines were returned to private ownership. The majority of the operators, of course, wanted nothing of the sort.[13] When federal control was relinquished in July, 1947, the Republican-dominated Congress would give only a one-year gutted extension of the UMW code.[14]

Four years later, 119 miners died in West Frankfort, Illinois, and Con-

---

10. Lewis admitted to this Faustian bargain in a congressional subcommittee hearing. U.S. Congress, House, *Welfare of Miners: Hearing before the Subcommittee on Welfare of the Committee on Education and Labor,* 80th Cong., 1st sess., 1947, 41.

11. As you can see, workers did not receive wage increases commensurate with the gains in productivity. Productivity data were drawn from U.S. Department of Energy, Energy Information Administration, *Annual Report to Congress, 1981,* vol. 2:135; U.S. Department of Interior and Insular Affairs, Bureau of Mines, *Minerals Yearbook, 1946,* 284. Wage and employment data come from U.S. Department of Labor, Bureau of Labor Statistics, *Employment and Earnings, 1909–1975,* 3.

12. See note 1.

13. U.S. Congress, House, *Welfare of Miners: Hearing before the Subcommittee on Welfare of the Committee on Education and Labor,* 80th Cong., 1st sess., 1947; U.S. Congress, Senate, *Investigation of Mine Explosion at Centralia, Illinois: Hearing before the Committee on Public Lands,* 80th Cong., 1st sess., 1947, 3.

14. PL80–328. Federal inspectors could use the code as a basis for informing states about violations. No penalties or enforcement powers were provided.

15. PL82–552.

gress mandated federal inspections the next year.[15] The northern operators and the UMW urged passage of the 1946–47 safety code, but to placate southern Democrats and their small-mine constituents, the enacted law had several escape clauses.[16] Mines employing fewer than fifteen miners were exempt from the law. Inspectors were given the power to close mines only if there was an imminent danger of explosion, and the law did not include any provisions regulating unsafe but non-explosion-threatening conditions.

The growth in small-mine production was spectacular after 1952.[17] Testimony from hearings during this era suggests that miners thrown out of work because of mechanization opened up small drift mines to survive, despite the fact that the rate of return was not at all adequate.[18] The UMW and large operators, of course, wanted to eliminate these threats to reorganization of the mining industry along modern capital-intensive, high-productivity, non-price-competitive lines. The independent miners resisted, and John Sherman Cooper in the Senate and several Republicans in the House became their champions. Legislation to repeal the small-mine exemption from safety inspections, repeatedly introduced in the House between 1958 and 1965, always died in the Rules Committee. The House reduced the power of the Rules Committee in the next congressional session, and the repeal passed.[19]

The deaths of 78 miners in 1968 in the Farmington, West Virginia, disaster prompted another, and this time successful, effort to enact a complete mine safety code. The Coal Mine Health and Safety Act of 1969[20] contained incredibly detailed safety regulations similar to those in the code the UMW had been promoting since World War II. The efforts of John Sherman Cooper and others to protect the right of small operators to engage in competition over safety finally collapsed.

The claims of the independent mine operators that the push for safety legislation by large union operators was, in part, an attempt to put them out of business appear to have been true. Neuman and Nelson (1982) report that the 1969 act caused small firms to cease production.[21]

---

16. See U.S. Congress, House, *Coal Mine Safety: Hearing before the Committee on Education and Labor*, 82d Cong., 2d sess., 1952, 208, 327, 459.

17. The output of the smallest mines (less than 10,000 tons annually) grew from 13.735 million tons in 1954 to 20.212 million tons in 1959, an increase of 50 percent; at the same time, total coal production increased by only 5 percent. U.S. Department of Interior and Insular Affairs, Bureau of Mines, *Minerals Yearbooks*.

18. U.S. Congress, Senate, *Federal Coal Mine Health and Safety Act: Hearing before the Committee on Labor and Public Welfare*, 85th Cong., 2d sess., 1958, 112–13. Moyer (1964, 175) reports a negative rate of return for mines producing less than 100,000 tons annually.

19. PL89–376.

20. PL91–173.

21. Lewis-Beck and Alford (1980) report that the 1969 act decreased fatalities even after changes in industry composition (small-mine closures) were taken into account. Neuman and Nelson find that controlling for industry composition cancels out the effect of the act. The

Small-mine bankruptcies did not result from governmental intervention per se, but from the particular form of intervention. Worker safety issues are not normally thought of as market failures as long as labor can choose between different packages of wage and safety provisions under conditions of informed consent. In Appalachia, however, labor choices are constrained. Coal mining is one of the few occupations available, creating unusual labor-market power for the mine owners. Policy intervention, therefore, can be justified. The particular form that policy intervention took in this case, though, hurt small mines.

The optimal solution would have been an injury tax. The isolation of coal firms presumably allows them to pay lower wages, given the industry's injury/fatality rate, than they would if they had to compete with safer occupations. An injury tax would capture the excess profits that result from this situation and recycle them to workers to equal the compensation they normally would have received for a similarly hazardous occupation in a competitive setting. If small mines really were as safe as the lobbyists claimed, then small-mine operators would not have been threatened by this policy. The enacted legislation, however, worked very much to the disadvantage of the small operators because it mandated the installation and use of equipment that would result in increased worker safety. Safety conditions may have improved because of the legislation, but a more certain result was an increased need for capital, something the independents did not have.

Black Lung
In addition to creating safety regulations that made life difficult for small-mine owners, the 1969 Health and Safety Act also socialized the costs of the major negative result from mechanization of the large mines—Black Lung disease (pneumoconiosis)—a chronic condition afflicting people exposed to dust particles too small in diameter to be trapped by the cilia and mucous membranes of the bronchial system. The particles come to rest directly in the alveoli and considerably reduce the transfer of oxygen from the lungs to the bloodstream. Those suffering from the condition progressively lose their ability to perform physical tasks. Coal mines have always been dusty, but the shift in production methods increased the potential hazard. Particles created by labor-intensive production methods are large enough to be trapped by the body's defensive mechanisms; mechanized production, however, creates particles too small to be captured.

---

contradictory results may stem from the different measures used in the two studies. The fatality rate is measured by fatalities per man-hour in the Lewis-Beck and Alford study and by fatalities per ton in the Neuman and Nelson article. Lewis-Beck and Alford measure industry composition in terms of the percentage of mines producing less than 10,000 tons annually, while Neuman and Nelson use the percentage of coal output produced in small mines. Similar differences exist for all the indicators used in both studies.

Worker's compensation programs are creatures of the states, and coal states never recognized Black Lung as an occupationally related disease in order to avoid raising the tax rates on coal operators. By attaching a federal program of Black Lung transfers to the 1969 act, Senator Jennings Randolph created the coalition necessary for the passage of this legislation.[22]

Surface Mining

Although underground mine operators concentrated their efforts on controlling small-mine competition, surface mine output had become the real nemesis.[23] Ironically, while underground mine operators were using safety policy to further their interests, other federal policies were threatening their market position.

The Tennessee Valley Authority was created to develop cheap hydroelectric power to encourage industrial development in the South.[24] As might be expected, energy-intensive industries (including the government's nuclear laboratories at Oak Ridge, Tennessee) located in the region and created electricity demands that exceeded hydroelectric capabilities. To meet the new demand, the TVA built numerous coal-fired electricity generating plants and swiftly became the single largest consumer of coal in the United States. Its policy of soliciting competitive bids for coal put tremendous downward pressure on prices.[25] The most obvious technique at coal operators' disposal to cope with these pressures was to surface mine.[26] Thus, an unanticipated consequence of the TVA's attempt to encourage Appalachian development was a reduction in underground mine employment and an increase in environmental degradation.

Surface mining began to grow rapidly in the mid-1960s. The struggle to enact federal regulation of surface mines began in earnest with the introduction of President Johnson's bill in 1968 and ended with the passage of the

22. Federal subsidy of Black Lung payments was limited to three years in the 1969 act, after which time responsibility was to revert to state worker's compensation systems and the coal companies. In 1971 and 1973, Congress twice delayed the day of reckoning. In 1978, responsibility for post-1973 claims finally was placed on a disability fund financed by a tax on coal (fifty cents per underground ton and twenty-five cents per surface ton, PL95–239). In 1981, PL97–119 doubled the tax rates.

23. In 1945, surface mining accounted for 19 percent of the nation's bituminous output; in 1963, 33 percent; and by 1970, 40.5 percent. See U.S. Department of Energy, Energy Information Administration, *Annual Report to Congress, 1981*, vol. 2:125.

24. See Vietor 1980 and Jacobs 1984.

25. In constant 1972 dollars, the average price per ton of coal in the United States was $8.62 in 1951 and $5.75 in 1969. See U.S. Department of Energy, Energy Information Administration, *Annual Report to Congress, 1981*, vol. 2:143.

26. The productivity of surface mines has been three times that of underground mines since 1970. See U.S. Department of Energy, Energy Information Administration, *Annual Report to Congress, 1981*, vol. 2:135.

Surface Mining Control and Reclamation Act of 1977.[27] In between, President Ford vetoed two bills, in 1974 and 1975. As in previous cases, the UMW and underground operators favored federal restrictions, while surface mine owners resisted them. By 1977, however, the UMW had organized numerous surface operations, and its attitude dramatically shifted toward opposition of regulation.[28]

Coal Transportation Issues: Railroads versus Slurry Pipelines

Price discrimination is an essential feature of railroad rates because marginal costs are much less than average costs. Low-value commodities that have high demand elasticities are shipped at rates close to marginal cost, while high-value commodities with low demand elasticities are charged rates far above costs. Price discrimination captures the consumers' surplus of the low-elasticity shipper to cover the large fixed costs of running the railroad (Friedlaender 1969, 63).

In general, coal operators benefit from this state of affairs, although publicly they carry the populist torch of the captive shipper, much like the traditional behavior of western grain farmers. Coal is a low-value commodity whose final demand elasticity is fairly high because of competition with residual fuel oil (Moyer 1964, 56). Rail-rate markups for coal are among the lowest of any commodity group (Friedlaender 1969, 56).[29] However, these markups vary by location. Rates are lower in regions where water transportation and petroleum competition are present than in inland regions far from barge traffic and oil pipelines. In the latter areas, slurry pipeline movements periodically appear. Railroad interests, however, have prevented them from receiving the necessary eminent domain authority from Congress.

Coal Conversion

Coal-conversion policy, the final aspect of coal policy I will discuss, is not rooted in the producer struggles that have dominated all the policies mentioned so far. Instead, it is a direct consequence of the petroleum policies adopted by

---

27. PL95–87.

28. See U.S. Congress, House, *Reclamation Practices and Environmental Practices of Surface Mining: Hearing before the Subcommittee on Energy and Environment of the Committee on Interior and Insular Affairs*, 95th Cong., 1st sess., 1977, pt. 3, 10–11; U.S. Congress, House, *Regulation of Strip Mining: Hearing before the Subcommittee on Mines and Mining of the Committee on Interior and Insular Affairs*, 92d Cong., 1st sess., 1971, 331.

29. Friedlaender modified her position somewhat in 1981, when she concluded that bulk commodities were charged rates equal to or slightly above marginal cost and manufactured goods were carried at rates below marginal cost (Friedlaender and Spady 1981, chap. 3).

Congress after 1973. In adopting oil price controls to eliminate rents and placate consumers, Congress gave itself no choice but to adopt regulations and subsidies to induce the substitution away from oil, which was essential, but not in anyone's pecuniary interest, given that prices were restrained.

The Energy Supply and Environmental Coordination Act of 1974[30] directed the Federal Energy Administration (FEA) to prohibit the use of oil or natural gas by electric utilities that could use coal (the FEA's authority was discretionary for other fuel-burning facilities) and authorized the FEA to require that new electric power plants be able to use coal.

The Energy Policy and Conservation Act of 1975 extended these powers from June, 1975, to June, 1977, and in a fairly blatant handout to the UMW, authorized $750 million in loan guarantees for new underground low-sulphur mines.[31]

President Carter, in his National Energy Plan, proposed to tax industrial use of oil and natural gas as part of his overall strategy to replace the framework of regulations and price controls with replacement-cost pricing and rent redistribution. Congress did not follow the president's request and, instead, continued the coal-conversion process (1) by mandating that existing utility boilers convert to coal by 1990 and that new utility and industrial boilers use coal immediately, and (2) by allowing the Department of Energy to order existing boilers to convert before 1990 if necessary.[32] Congress, however, backed down from this stance in some provisions tucked away in the mammoth Omnibus Reconciliation Act of 1981.[33] Existing utility users of natural gas, located mainly in the Southwest, would only have to file conservation plans, and not actually discontinue use, in 1990. In 1987 Congress backed down and repealed the coal-conversion requirements altogether even for new power plants.[34]

Summary

Coal's policy history, like petroleum's, has been a series of struggles between high-cost original producers (northern unionized mines) and their lower-cost substitutes (southern and western mines). Unlike petroleum producers, however, coal operators and unionized miners have had great difficulty in securing legislation beneficial to their interests. The large increase in the price of oil and the subsequent increase in coal prices during the 1970s aided the industry much more than stabilization through policy.

---

30. PL93–319.
31. For an account of the odd coalition between eastern coal operators, the UMW, and environmentalists, see Ackerman and Hassler 1981.
32. PL95–620.
33. PL97–35, Title X, sec. 1021.
34. PL100–42

From the 1930s until 1970, the coal industry was plagued with chronic excess capacity. Disinvestment was slow because of the reluctance of marginal workers and operators to migrate from Appalachia. The struggle over safety legislation after World War II was a manifestation of the struggle between the modern and marginal sectors over excess capacity. Ironically, the 1969 Coal Mine Health and Safety Act not only caused the exodus of small mines, but also resulted in a drastic decrease in productivity in those underground mines that remained open, eliminating any competitive advantage created by the small-mine exodus.[35]

During the Carter administration, unionized coal operators and miners were more successful in stabilizing their markets through policy. Since the mid-1960s, the threat to established underground mines has come from western surface mining of low sulphur coal. The passage of the Surface Mine Reclamation and Control Act of 1977 and the new source performance standards in the Clean Air Act Amendments of 1977 decreased both the productivity and pollution advantages held by western coal.

The Origins of Natural Gas Market Problems

Natural gas markets possess characteristics that are similar to petroleum, with two exceptions (MacAvoy and Pindyck 1975; Sanders 1981). Natural gas producers have been immune to import competition, and the retail segment of the industry has been a regulated monopoly since its coal-gas origins. Consequently, two sources of income variation that have had large consequences in petroleum economic history have been absent in the natural gas context. The determination of producer prices, however, has generated political struggle. Congress correctly decided in 1938 that production of natural gas did not suffer from market failure and could not be improved by public policy. Later court decisions imposed such regulation, however, and a struggle ensued over the proper distribution of excess profits, although it was disguised as a struggle over "proper prices." As long as price controls did not create shortages, natural gas politics were quiescent. However, when the difference between the controlled price and market-clearing price became large, as it did after 1973, the struggles between producers and consumers over the distribution of excess profits became prominent.

Natural Gas Market Problems: The Congressional Response

Two issues have been central to natural gas policy. Do pipeline and producer prices suffer from market failures that warrant public action? Congress cor-

---

35. See Neuman and Nelson 1982; U.S. Department of Energy, Energy Information Administration, *Annual Report to Congress, 1981,* 135.

rectly decided initially that pipelines were natural monopolies and thus deserved public-utility regulation, while natural gas production did not suffer from market failure and, consequently, could not be improved by public policy. Later court decisions imposed producer-price regulation, however, and Congress has experienced great difficulty in repealing the price controls that benefit so many urban consumers, although total decontrol finally became law in the summer of 1989.[36]

The Natural Gas Act and the Supreme Court

Congress passed the Natural Gas Act[37] in 1938 to remedy the problem of monopoly power exercised by the interstate pipelines. The Federal Power Commission (FPC) was granted the authority to regulate pipeline rates.

All was well until 1947, when the Supreme Court suggested in *Interstate Natural Gas Co. v. Federal Power Commission* that the congressional exemption of "production and gathering" in the 1938 act only applied to regulation of the physical processes of production, not the sale of the product. This language spurred southwestern congressmen to action. Senator Moore (R–Okla.), and Representatives Rizley (R–Okla.) and Priest (D–Tenn.) introduced bills specifically declaring that Congress, in the 1938 act, had no intention of ever regulating producer prices. Unlike petroleum conflicts, in which domestic, international, integrated, and nonintegrated firms had different market positions and policy preferences, natural gas disputes did not exhibit cleavages among producers.[38] Natural gas already had become a producers-versus-consumers battleground. President Truman, responding to consumer fears, vetoed an exemption bill in 1950.

The election of President Eisenhower pleased natural gas producers, who reasonably assumed that under a Republican administration passage of an exemption would be obtained easily. The legislation was made all the more urgent by a 1954 Supreme Court decision. In *Phillips Petroleum v. Wisconsin*, the Court ruled that the FPC must regulate natural gas prices at the wellhead. Legislation exempting independent producers passed both the House and Senate in 1956. Before the president had signed, however, Senator Francis Case reported that he had been offered a bribe for his favorable vote. President Eisenhower vetoed the legislation to avoid a scandal. In the next few congresses, Oren Harris of Arkansas dutifully introduced exemption bills, but they never left committee.

---

36. PL101–60. This section of chapter 4 draws on MacAvoy and Pindyck 1975 and Sanders 1981.

37. PL75–688.

38. Natural gas distributors, of course, did want price controls so as to encourage consumption, as long as shortages did not result.

Natural Gas Policy during the Energy Crisis

In the 1970s, natural gas became involved in the same conflicts as petroleum, but with an additional twist. Federal price controls applied only to natural gas sold in interstate commerce. Intrastate gas was exempt. Policymakers thus faced two dilemmas. As the gap between the interstate and intrastate prices grew, producers sold their product within the state and did not dedicate new supplies to the interstate pipelines. Second, as the BTU equivalent prices of natural gas and oil diverged, consumers switched to natural gas. Shortages were the predictable result. From 1973 to 1978, consumer-state Democrats fought brutal battles over natural gas pricing, similar to those over petroleum pricing, with producer-state Democrats allied with the administration. Again, the underlying issue, although no one ever publicly proclaimed it as such, was the allocation of rents. Oil shortages made natural gas more valuable, much like the effect of coffee shortages on tea prices. Higher natural gas prices have a legitimate allocative role to play, but low-cost producers receive excess profits (inframarginal rents) as a result.

Both Presidents Nixon and Ford favored the decontrol of new natural gas prices, the same policy Congress had enacted for petroleum prices in the EPAA, but northeastern Democrats favored continued controls on all natural gas.[39] President Carter, during his 1976 campaign, made the same promise as Nixon and Ford; but once elected, Carter, in his National Energy Plan, called for the merger of the interstate and intrastate markets at a new controlled price of $1.75 per million BTUs for new gas.[40]

In a convoluted attempt to provide producers with prices that equaled marginal cost but did not generate excess profits (very similar to what the EPAA did for oil), the Natural Gas Policy Act of 1978[41] created various categories of natural gas, each of which received different prices. New natural gas was set at $1.75 per million BTUs. The price rose at the rate of the GNP deflator plus approximately 6 percent per year until 1985, when it was deregulated. Old interstate gas received the current contract rate plus the GNP deflator. When the contracts were rolled over, they would receive $.54 or the "just and reasonable" rate if they were already above $.54. Old intrastate gas received the contract price or $1.00, whichever was higher, plus the GNP deflator. Old intrastate gas selling for more than $1.00 also was deregulated in January, 1985. The most interesting provisions of the act pertained to the distribution

---

39. In 1974, Congress raised prices from the $.20 per million BTU range to $.42. In 1976, it raised the level to $1.42.

40. This price was chosen because it made oil and natural gas equivalent in terms of the heat (BTUs) available from each and ended the incentives for consumers to switch from scarce fuel (oil) to scarce fuel (gas). This price compared with the then current Federal Power Commission level of $1.42 and the unregulated intrastate level of over $2.00.

41. PL95–621.

of the price increases. The act mandated that residential customers would be charged as if they had received nothing other than old gas. Only industrial and commercial users would face the new marginal cost. Home heating customers would still face tremendous incentives to use or convert to natural gas.

The ironic effect of "protecting" residential consumers from marginal-cost pricing was to raise the cost of new gas in the 1980s above market-clearing levels (Williams 1985). Price controls on old gas and average-cost pricing for residential consumers ensured that the natural gas market would clear if and only if the price of new gas were bid up above the spot-price level. The resulting average price of overpriced new gas and underpriced old gas cleared the market initially, but because the only users to directly pay the excessive price for new gas were the most elastic industrial and commercial users, the initial average-price equilibrium was not stable. These elastic users switched to oil or coal (or shut down because of the 1981–83 recession), and demand for natural gas dropped. Pipeline companies, however, had signed contracts for the new gas with take-or-pay clauses in them, so they had to pay for the new gas even though they did not use it. Pipelines raised their rates to cover these costs, and many members of Congress mistakenly believed that the take-or-pay contract provisions were the source of the problem, rather than the average-cost pricing policy. In 1984, the House Energy and Commerce Committee approved a measure that would have allowed an arbitrator to renegotiate the provisions of take-or-pay contracts and would have capped escalator clauses at their December 31, 1984, levels, but House Speaker O'Neill never brought the measure to the floor to prevent open divisions in the Democratic party during a presidential election year.

By 1989, gas under price controls had become such a small share of the market (6 percent) that the differences between a controlled and decontrolled world had become largely semantic, and a bill ending all controls by 1993 became law (Hager 1989).[42]

The Origins of Nuclear Power Market Problems

Commercial nuclear power differs from the other markets I have discussed because private firms never would have produced nuclear electricity without subsidies. The nuclear industry did not suffer from volatile incomes, but rather from no income at all. Two features of nuclear technology inhibit the development of commercially viable power production, while a third drives entrepreneurs to ask Congress to ameliorate the first two.

First, the immense expense and long lead times inherent in the development of nuclear technology make it unlikely that private research and development expenditures will be optimal. Even if reasonable calculations show

---

42. PL101–60.

that forty years of development, for example, would result in a technology with net benefit to society, private firms might not undertake the necessary research because of the lag time between their investment and first revenues and because of the difficulty in restricting use of the resulting knowledge to those who pay. Commodities that possess these characteristics warrant public subsidy of accompanying research and development. The main question in the case of nuclear power, of course, is whether long-term net benefits will result and thus warrant the use of state subsidies to overcome the research and development problem. The answer provided by public-goods auctions (had they been held) would have varied across the last forty years as citizen assessments of nuclear power changed.

The externalities imposed by the hazards of radiation exposure constitute the second characteristic of nuclear power that inhibits development. The lack of private insurers willing to indemnify owners of reactors against radiation effects eliminates interest in ownership. Well-known solutions for dealing with risk and third-party harm exist, but nuclear power creates unusual problems because accidents, while very unlikely, will have large negative consequences should they occur. An additional complication exists because these externalities involve future generations. The determination and weighting of costs and benefits in problems of social choice are difficult even when only the current generation is affected. Once the preferences of future inhabitants become germane, the problem grows intractable.

The standard remedy for this type of externality condition is the creation of a market-like situation for the commodity that is overused (underpriced), so that an optimal amount of harm is created by the production activity. In the case of nuclear power, adequate markets do not exist for exposure to radioactive substances. An unlikely, but theoretically correct, solution to this problem would be to inform the public of the increased likelihood of radioactive exposure that would result from both plant operation and waste-disposal methods and the consequences of such exposure, and then ask the public how much compensation they would require before they would consent to nuclear power.[43] In practice, the best that can be expected is the creation of an exposure standard, with an auction to allocate the hazard rights to firms. Since the realistic outcome of such a procedure would be severe limits on the number of plants in operation, this may explain why existing policies do not use these procedures.

Despite the impediments to nuclear power, utilities favor capital-intensive nuclear production strategies because they receive a guaranteed rate

---

43. The EPA, in fact, has conducted such a policy exercise with an arsenic smelter in Tacoma, Washington. The public was informed of the likely risks associated with ambient arsenic and the likely reduction in employment that would occur if pollution-reduction investments were carried out. See Kalikow 1984.

of return on invested capital (Kahn 1971, vol. 2, chap. 2). As a consequence, they have strongly supported public policies that underwrite the cost of nuclear development and limit radiation liability.[44]

Nuclear Power Problems: The Congressional Response

Congressional action on the microeconomic choices presented by nuclear power can be divided into two distinct phases.[45] In the first phase, from 1954 to 1974, Congress treated nuclear plants like dams and post offices—shiny new toys that make life better and allow credit taking. Democrats and liberal interest groups, especially the AFL-CIO, promoted nuclear power, while Republicans and private utilities were more skeptical of the need to subsidize the rush into the nuclear age. Labor and public-power groups saw nuclear power as the little people's panacea, another in the line of New Deal inventions that made working-class incomes higher without directly tackling the issue of how incomes should be distributed. In their view, the only obstacle to the land of milk and honey was the intransigence of the private utilities.[46]

The policy results of these viewpoints were programs to subsidize the development of commercial nuclear power and to ignore the social costs despite the objections of coal representatives.[47] Republicans succeeded in preventing an all-out, publicly funded campaign to build nuclear reactors, but shortly

---

44. Industry supports nuclear power because of its high capital and low marginal costs, not because it is the cheapest source of enthalpy (heat) at the margin. Lovins (1977, 134) has shown convincingly that nuclear electricity is the most expensive marginal source of delivered energy.

45. For a concise history of commercial atomic energy, see Bupp and Derian 1978.

46. See U.S. Congress, *S. 3233 and H.R. 8862 to Amend the Atomic Energy Act of 1946: Hearing before the Joint Committee on Atomic Energy,* 83d Cong., 2d sess., 1954, 303 (rural cooperatives), 445 (Cooperative League of the United States); U.S. Congress, *Accelerating Civilian Reactor Program: Hearing before the Joint Committee on Atomic Energy,* 84th Cong., 2d sess., 1956, 187, 204 (comments of Walter Cisler, chairman of Detroit Edison); U.S. Congress, *Development, Growth, and State of the Atomic Energy Industry: Hearing before the Joint Committee on Atomic Energy,* 86th Cong., 1st sess., 1959, 279 (AFL-CIO); U.S. Congress, *Development, Growth, and State of the Atomic Energy Industry: Hearing before the Joint Committee on Atomic Energy,* 87th Cong., 1st sess., 1961, 243 (Craig Hosmer (R–Ca.) can't understand the rush). The most consistent pessimist regarding the costs of nuclear power was Phillip Sporn, president of American Electric Power, the largest private coal-fired utility in the nation. For a compilation of this exchange of views, see U.S. Congress, Joint Committee on Atomic Energy, *Nuclear Power Economics, 1962 through 1967,* 90th Cong., 2d sess., 1968.

47. Three primary subsidies were enacted during this time. First, in 1957, Congress created a cooperative program in which the Atomic Energy Commission subsidized the construction of reactors sponsored and operated by private utilities (PL85–162). Second, starting in 1958, NATO allies received subsidies to purchase American light-water-reactor technology under the Euratom Program. Finally, government charges for the supply and enrichment of uranium did not take into account capital or inventory costs. Two episodes illustrate the lack of effective policies for externalities. In 1957, the Price-Anderson Nuclear Insurance and Indemnification Act (PL85–

thereafter the private utilities forgot their earlier sentiments and embarked on a nuclear orgy.

The stampede toward nuclear power started in December, 1963, when General Electric signed a turnkey contract with Jersey Central Power and Lighting Company.[48] The contract guaranteed the ultimate price of the power plant at a figure quite competitive with coal. Eight more turnkey contracts were signed in 1964, and between 1966 and 1967, forty-nine orders for plants were placed without price guarantees. These latter purchases were predicated on the belief that the turnkey prices were credible and that economies of scale from larger reactors and the learning process would decrease costs, in much the same way that coal-fired electricity had become progressively cheaper since World War II. As the first plants opened in the early 1970s, the fact that they cost three times their estimates did not discourage nuclear proponents, but by 1978, the ever-increasing costs of nuclear power were an inescapable fact. No orders have been placed since.

From 1974 on, Congress no longer uniformly viewed nuclear power as innocuous pork barrel. In 1974, the renewal of the Price-Anderson Insurance Act ran into some heavy opposition. The subsidy was eliminated, and the cap on liability was almost removed.[49] That same year, the responsibility for regulation and subsidization of atomic energy, previously vested in the Atomic Energy Commission, was divided between the Energy Research and Development Administration and the Nuclear Regulatory Commission.[50] In 1976, the Ford administration proposed that future uranium-enrichment capacity be provided by private firms. This, of course, implied an end to the below-market charges to which the utilities had become accustomed. The bill did not succeed, but the fiscal 1978 Energy Research and Development Administration (ERDA) authorization legislation stipulated that federal enrichment services should be priced at levels not detrimental to private efforts.[51]

The final blow to nuclear subsidies occurred in October, 1983, when the Senate refused to continue funding the Clinch River breeder reactor. When the Senate majority leader (Howard Baker) cannot maintain funding for a project

---

256) limited the liability of commercial reactor owners to $500 million for each reactor incident and subsidized the difference between the amount of insurance privately available and the $500 million ceiling. Second, attempts by the American Federation of Labor to enact radiation regulation and research in the Department of Health, Education, and Welfare to counter the laissez-faire Atomic Energy Commission approach went nowhere in 1957 (S. 1228), 1959 (H.R. 7612), 1962 (S. 3472), 1963 (S. 1754), and 1967 (S. 2067).

48. The contracts between the utilities specified that for a fixed price the manufacturer (General Electric or Westinghouse) would provide a nuclear power plant. All the utility had to do was turn the key and start it up.

49. PL94–197.

50. PL93–438.

51. PL95–238.

in his own state, one can safely say that policies to subsidize nuclear power research and development are on their last legs.

Summary

Despite its apparent complexity, nuclear policy involves very simple issues. Commercial nuclear power requires two types of policy support: research and development subsidies and externality regulations preventing vetoes of plant operation by those who may suffer harm as a result of nuclear radiation. Since 1974, the Joint Committee on Atomic Energy and its successors have been increasingly unable to deliver those two policy outcomes. Consequently, the market for nuclear power has disappeared.

Conclusion

Coal and natural gas policy conflicts (like petroleum conflicts) typically involve attempts by consumers or firms to protect their incomes from market forces that would erode them. The congressional response, however, has differed from the response exhibited in the petroleum context. Congress ignored the demands of unionized coal firms for protection against their surface and nonunion competitors from the end of World War II until the passage of the Clean Air and Surface Mining Control Acts in 1977. Moreover, Congress actually enacted sound natural gas policy in 1938, but once the Supreme Court controlled consumer prices in its 1954 *Phillips* decision, Congress was most reluctant to force voters to experience market (higher) prices. The Natural Gas Act of 1978 decontrolled the price of new natural gas in 1985, but the reluctance of Congress to force consumers to pay marginal costs actually raised prices of new natural gas above the spot-market level and distorted the decisions of industrial and commercial users. By 1989 controlled gas was such a small portion of natural gas sales that total decontrol became law quite easily.

Nuclear power problems exist because Congress overrode market forces that inhibited nuclear power development—radiation risk and long research and development lead times. Ironically, the use of command-and-control regulation to solve the safety and radiation externality issues has increased the cost of power plants so much that nuclear power is effectively dead for the time being, although the incentives that cause utilities to favor nuclear power in the first place (guaranteed return on a capital-intensive investment) will cause the pronuclear bandwagon to roll again when the next oil shock occurs.

Part 2
Determining the Causes of
Congressional Policy Choices

CHAPTER 5

Positive Theory

When Congress has made energy-policy choices, why have misguided and counterproductive proposals so often defeated economically sound alternatives? A complete answer to this question and, more generally, a complete theory of the policy process, would explain both where the proposals came from (agenda formation) and why Congress enacts some proposals and not others (legislative action). In accounting for requests, the theory would explain what factors cause actors to object to particular social conditions and seek redress from the government. In accounting for responses, it would explain the distribution of support for the various alternatives on the agenda and why only some of these proposals become law.

In the case of energy policies, for example, a full explanation would begin by specifying which factors cause citizens to view energy-market conditions as a problem and cause them to intensify their beliefs. It would go on to account for the differing support for different classes of proposals and conclude by explaining why research and development proposals, for example, have enjoyed more legislative success than proposals to price petroleum at replacement cost.

Agenda Formation

The importance of agenda formation in the overall policy process is a variable bounded by two extreme theoretical possibilities. At one extreme, agenda formation is completely determined by the likelihood of enactment success; that is, no ideas are introduced as legislation unless they are certain to become law. Under this scenario, policy outcomes are determined solely at the agenda formation stage because all ideas introduced into the legislature are enacted into law. At the other extreme, agenda formation is driven by issue relevance; that is, all ideas relevant to policy problems are introduced as legislation. Factors affect the policy process only through legislative action. Agenda formation, per se, has no independent effect on policy outcomes. In between these two theoretical extremes, of course, agenda formation and legislative action would vary in their relative importance to the determination of policy outcomes.

A theory of agenda formation would answer two questions: why proposals are introduced in Congress at some times and not others (issue salience), and why some ideas relevant to a policy problem are introduced as legislation while others remain just ideas (bias in the idea selection).[1] Both questions need to be considered because some factors affect whether the legislature pays attention at all to a policy problem (issue salience) rather than which ideas, among those that are relevant to a policy problem, are introduced as legislation.

Scholarly attention to agenda formation has focused largely on idea selection and not issue salience. Bachrach and Baratz (1962), for example, argue that certain (usually radical) solutions to policy problems are never introduced as legislation in Congress. Our ability to develop and empirically validate the theories of salience and bias, however, is exactly opposite their importance and the amount of scholarly attention they receive. A theory of agenda salience can be developed and verified but is not that important, whereas bias in idea selection is the heart of the agenda controversy but theoretically and empirically difficult to develop.

Issue Salience

Why do market conditions vary in their political salience across time? In chapters 3 and 4, I developed a theory of the timing of topic salience within the energy-market context. Energy commodities possess certain features that cause both producers and consumers to be dissatisfied with market outcomes. This dissatisfaction can be the product of market failures or income (equity) concerns. In my view, the majority of energy proposals arise from producer and consumer attempts to stabilize and increase their incomes and not from genuine market failures. When consumer and/or producer incomes come under stress because of energy-market conditions, the salience of energy-policy proposals increases.

Idea Selection

Idea selection, the second component of the agenda process, is usually explained in a manner similar to that employed in the context of legislative action. The probability that an idea will be formally introduced as legislation is dependent on the policy positions of the usual gamut of actors in American pluralism—members of Congress, the president, leaders of executive agencies, organized interests, and the general public. I do not fully develop and empirically validate this theory because I believe there is little bias in idea selection, at least for energy issues. In my view, very few ideas are not

---

1. See Kingdon 1984 for a discussion of both timing and bias.

introduced in Congress simply because they are unlikely to pass or because they threaten the prerogatives of important institutions.[2] In short, little leverage would be gained by developing a theory of which ideas do not get on the agenda because in energy policy, at least, almost all ideas do.

Even if the proposals introduced in Congress were a biased sample of the universe of ideas and even if important political actors exerted their influence at the agenda formation stage and not in legislative selection, validating an explanation of this process would be extremely difficult. The largest problems occur in specifying the unit of analysis. In particular, whose suggestions would be included as cases? Should the ideas be limited to those originating in academic sources or should the legislative agendas of unions, corporations, political organizations, and press editorials be cases as well? It seems reasonable to ask why certain solutions to the problems of the steel industry have become congressional bills while others have remained only as ideas in books or memoranda, but what are the boundaries of ideas affecting the steel industry? How would one find all the proposals or ensure that the sample was random? How would one determine the positions of actors toward these cases?

I cannot ignore agenda formation and still claim to have explained the complete process of public policy enactment. In the energy-policy area, however, the consequences of my downplaying agenda formation and concentrating on legislative action are minor. I find no systematic difference between the energy-policy solutions available to society and those ideas actually introduced into Congress.

Legislative Action

A proposal becomes law when a majority of lawmakers vote in favor of it at each stage in the policy process (committee, floor, and conference) and the president signs the resulting legislation. About this aspect of legislative action, there is little controversy. Instead, the focus of debate centers on why members of Congress favor certain proposals over others.[3]

If members maximize their probability of reelection, then they favor proposals until the expected value of marginal gains in votes that would come from proposal supporters is equal to the expected value of marginal losses in votes that would come from those who oppose proposals (Becker 1983). Analysts often classify the causes of these vote gains and losses into two categories. Members' own policy views can affect policy choices in situations in

---

2. I will elaborate on the evidence for my view in later chapters, after I formally operationalize the unit of analysis and sample-selection procedures.

3. See Kingdon 1973 and Jackson 1974 for two previous attempts by political scientists to explain legislators' decisions. See Peltzman 1984 for an overview and update of economists' attempts to explain congressional voting behavior.

which interest-group, executive-branch, and voter policy preferences do not affect the vote-gain and vote-loss functions. Actors with a stake in policy outcomes also may influence members' policy behavior in a variety of ways, including persuasion, exit, cue effects, and anticipated reactions.[4]

Legislators' Preferences

Members of Congress certainly have policy beliefs, but under what conditions can they implement them? Some scholars believe that if all potential winners and losers are represented by well-organized groups, the ability of members to implement their own views is enhanced because the various pressures cancel each other out, creating room for individual discretion (Bauer, Pool, and Dexter 1963, chap. 5). Others simply argue that the beliefs of members have more of an effect on outcomes than do other actors' preferences (Wilson 1977, chap. 8). Both claims depend on the slopes of the expected vote-gain and vote-loss functions. If the slopes are large, then any small perturbation from the policy equilibrium results in large changes in voter support. Under these conditions, all preferences have large effects on outcomes. If the slopes are small, then large changes in outcomes have little effect on expected vote gains and losses. Only under the latter circumstances can members implement their own policy preferences because policy outcomes do not cause citizens to change their voting behavior significantly.

Asking whether members of Congress have discretion to implement their own policy views is directly analogous to asking how closely firms have to follow consumers' preferences. In the latter case, the answer depends on two factors—the ease with which other firms can enter the industry and the demand elasticities of the goods produced by the firm. If entry is difficult and demand elasticities are low, then the firm has more discretion than in situations in which entry is easy and demand elasticities are high. In the case of elected officials, the reasoning is comparable. If political entry is easy and changes in policy outcomes have large effects on challenger and voter behavior, then legislators have little discretion. If entry is difficult and large changes in policy outcomes have small effects on challenger and voter behavior, then legislators have much discretion.

Influence Relations

Legislators' positions[5] may be affected by the positions of other political actors such as the president, leaders of bureaucracies, organized business and

---

4. See Nordlinger 1981 for a review of various empirical democratic theories.

5. I use the term *preferences* to describe actors' private dispositions toward policy proposals and the term *positions* to refer to the public act they carry out in support of or in opposition to proposals. Positional behavior may differ from preferences for strategic or other reasons.

citizen groups, and members of the general public. Legislators actually may be persuaded by the intellectual soundness of the policy positions of these actors, or they may simply defer to lobbyists' viewpoints because the lobbyists possess resources that could affect reelection much as consumer tastes alter the behavior of firms in product markets. Of the two modes of explanation, the "resources" version dominates.[6] Under this view, members of Congress have various real and symbolic policy "products" to sell.[7] If members' policy products do not match their constituents' preferences, the legislators run the risk of being put out of business by competitors whose beliefs match those of the constituents.[8]

Different authors within this tradition emphasize the effects of different actors. Jones (1975), for example, focuses on the affect of the public. He claims that during the passage of the Clean Air Act Amendments of 1970, many actors, including President Nixon and leading presidential contender Edmund Muskie, engaged in a bidding war over who could offer policies to clean up the environment most thoroughly and satisfy an aroused citizenry.[9]

While public opinion plays a role in the passage of legislation, discrete groups also have an impact on Capitol Hill. The ability of organizations to delay or prevent the passage of bills they oppose, as well as secure the enactment of legislation they desire, led scholars to revise their pluralist notions to account better for the influence of interest groups.[10]

Interest groups control money and can generate publicity about members' actions on legislation. Both of these resources can create electoral fear among legislators and prompt them to vote in accord with interest-group positions. One prominent example involved the banking industry's extensive publicity campaign to arouse citizen opposition to the withholding of taxes from interest and dividends.[11]

Bureaucrats, the chief executive, and fellow legislators also control resources that individual legislators might find helpful in fulfilling their goals.

---

6. A prominent exception to this view is Kingdon 1973.

7. Real policies actually affect constituent welfare (Downs 1957), while symbolic policies merely convince constituents that public actions improve their lives or, at the very least, show that the public sector cares (Edelman 1967; Mayhew 1974).

8. These propositions are, of course, the heart of original pluralist theory. For the classical literature, see Truman 1951; Latham 1952, chap. 2; and Gross 1953, chap. 2. See Fiorina 1981 for a contemporary empirical assessment.

9. The public-interest theory of economic regulation also holds that changes in public opinion are a sufficient condition for Congress to respond. Market failure causes the public to demand ameliorative policies, and Congress, in turn, passes remedies (Posner 1974, 336–40).

10. The oil depletion allowance, for example, was passed in 1926 and was not altered until 1969, despite continual attempts by liberals in the post-war period. In contrast, within a month of its introduction, Congress passed the Emergency Petroleum Allocation Act of 1973 (PL93–159) to aid independent gasoline stations and refineries.

11. See "The Death of Withholding, or How the Bankers Won a Big One," *Washington Post*, July 31, 1983, sec. A.

Administrators, for example, decide whether military installations are opened or closed, and how water and sewer grants are distributed. When they have discretion, bureaucrats often allocate a disproportionate share of benefits to the districts of committee members who vote to maintain or increase their agencies' budgets (Arnold 1979; Faith et al. 1982). The president can ensure that friendly legislators get appointed to special commissions; that they get invited to state dinners, retreats, and junkets; and that their supporters receive patronage. Congressional leaders also appoint legislators to special commissions and can send them off to Caribbean islands in the middle of the winter on "fact-finding" missions. The leadership also has a strong say in the determination of members' committee assignments, office space, and opportunities to give their party's response to presidential television and radio statements. And committee chairs can either assist or obstruct other legislators' bills as they pass through their domains.

Exit

Exit, an indirect influence relation, aligns extracongressional views and legislators' positions through elite competition and succession rather than through alteration of legislators' votes. Incumbents merely are replaced by challengers whose views are in closer agreement with the electorate's. Policy outcomes are caused directly by the legislators' own preferences and indirectly by the positions of those actors who marshall resources to defeat incumbents. Examples include the 1982 defeat of Representative Bob Eckhardt (D–Tex.)—an iconoclastic, anti-oil liberal very out of step with his district—and the replacement in 1980 of four out of six liberal senators who were targeted by the National Conservative Political Action Committee (NCPAC).[12]

Cue Effects

Many authors discuss cue effects as a separate cause of legislators' decisions (Kingdon 1973; Heclo 1975). The cue, however, is not a cause but an informational device compatible with all modes of policy explanation—legislators' preferences, and both direct and anticipated influence relations (discussed later). Since it requires time to collect and analyze information about policy proposals, lawmakers may often choose not to formulate their own preferences but to rely instead on the judgment of actors with similar beliefs. On a particular civil rights bill, for example, some legislators might inquire about the position of a knowledgeable colleague or the American Civil Liberties Union and vote accordingly. Members can utilize this information as if it represented their own preferences or to make decisions according to either the direct or anticipated-reactions resource mechanisms.

---

12. They were Bayh of Indiana, Church of Idaho, Cranston of California, Culver of Iowa, Eagleton of Missouri, and McGovern of South Dakota. Cranston and Eagleton survived.

Anticipated Reactions

Anticipated reactions is merely a form of "resources" explanation in which no muscles are actually flexed. Instead, legislators fear prospective attempts by interest groups, the president, bureaucrats, and the public to affect electoral success. For example, when voting on proposed legislation, members of Congress may sometimes ignore their own preferences and support an organization's position in hopes of appeasing its followers. Many legislators, for example, disagree with the positions of the National Rifle Association but oppose handgun control to avoid the possible effects of the NRA's wrath.

Income Effects

An important type of anticipated-reactions argument emphasizes the income and wealth redistributions that result from the enactment of policies.[13] Most congressional policy proposals, if enacted, would alter the distribution of income and wealth. Economists simply note this fact and claim that members of Congress anticipate which constituents gain and lose from the redistribution and the probability that these shifts will create a net change in electoral opposition. The probability that income and wealth changes will create political opposition is, in turn, related to the distribution and concentration of gains and losses.

Established business organizations can easily develop lobbying efforts to attempt to secure policies that augment or prevent redistribution of their incomes because the benefits of these policies are likely to outweigh the marginal costs of the lobbying effort. On the other hand, groups lobbying for policies that seem reasonable only from a collective perspective will find it difficult to create and maintain viable political organizations because the pecuniary benefits for each individual are less than the costs of developing a successful organization (Schattschneider 1960; Olson 1965).

Many argue that congressional reluctance to pass efficient policies that take into account market-failure, public-goods, and equity problems results from the lack of organizational resources exerted on behalf of these viewpoints (Surrey 1957; Dunham and Marmor 1978; Wilson 1980). Because most socially rational policy proposals would create noticeable income losses for politically organized firms and individuals and disperse the benefits widely

---

13. Chicago economists have played prominent roles in the development of this perspective (Stigler 1971; Posner 1974; Peltzman 1976). In addition to making income and wealth redistributions the central variable in policy struggles, the economic theory of regulation goes on to specify the factors that determine which firms will possess more politically relevant resources to augment their policy positions. The less elastic the demand for the product in question and the more asymmetrical the interests of the firms that produce it, the more likely that legislation benefiting those firms will pass because they will solve free-rider problems. Since even Stigler and Posner do not think data can be gathered on such concepts and since I cannot measure other resources anyway (see chap. 7), these elaborations will not enter into my model.

across a less well-represented populace, legislators feel greater pressure to oppose these reforms than to support them. Moreover, special interests advocating policies with pernicious allocational and equity consequences have been adept in formulating them in ways that obscure the losses to society (Altshuler 1979, 84–85; Thurow 1980; Arnold 1990).

Many authors claim that the allocation of costs and benefits can account for the passage and persistence of many economically inefficient policies, including oil price controls (Kalt 1981), resource depletion allowances (Nash 1968; Blair 1976), and the deductibility of mortgage interest (Aaron 1972). However, recent reforms in petroleum, banking, airline, and railroad policies are difficult to explain from this perspective.[14]

In addition to the legislative rank and file, the president and congressional leaders also are unlikely to put themselves on record as favoring proposals whose income effects create political dangers and few advantages. Only the politically insulated bureaucrats seem to react differently to the distribution of costs and benefits because they are often concerned, from a professional standpoint, about whether policies improve economic efficiency. The Treasury Department, for example, almost always opposes tax changes that would benefit one or two industries but would detract from the horizontal equity of the tax code.[15]

Strategic Considerations

Political actors do not make individual decisions in isolation, of course, but rather with an eye toward the collective outcome. In any collective decision-making process, one may publicly oppose proposals that one privately favors in order to enhance the probability that the final collective decision will more nearly coincide with one's preferences (Farquharson 1969). Legislators also might engage in logrolling and thus vote against bills they like in hopes of securing passage of bills they consider more important. Positions, furthermore, also may vary as the probability of passage varies. If the probability of passage is near 50 percent, for example, then individual members become pivotal to the outcome and will behave accordingly (Shapley and Shubik

---

14. Congress has passed much legislation since 1975 that enhances economic efficiency in many regulated markets. Examples include the Securities Act Amendments of 1975 (PL94–145); the Railroad Revitalization and Regulatory Reform Act of 1976 (PL94–210); the Airline Deregulation Act of 1978 (PL95–504); the repeal of the federal income tax deduction for state gasoline taxes in 1978 (PL95–600); the Depository and Financial Institutions Deregulation and Monetary Control Act of 1980 (PL96–221); and the Staggers Rail Act of 1980 (PL96–448). Teske (1990) argues that these apparent anomalies are not so difficult to explain once one realizes that politically organized corporations are the largest consumers of products from all the deregulated industries.

15. An example of this ethos was the comprehensive tax reform proposal put forth by the Treasury Department in December, 1984.

1954). But if support for the legislation is already at 90 percent, undecided legislators have the freedom to oppose a proposal if such behavior would curry favor with voters or contributors (Fenno 1978).

For governmental actors, politics is a process in which they simultaneously make decisions that cause outcomes and examine outcome likelihood in order to make decisions. This complicates the study of congressional action.

Contextual Factors

Economic conditions modify the nature of both anticipated and direct influence relations.[16] The economic fitness of owners, workers, and consumers in particular sectors of the economy affects the passage of proposals relevant to these sectors through two different mechanisms. First, economic factors may modify the influence of other actors' positions on legislators' behavior. Because citizens appear to take economic conditions into account when they vote, the effectiveness of pleas for legislation is determined, in part, by whether the requests are warranted by economic realities.[17] It is quite probable, for example, that Chrysler's plea for federal loan guarantees had more of an effect on lawmakers than the oil producers' requests in 1975 to preserve the existing oil taxation structure because Chrysler's economic condition made its request credible, whereas the oil industry's record profits "proved" that its contentions had no basis in reality.

Second, conditions within sectors of the economy affect citizens' and firms' incomes, which, in turn, may induce electoral mobilization. Elected officials understand this and observe economic conditions directly in order to anticipate possible negative election results. When owners, workers, or consumers are in economic difficulty, members of Congress and the president are likely to support legislation that would benefit the relevant industry. Conversely, when an industry is performing well, bills that would tax its surplus and reallocate it elsewhere have a higher probability than normal of becoming law.

Traceability

An important link between the flow of costs and benefits created by policy decisions and the probability that voters will shift support from incumbents is

---

16. Political conditions such as issue salience and size of majority in Congress do not have the same explanatory status as economic conditions. The former are not really separate causes of outcomes but are simply endogenous intervening variables that come between actor positions and outcomes.

17. For differing views of the relationship between macroeconomic conditions and voting behavior, see Tufte 1978; Kiewiet and Kinder 1979a, 1979b; and Kramer 1983. To my knowledge, there is no literature on microeconomic conditions and voting.

the extent to which explicit policy outcomes can be attributed to individual legislators through roll call votes (Arnold 1990). If members of Congress decide to enact policies with explicit costs and vague benefits (policies that normally would create losses in voter support that exceed gains), they have a wide variety of parliamentary tactics at their disposal to avoid explicitly supporting the imposition of costs on voters. Omnibus bills, closed rules, voice votes, conference committees, and delegation of tough decisions to the executive branch or prestigious commissions all allow legislators to disassociate themselves from policies that impose costs on voters.

The success of these shielding techniques depends on voters' decision rules. If adverse outcomes occur for which governmental action is responsible (in the voters' opinion), and if voters support challengers in such situations regardless of whether incumbents can be explicitly linked to the imposition of costs, then parliamentary techniques cannot sever the link between policy outcomes and voter behavior. Even if voters' decisions are affected by traceability, the parliamentary techniques that reduce traceability are not really causes of congressional behavior. Instead, they have the same explanatory status as issue salience and the size of the majority—endogenous intervening variables that come between fundamental causes of decisions and policy outcomes (see note 16).

Conclusion

Theories of public policy outcomes should explain why ideas become actual legislative proposals and why Congress enacts some proposals and not others. Agenda formation consists of two discrete phenomena—issue salience and bias in idea selection. Issue salience refers to the timing of political concern over conditions such as energy markets or Central American relations. Idea selection refers to the process of choosing which ideas get introduced as legislative proposals once the issue area is politically salient.

Those scholars who study agenda formation emphasize idea selection as the more important problem. Of great political interest is whether some proposals to deal with nuclear or petroleum conditions, for example, are not formally introduced in Congress when energy conditions are salient because the proposals would interfere with the prerogatives of existing firms. Unfortunately, anyone who wishes to empirically validate such power relationships in idea selection must solve difficult and, in my view, intractable methodological problems. The explanation of issue salience, while more amenable to empirical analysis, is less important theoretically. When energy-market conditions, for example, cause consumer, firm, or worker incomes to fall, energy issues become more salient. Although often overlooked, this argument is not politically startling. Because of the problems in the study of agenda formation, the remaining chapters develop and test different theories of legislative action.

Once formally introduced, proposals cannot become law until a sufficient number of legislators vote in favor of them. Formal theorists have demonstrated that members will support policy proposals until the expected value of gains in voter support equals the expected losses. The literature on the U.S. Congress suggests that the positions of constituents, interest groups, bureaucrats, the president, and colleagues directly affect the calculation of expected vote gains and losses by members. In addition, all of these actors attempt to influence one another and thus also have indirect effects on members' policy choices. Under some circumstances, members' own policy views may be an important determinant of outcomes. Finally, the political and economic context, the use of political resources, the cost-benefit allocation created by the proposal, and strategic considerations also play a role.

CHAPTER 6

Research-Design Theory

In the previous three chapters, I have discussed the sources of energy-market conflict, congressional reactions to those conflicts, and theories of congressional behavior that scholars have invoked to explain both general and energy-policy results. The next step, of course, is to determine which alternative theories have more explanatory power. In this chapter, I will clarify the characteristics that an ideal empirical study would possess, and then illustrate how research designs traditionally used in the study of public policy do not satisfy these criteria. In chapter seven, I will describe the research design and methodologies used in this study.

An Ideal Empirical Study

To establish the validity of any explanation of natural outcomes, be they epidemiological, political, or economic, a study must accomplish the following tasks:

- Specify the events to be explained (the dependent variable).
- Decide which alternative theories are to be tested, taking care to distinguish aggregate- from individual-level phenomena.
- Define the unit of analysis.
- Choose the population of cases and gather an appropriately drawn sample.
- Gather data for each of the cases that satisfactorily represent the theories.
- Establish the marginal effect of various factors, controlling for alternative theories.

What I am proposing is hardly revolutionary. A political scientist studying voting behavior, an economist interested in the effect of property taxes on firm location, or a marketing researcher concerned with the determinants of Coca-Cola consumption would structure his or her work along the lines I have suggested. Policy analysts have not, however, and the consequences are severe. Case studies, policy histories, and, even more explicitly, quantitative studies all have research-design characteristics that undermine the validity of their results. They do not distinguish between aggregate- and individual-level explanation; they often do not test alternative theories; and they frequently suffer from selection bias and other research-design problems. I will examine each in turn.

Aggregate- versus Individual-Level Explanation

The inability of existing studies to adequately explain public policy outcomes can be attributed, in part, to their failure to distinguish between aggregate- and individual-level explanations. Scholars typically do not explain individual events. Instead, they develop theories about the effects of certain factors on the central tendencies of populations of events or individuals. Epidemiologists, for example, do not attempt to explain the death of an individual; rather, they develop theories about the effect of factors on the death rate of groups of individuals. After population effects have been determined, probability predictions can be made for an individual based on the values of the causal factors in his or her particular case. For example, assume that studies determine that the death rate for those age sixty who have smoked two packs a day for twenty years is six times the rate for those who have never smoked. Given this populational data, all we can do for a specific individual is assign him or her a probability of living one more year based on age and smoking history.

The accuracy of predictions about any individual's longevity depends on how much the effects of smoking behavior on health vary across individuals. The smaller the variance, the more similar the response of individuals to causal factors. When the variance is large, no specific individual's fate can be predicted with much certainty. As long as the variance in the effects of smoking on health is greater than zero, some heavy smokers will live long lives. Such individuals, however, do not disprove the claim that smoking adversely affects life expectancy because the theory refers to the effects on the central tendency of a group of individuals and not on any single person. At the level of the single event, one can explain only the probability of occurrence and not whether a specific individual will actually experience the event in question.

Case/Counter-Case Approach

Empirical studies of public policy have *generally* not been conducted at the level of populational explanation. Instead, they have used a case/counter-case approach. Typically, Scholar *A* presents a theory and uses historical events as evidence in support of the theory. Scholar *B*, in a later work, will then argue that one must consider other events for which Scholar *A*'s theory does not account. Scholar *B* then proceeds to develop a new theory to explain the cases *A* considered, as well as the additional cases subsequently discovered by *B*.[1] In general, our confidence in hypotheses increases if the same relationship is observed in additional cases not under study and decreases if cases can be found that refute the relationship; the normal pattern in public policy is to discover counter cases. Over the years, this scholarship process creates evidence that supports numerous competing public policy theories.

Many scholars have despaired over the morass of theories and over what appears to be a very primitive understanding of the policy process (Elkin 1974, 404–5; Simeon 1976, 548). Two mistaken views lie at the source of this pessimism. First, we ask whether theories are correct or incorrect (a mechanistic view), instead of asking how much confidence we have in their estimates of relationships (a probabilistic view). Second, and more important, public policy theories do not typically distinguish between explaining the enactment of a proposal (which they cannot do) and explaining the probability of enactment (which they can do). I will illustrate my argument by examining two similar policy cases with divergent outcomes.

Two Examples: Coal Emissions and Uranium Enrichment

The first case involves a policy event studied by Ackerman and Hassler in their work *Clean Coal/Dirty Air* (1981). In 1977, Congress passed an amendment to the Clean Air Act requiring that new source performance standards issued by the Environmental Protection Agency (EPA) reflect "a degree of emission reduction achievable through the application of the best technological system of continuous emission reduction."[2] In practical terms, the standards mandated the use of stack scrubbers by new coal-fired electric generating plants, and thus ensured that the demand for high-sulfur, union-mined underground coal would not fall as a consequence of the latter's compliance with the Clean Air Act. Among the supporters of this legislation were the United Mine Workers (UMW), underground coal mine owners, environmental groups, President Carter, the EPA, and the relevant congressional committee chairs.[3] The electric utility companies adamantly opposed it. The implication of legislative passage in this case is that the UMW, coal operators, and environmentalists have a large effect on outcomes, while electric utilities do not.

A policy episode not taken into account by Ackerman and Hassler, but

---

1. For an exchange of views along these lines, see Olson 1982 and Thurow 1983a.
2. PL95–95, sec. 109, pt. 111 (a)(1)(c). See Ackerman and Hassler 1981, 29.
3. Senate Republicans—chiefly, Senator Domenici—led the opposition.

involving actors and positions identical to the coal-emissions case, appears to support different conclusions, however. Its results suggest that electric power companies have a large effect on the policy process, while coal interests do not.[4] Since the advent of the nuclear age, uranium enrichment—the process that increases the U_{235} isotope percentage from its naturally occurring 0.7 percent to the 3.3 percent necessary for sustained nuclear fission in light water reactors—has been a U.S. government monopoly. By the mid-1970s, the Atomic Energy Commission thought that shortages of uranium would soon develop if modernization and expansion were not carried out. President Ford, disliking the prospect of large federal expenditures to bring the plants up to snuff, proposed that private investors be allowed to enter the industry and supply the increasing demand. A consortium headed by the Bechtel Corporation was prepared to construct a plant, but only if Congress guaranteed that its approximately $4 billion investment would not be at risk should enrichment prove to be unprofitable.

In addition to its effect on ownership, the Ford administration's proposal also would have had allocative effects. The price of private uranium enrichment would have been higher than the price of the publicly provided service because the government did not include the cost of capital or uranium inventory in its charges. Because nuclear power's alleged advantage over fossil-fired electric plants depends on marginal fuel-cycle costs that are lower than coal to compensate for nuclear power's higher capital costs, electric power companies were threatened by this proposal. Coal interests favored it because it would end subsidization of their chief competitor. Environmentalists also favored the proposal because they wanted to eliminate nuclear power's cost advantage.

The political lineup, then, was identical to that in the Clean Air Act case—electric power companies opposed the proposal and administration, coal, and environmental actors favored it. The outcome, however, was different. The bill failed. What conclusions should one reach about the causes of proposal enactment?

If one considers these two cases in terms of probability of passage, instead of actual passage, their contradictory implications disappear. Saying that coal operators, union miners, and environmentalists strongly affect the probability of passage is very different than saying that the pro-coal coalition causes policy outcomes. Under the probabilistic view, the events of the uranium-enrichment case, far from disconfirming the implications of the coal-emissions case are quite compatible with the finding that the pro-coal coalition (probabilistically) causes policy outcomes.

Even if coal-coalition support creates a high probability of enactment,

4. This section is summarized from the *Congressional Quarterly Almanac* (1976, 162–66).

some policy proposals that are virtually identical to that discussed in *Clean Coal/Dirty Air* will fail to become law just as some two-pack-a-day smokers will defy the group norm and live long lives. For example, because the positions in both are identical, let us assume that the coal-emissions and uranium-enrichment cases each have a probability of passage of 80 percent. We would expect that, on average, two cases out of every ten that have characteristics identical to these episodes will fail to become law. Only if the events of the uranium-enrichment case occurred significantly more than 20 percent of the time would the validity of a theory that rated the probability of passage of the coal-emissions case at a likelihood of 80 percent be in jeopardy.

Testing Alternative Explanations—Case Studies

Investigators who study a very small number of cases can uncover rich details and subtle nuances that necessarily are overlooked by those engaged in broader, but less intensive, analyses. Careful scrutiny of a few events provides a clear asset to researchers—an excellent opportunity to gain insights into the regularities they observe and formulate hypotheses that might explain them. Case studies, however, have at least one major limitation. Since investigators look at just a case or two, they can propose only possible explanations.[5] They cannot judge the validity of these explanations because alternatives cannot be tested.[6] An example will illustrate this limitation.

Consider again the coal-emissions case from the previous section, involving the setting of emissions standards for new pollution sources. The Carter administration and key coal-state Democrats in the House fought successfully to mandate the use of scrubbers on new coal-fired electric plants. After thoroughly examining the politics surrounding the passage of this proposal, one might conclude that the pressure the coal interests and environmentalists brought to bear on the political process was sufficient to overwhelm that applied by the electric utilities. A more institution-minded observer, however, might argue that Jimmy Carter's support determined the amendment's fate. Perhaps the first answer is correct, perhaps the skeptic is right, or perhaps both explanations are true to a certain extent.

---

5. Heclo (1972, 95, 97) noted that the primary problem inevitably facing any case study is that of establishing external validity for its results. "While case studies may be the most established and frequently used mode of academic policy analysis, there is no generally agreed-upon framework or mold in which to compare and incorporate the variety of case-study findings."

6. When cleverly designed, however, case studies can disprove explanations. Goldthorpe et al. (1969) studied the thesis that workers become conservative voters when their earnings become high by examining only the highest paid autoworkers in England. If these workers still voted for the Labour party, exactly what Goldthorpe discovered, the validity of the general thesis is doubtful.

To determine how much of an effect a particular factor has on the passage of legislation, one must control for the influence of other factors that also may be contributing causes—first by observing enough cases so that these factors vary, and then by calculating their effects with the appropriate statistical techniques. One can never ascertain the importance of various potential causes if they do not vary, and in case studies most of them remain constant. In very simplified terms, by looking at additional cases, we might find instances in which the pro-coal group and the president took opposite positions; and by comparing these positions against the proposal outcomes, we should be able to determine how much power each of these actors possessed.

Some might argue that one can control for other causal variables by looking at a case as it develops. This strategy, however, will not resolve the difficulties. Consider, for example, the idea of raising the ceiling price of natural gas found by independent producers. This proposal was introduced in every Congress from 1947 to 1977 and enjoyed the support of petroleum and natural gas producers and other business organizations. But successive presidents and Democratic congressional leaders and presidents opposed any changes in natural gas regulation, and none occurred until Jimmy Carter was elected. In 1977, Carter successfully proposed that new natural gas prices be gradually decontrolled and that intrastate prices be placed under federal jurisdiction for the first time.[7] In studying these phenomena Sanders (1981, 187–90) claims that presidential support must have had an important effect on the passage of legislation involving natural gas pricing because no other actors' positions changed.

This deduction could be wrong for either of two reasons. First, though major actors' positions might not have changed, other factors might have. The 1974 oil crisis altered public opinion about America's energy policies; legislators had become more independent of the leadership; and natural gas shortages made many believe the previously ignored alarms issued by the industry (MacAvoy and Pindyck 1975; 1983). Perhaps these contextual changes are primarily responsible for today's higher natural gas prices.

Second, even if one was certain that only a single variable had changed, the magnitude of that variable's importance still would be unknown. Both the natural gas lobby and congressional leaders could have been immensely powerful but very evenly matched, and the president's influence might have been relatively small but enough to have tipped the balance from one side's favor to the other's.

A well-done empirical study must compare alternative explanations. Case studies of congressional action on policy proposals rarely can meet this

---

7. Natural Gas Policy Act of 1978 (PL95–621).

criterion because comparison of alternative theories requires variance, and by restricting examination to just a case or two, the values of variables representing different theories will most likely have little variance.

Testing Alternative Explanations—Policy Histories

Investigators who develop policy histories study numerous policy proposals, can obtain variance in the values of possible explanatory variables, and are therefore in a position to resolve many of the problems facing case studies. Observing numerous cases, however, is not enough. To develop accurate, generalizable explanations, researchers also must ensure that all cases have an equal chance of selection and must attend to all the complications that accompany empirical analysis.

Selection Bias

Selection bias occurs when cases with different values for the dependent variable are not equally likely to be selected for study. Two examples would be a study of Coca-Cola consumption that examined only individuals who drank Coke or a study of the effect of coffee consumption on health that examined only sick people. In each case, one might conclude incorrectly that a certain factor has effects—that coffee consumption does cause health problems or that age does predict cola consumption, for example—because those who do not drink Coke also might be young and those who are healthy also may drink large amounts of coffee.

In the study of public policy decisions, selection bias frequently occurs when proposals that become law are the focus of study. The most common question in public policy is, Why did Congress pass a given piece of legislation? For example: Why did oil price controls pass? Why did banking deregulation pass? Investigators asking these questions often conduct their research using an intuitively natural but, nonetheless, fundamentally unsound research design. They examine the legislative history of the law or laws that pass—the Emergency Petroleum Allocation Act of 1973 or the Depository and Financial Institutions Deregulation and Monetary Control Act of 1980, for example—and conclude that the positions of actors such as the president or an interest group were crucial. The problem, of course, just as before, is that the factors related to passage in the laws examined could be equally present in the history of policy proposals that did not pass and hence were not examined. If this were the case, then conclusions about the effects of actors' positions would be wrong because the alleged causal factors also were present in cases that did not become law. One cannot validate a theory of policy outcomes by examining only those bills that become law. One also must examine proposals that are not enacted. I will further illustrate selection bias with energy cases.

Coal Emissions versus Nuclear Liability
In the case-studies section, two possible theories were offered to explain enactment success. The first attributed the result to interest-group positions, while the second gave credit to the positions of successive presidents. The examination of additional energy cases involving these same actors might aid us in validating these theories. One episode that comes to mind deals with the liability of nuclear power plants for radiation damage.[8]

Legislation to limit the liability of nuclear power plants was first introduced in 1956 but failed to pass in that session because President Eisenhower and the Democratic Congress were engaged in a dispute over public versus private development of nuclear power. The president did not support the aggressive public-subsidy program envisioned by the Joint Committee on Atomic Energy, and the Democrats, in turn, refused to consider Eisenhower's proposal to limit the liability of private nuclear plants. In 1957, President Eisenhower agreed to a government-subsidized development program. The Price-Anderson Nuclear Insurance and Liability Act[9] was enacted soon thereafter, despite the opposition of coal operators and union miners, who opposed subsidies for a competitor. By 1975, liberal Democrats and conservation groups had joined coal interests in opposing nuclear power. Nevertheless, the Price-Anderson Act was renewed with the solid support of President Ford and the Joint Committee on Atomic Energy, whose members still favored nuclear power.

After taking this case into account, one might start to have more confidence in the effect of presidents on policy outcomes and less in the effect of interest groups. In fact, if I were to list ten more examples detailing how various presidents defeated the environmental and coal interests, one might be so bold as to assert that President Carter, indeed, was more influential than the pro-coal lobbyists in the coal-emissions case.

Such a contention easily could be wrong, however, for I purposely have presented only those examples that support the institutional explanation. If, instead, I had listed a dozen cases in which the pro-coal group beat the chief executive, one would have been tempted to leap boldly in the opposite direction. Only if analysts choose their cases in an unbiased manner can we have confidence in their conclusions.

---

8. The details are summarized from the *Congressional Quarterly Almanac* (1956, 542–55; 1957, 587).

9. PL85–256.

Policy Studies in General

Public policy analysts generally pick cases involving legislation that has been voted on by a full chamber, is substantively significant, or has received much public attention. Since many observers of the U.S. Congress believe committee chairs can prevent committee approval of most legislation passing through their domains, researchers who study just those bills that get to the floor run the risk of underestimating both the direct influence of committee chairs and the indirect influence of actors (e.g., the president) who might affect the behavior of these committee leaders. The estimates of factor influence in roll call studies also will be biased because one of the main effects of actors such as committee chairs may be to prevent bills from going to a roll call vote, that is, from leaving committee. Similarly, because legislators probably are less likely to support the president if they or their constituents have strong views on a proposal, investigators who examine only substantively important or publicly salient issues cannot accurately assess the chief executive's overall power.

In addition to improving the accuracy of findings, the random selection of cases also allows researchers to generalize their findings. Investigators usually have limited interest in understanding what factors cause a particular outcome to occur; instead, they seek hypotheses that explain numerous outcomes. Learning that the UMW played but a minor role in the passage of a Clean Air Act amendment is not terribly exciting; discovering it is one of the weakest lobbying groups on Capitol Hill is. A few public policy analysts might like to know why the government limited the liability of nuclear power plant owners; almost all of them want to understand why Congress passes some bills and not others. Are committee chairs more powerful than the majority leader? Does the Sierra Club wield more clout than the Seven Sisters? How closely do representatives listen to constituents' opinions? These are interesting questions that can be answered only if researchers are able to generalize their conclusions.

Additional Research Problems

Formulating a logical, testable explanation is terribly difficult to do. Among other things, findings must be consistent across cases, be deductive and non-tautological, control for other factors, deal with other plausible hypotheses, and be expressed precisely. While attaining the ideal is probably impossible, the modal policy history, in addition to suffering from selection bias, has other methodological flaws. An otherwise well-done and detailed study of natural gas regulation (Sanders 1981) illustrates that policy histories often do not compare alternative explanations across cases. Instead, arguments are invoked that are consistent with the facts of a particular case. We have many explanations of many events, instead of a comprehensive explanation of events.

Sanders' initial claim is that the positions of pipeline owners have a large effect on natural gas policy, while producer groups and House committee chairs do not. Regarding a 1935 proposal to place pipeline prices under federal control and make the pipelines common carriers, she writes

> Independent producers, particularly on the Panhandle and Hugoten fields, stood to benefit most from the common carrier provisions. These beneficiaries, however, were too geographically concentrated to exert political pressure to overcome the bills' perceived liabilities (even though [House Commerce Committee Chair] Sam Rayburn was an influential friend). . . . However, as long as the pipelines remained opposed, Congress had little appetite for a regulatory battle.[10]

At other times in the narrative, Sanders provides us with different explanations. The Natural Gas Act of 1938[11] "was the result of a political consensus achieved on the basis of the extraordinary economic conditions of the 1930s" (71). The Murphy-Hollings bills of 1971–72 failed because consumer groups and bureaucrats opposed them (130). In 1973, she observes, the House and Senate Commerce Committees were crucial to the formulation of natural gas policies (132).

In her formal conclusion, Sanders fails to incorporate alternative explanations. She argues that "the position of congressmen and presidents on natural gas regulation depended on the importance to their electoral constituencies of gas production or consumption" (196). If we look at districts where over three-quarters of the households used natural gas, we find that in 1955 and 1976, respectively, 92 and 96 percent of the Democratic members voted to retain price controls—compared to 48 and 20 percent of their Republican counterparts (160, table 21). I suggest, to play devil's advocate, that legislators considered not only their constituents' views when making their voting decisions, as Sanders argues, but also their own beliefs about the appropriate role of markets.

Unfortunately, most policy histories utilize a similar style of analysis. In reviewing James Q. Wilson's (1980) comprehensive examination of regulatory policy, Shepsle (1982, 216–17) notes:

> Although not explicitly coordinated by an overarching theme or approach, all the essays, save one, share an aversion not merely to a

---

10. Sanders (1981, 37, 40).
11. PL75–688.

common theoretical orientation but to any theoretical orientation at all. . . . Much of the argument in these essays takes [a] *post hoc, ergo propter hoc* form. History, after all, is just "one damn fact after another."

While some policy histories address their topics somewhat more systematically, the residual ambiguities still leave readers wondering how much confidence to place in the findings.[12] Heclo (1975), for example, concludes that bureaucratic preferences account for the "major transformations" in English and Swedish social policies over the last century. He generates straightforward nontautological conclusions, and he controls for other important factors such as interest-group positions and public opinion. But Heclo never defines what he means by major social policy transformations, making it difficult for anyone to come up with counterexamples. Nor does he explain how he treats cases in which bureaucrats hold a mixture of differing opinions. And he never tells us whether other actors' positions have no effects or just small ones.

Problems in Quantitative Work

Even when policy scholars precisely specify their units of analysis, their hypotheses, the measurement of their variables, and the population of events across which the theories are tested, and even when they use econometric techniques to determine the magnitude of effects, the logical rigor necessary to ensure valid conclusions often is absent. For example, studies of the determinants of state policies generally have operationalized the dependent variable (i.e., policy) as different types of expenditure and taxation.[13] Although these are convenient measures, they do not represent all aspects of policies that assist the poor and are not good measures of the redistributive character of state expenditures. In addition, state policy analysts often oversimplified their models by using bivariate rather than multivariate techniques, made dubious causal deductions by examining cross-sectional instead of time-series data, and did not consider the possibility that some of the variables they treated as causes were in fact spuriously related to or caused by the dependent variable.

In more recent quantitative policy literature, scholars frequently use individual-level data on roll call votes to ascertain the causes of congressional behavior. Political scientists, including McRae (1958, 1970), Clausen and Cheney (1970), Clausen (1973), Clausen and Van Horn (1977), and Poole and Rosenthal (1985a, 1985b), utilize roll-call vote data to demonstrate that members have relatively stable positions (relative to one another) on a small

12. See Heclo 1975 and G. Wilson 1977.
13. See Dawson and Robinson 1963; Dye 1966; Hofferbert 1966; and Sharkansky 1968. This problem is not peculiar to political science. For a recent, statistically supported economic argument and logical refutation, see Feldstein 1983 and Thurow 1983b.

number of basic policy choices such as public intervention in the economy, civil rights, and foreign policy.[14] These policy positions, in turn, are used to forecast future aggregate congressional decisions once the cutting line (the division between those members in the conflict space who vote yes and those who vote no) is known.

Some analysts in this tradition (McRae 1958; Clausen 1973) also attempt to separate from other factors the effects of constituents' preferences on the variation in members' relative policy positions. Clausen (1973, 149), for example, concludes that constituents strongly affect members' positions in policy areas such as foreign policy and civil liberties, but do not affect positions in the areas of agricultural and social-welfare policy.

Other researchers, mainly economists, also have used roll-call vote data to determine the effect of constituents on members' voting behavior.[15] These studies regress roll call votes against constituents' preferences, as measured by the income and wealth flows that would result from policy enactment, and measures of legislators' preferences. Authors conducting this research disagree about whether legislators' private preferences (ideologies) are a significant cause of the variance in their roll call behavior. Peltzman (1984) argues no, while Kalt and Zupan (1984) argue affirmatively.

Despite their differences, these two prominent empirical approaches to the study of Congress share methodological characteristics that limit the utility of their findings. First, the explanation of policy-preference variation across members does not explain aggregate policy decisions by Congress. Members' policy views relative to one another may remain relatively constant, while aggregate congressional decisions may change dramatically over time as the policy views of the whole distribution of members shift. For example, Congress approved oil price controls in 1973 and failed to renew them in 1979 even though the economic stakes for oil-producing districts in Oklahoma and oil-consuming districts in Massachusetts (the cross-sectional variance) remained basically constant.

Second, while individual-level roll call data are appropriate to explain the causes of policy-position variation across members, the separation of constituency-preference effects from other causes, such as members' private policy preferences (ideologies), is difficult. Clausen (1973, chap. 6), to his

---

14. The authors in this tradition disagree on how many distinct policy dimensions must be utilized to adequately fit the data. Clausen (1973) and Clausen and Van Horn (1977) argue five to seven, while Poole and Rosenthal (1985a) argue that one dimension accounts successfully for 80 percent of the votes cast. Koford (1989), however, argues that the techniques used by Poole and Rosenthal (and, implicitly, the others) would "detect" policy dimensions even if legislators' preferences were randomly distributed and had no actual structure at all.

15. See Bernstein and Horn 1981; Kalt 1981; Kau and Rubin 1978, 1979; Carson and Oppenheimer 1984; Kalt and Zupan 1984; and Peltzman 1984, 1985.

credit, utilizes a time-series intervention approach. He compares the relative policy-position scores of representatives from districts that undergo party change with the scores of representatives from districts that have constant party representation during six years of the Eisenhower presidency. Clausen is very cautious about his results and understands that their power depends on variables other than party affiliation remaining constant in those districts that experience party turnover.

Ideology as an Explanatory Variable
The approach used in the newer roll call studies, conducted mainly by economists, is to isolate econometrically members' ideologies from the other causes influencing group ratings of legislators (such as ratings by Americans for Democratic Action). This research approach has not been successful, in my view, because important causes of decisions have not been included in the regression equations.

A legislator's policy behavior is determined by three generic classes of factors—his or her own policy preferences, influence relations carried out by other actors within and outside the government, and the anticipation of influence relations that would be caused by the cost and benefit flows generated by enacted policies.[16] These factors can be represented formally as follows:

$$\mathbf{d} = \beta_1\mathbf{pp} + Ip\beta_2 + Op\beta_3 + Econ\beta_4 + \beta_5\mathbf{lk} + \mathbf{u}, \tag{1}$$

where $\mathbf{d}$ is a column vector of individual member's decisions to support legislation; $\mathbf{pp}$ is a column vector of individual member's personal preferences (ideology) with respect to the legislation; Ip is a matrix of the positions of all other relevant intragovernmental actors interacting with both intensity of position and political resources; Op is a matrix of the positions of all other relevant extragovernmental actors interacting with both intensity of position and political resources; $Econ$ is a matrix of the policy-induced cost-and-benefit flows; and $\mathbf{lk}$ is a column vector of the likelihood of passage of the policy proposals. The various betas are vectors of coefficients, and $\mathbf{u}$ is a random disturbance vector.

When causal variables of interest cannot be measured directly and a model is actually estimated with proxies that only imperfectly measure the variable of interest, severe bias can result. For example, in sorting out the differences between cross-sectional and time-series analyses of the relationship between economic conditions and electoral behavior, Kramer (1983) demonstrates that the use of the change in an individual's total income as a proxy for the real causal variable—governmentally induced income change—

---

16. See chapter 5.

generates biased estimates of the relationship between the economy and voting behavior. Because the variation in the governmentally induced component across individuals at any one point in time is near zero, the coefficient on total-income change is simply picking up the relationship between all the other causes of income variation, other than government policy, and an individual's partisanship (the intercept of the vote equation).

The roll-call vote studies conducted by economists have an analogous problem because they do not estimate equation (1), the true behavioral model. Instead, they estimate equation (2),

$$\mathbf{d} = \beta_1\mathbf{pp} + Econ\beta_2 + e, \tag{2}$$

where $\mathbf{d}$ again represents an individual legislator's decision to support legislation; $\mathbf{pp}$ is personal preferences (ideology); $Econ$ is a matrix of the policy-induced income flows as a percentage of district income; and e represents random error. The actual variable of interest, a legislator's individual ideology, is not used in the equation. Instead, a surrogate for ideology such as an ADA ranking is used:

$$\text{ADA or Other Ranking} = \beta_1\mathbf{pp} + e, \tag{3}$$

where $\mathbf{pp}$ equals a member's personal preferences (ideology) and e represents all the other causes influencing an ADA or similar ranking index.

Two sources of bias may result from the use of an ADA ranking as a surrogate for legislators' ideologies. If the explanatory power of the error term in equation (3) overwhelms ideology in a cross-sectional estimate (because the variance in ADA and other vote ratings across members is determined more by constituency variation than by variation in members' personal beliefs), Kramer's argument becomes very important. To the extent that the covariance between the ideological component ($\mathbf{pp}$) and the ADA or equivalent rating is relatively small compared to the total variance in the rating, then the coefficient on $\mathbf{pp}$ in equation (2) is largely affected by the irrelevant relationships between all the other causes of the ADA rating and the intercept and variables in equation (2).

Because ranking indexes such as that used by the ADA are nothing more than summary measures of previous roll call votes, all the other causes of the rating in equation (3) besides ideology are precisely all the other terms in equation (1). Thus, the coefficient on $\mathbf{pp}$ in equation (2) probably will not represent the effect of ideology but instead will represent the effect of all the terms in equation (1) other than $\mathbf{pp}$.

Are Residuals a Solution?
Many of the authors of roll call articles are aware that the roll call rankings

they utilize as indicators of personal ideology are contaminated by all the causes of congressional decisions besides personal beliefs (Kalt 1981; Kau and Rubin 1982; Kalt and Zupan 1984; Carson and Oppenheimer 1984). To control for the problem, they regress the ADA or equivalent rating against numerous economic, demographic, and regional dummy variables. The unexplained residual variance in these equations, a combination of a member's personal ideology and whatever error remains, is then utilized as an explanatory variable.

Those who utilize this technique obviously hope that these residuals largely represent personal ideology and not the other possible causes of voting decisions. The veracity of this assumption depends on whether the variables regressed against the ADA rating capture all the other causes of congressional behavior. To the extent that the theories of congressional behavior I formally represent in equation (1) are accurate, the variables used by Kalt and Zupan (1984, 293), Carson and Oppenheimer (1984, 172), and Kau and Rubin (1982, 64) do not include three important classes of variables—the positions of interest groups and executive-branch actors and the likelihood of proposal passage, which, in turn, affects those preferences that are endogenous. This exclusion increases the probability that the residuals in the ADA equation do not simply represent personal ideology but also represent deviations from district-specific economic and demographic characteristics caused by the ability of executive-branch and interest-group actors to affect reelection.[17]

Even if the additional three classes of variables were used to purge the ADA ratings of additional causes and the residuals were then utilized as explanatory variables, I would not label the residuals as personal ideology, as the authors in this tradition do, for two reasons. First, under this scheme a legislator has an ideology if and only if his ADA rating is not predicted accurately by other variables representing the interests of constituents. If Edward Kennedy, for example, behaves as one would predict a Massachusetts senator would behave, then he is not ideological under this methodology. Second, using this reasoning, Edward Kennedy could be deemed more conservative than Senator Strom Thurmond if Kennedy's actual voting record were less "liberal" than Massachusetts variables would predict and Thurmond's voting record were more "liberal" than South Carolina variables would predict. Such characteristics are so contrary to the usual meaning of the word *ideology* that I feel another term, perhaps *discretion*, would be more appropriate.

Even discretion may not be the appropriate term, however, because under this methodology constituent preferences do not directly enter the equa-

---

17. Peltzman (1984, 208) recognizes this possibility and finds that the residuals from his equations are correlated for senators in the same state. He concludes that "the ADA variable works in the voting regressions [because] it captures some common interests of the constituency."

tion. The fact that the variance in voting behavior cannot be explained by economic and demographic characteristics does not necessarily imply that legislators are shirking their duties because their constituents' views also may not be well predicted by the same variables.[18] Logically, a legislator's votes could represent the views of his or her district accurately yet still not be predicted very well by economic and demographic data.

Roll Call Votes and Sample-Selection Bias

A possible solution to the problems I have raised so far is to estimate equation (1) with a pooled data set of aggregate congressional roll call decisions where both issues and time vary. This strategy also will not succeed, however, because roll call votes are not a random sample of congressional decisions.

Inferences made from roll call data will likely be contaminated by three types of errors. Only a small fraction of legislative decisions are subject to roll call votes. Many proposals don't leave committee, and of those that reach the floor, less than one-half receive roll calls in both the House and Senate. Inferences gained from roll-call vote models can be generalized to other types of congressional decisions only if the processes that govern the different types of decisions are similar. Models of congressional decisions in which coefficients are allowed to vary across floor, roll call, and voice-vote samples fit the data significantly better than models in which the coefficients are constrained to be identical across the different samples. The processes that determine committee and voice-vote decisions are different than those that determine roll call decisions (VanDoren 1990).

Even if the processes affecting committee approval and roll call occurrence do not differ from roll call passage, a second difficulty occurs because the parameters estimated from roll call data do not take the probabilities of the prior events—committee approval and roll call occurrence—into account. When I compare estimates of factor effects calculated from roll call data (that are not corrected for committee approval and roll call occurrence) with estimates derived from cases that include all policy decisions (and not just roll call votes) the results differ by 70 to 90 percent (VanDoren 1990).

A third and more technical source of bias occurs because the error terms of the equations that explain why cases become roll calls and the error term of the actual decision equation covary. While I cannot explicitly detect this problem, I do compare roll-call parameter estimates corrected for the probability of prior events with parameter estimates generated directly from a full sample of policy proposals. The estimates are wildly different with no consistent pattern of over- or underestimation.

---

18. Constituents who had these preferences, of course, would not be maximizing their own incomes.

Conclusion

Conventional methods of policy inquiry do not provide for adequate comparison of alternative explanations, random selection of cases, or systematic analysis. Although case studies allow researchers to formulate plausible hypotheses about the events they observe, these hypotheses can be validated and generalized only if one examines many randomly selected events and then fairly compares alternative explanations. Neither previous policy histories nor statistical policy studies—two research styles capable of overcoming the limitations of case studies—have satisfied these conditions. Because one can explain only the probability of events and not the events themselves, case studies and policy histories that support and refute hypotheses through the use of case/counter-case evidence are flawed even further. Only by examining patterns in the occurrence of equally probable policy events can one judge the validity of hypotheses about policy behavior.

CHAPTER 7

The Selection of Energy-Policy Cases

As set forth in chapter 6, an ideal empirical study must accomplish six tasks:

- Specify the events to be explained (the dependent variable).
- Decide which alternative theories are to be tested, taking care to distinguish aggregate- from individual-level phenomena.
- Define the unit of analysis.
- Choose the population of cases and gather an appropriately drawn sample.
- Gather data for each of the cases that satisfactorily represent the theories.
- Establish the marginal effect of various factors, controlling for alternative theories.

Previous studies of congressional policy decisions have not paid equal attention to all six problems. As a consequence, the determinants of congressional policy decisions are not known with any certainty. A satisfactory research design can be created, however, if careful attention is paid to all six criteria.

The Events to Be Explained

Four issues complicate what would otherwise appear to be a simple decision to explain the enactment of energy proposals into law. First, can one explain energy policy separately from other policy areas? What policy categories are acceptable for purposes of explanation? Second, must one explain both agenda formation and legislative action in order to avoid selection bias? Third, given that the dependent variable is the probability of an individual event rather than the event itself, how does one statistically estimate the effect of factors on the probability of an occurrence? Finally, the enactment of policy proposals into law is typically a multi-step process, including committee and floor consideration and approval, conference, and presidential approval. Must one explain all the stages in order to explain policy outcomes?

Energy Proposals

I have limited my study to the causes of energy policy only because of time constraints and substantive interest, not because I believe the politics of energy are theoretically distinctive. In fact, in chapter 5, I offered only three generic types of explanation for policy results—legislators' own preferences, context-dependent influence relations carried out by actors with a stake in policy outcomes, and the anticipation of influence relations. Policy areas differ in terms of the actual actors and contextual factors involved and the relative importance of these variables to outcomes. The United Mine Workers, for example, might affect outcomes in coal-policy cases but would probably not even participate in farm-policy struggles. The National Farmers Union conceivably might influence neither coal nor farm politics because it would not participate in the former and because the anticipation of economic events might be more important in the politics of the latter than actual group positions.

These differences do not lead me to conclude, however, that the study of public policy should be as segmented and subject-specific as is currently the case. Isn't it likely that constituents' influence on legislators, for example, varies according to how loudly they scream and not which policy topic they scream about? Similarly, won't the level of concern the Congress has for an ailing industry depend on the sector's economic condition and importance and not on whether the industry produces cars or coal?

I would like to have been able to identify all of the policy proposals introduced into Congress during a relatively long time period, for such a population would have allowed me to test how similar the determinants of outcomes in various policy areas actually are. Because of obvious time constraints, however, I limited my research to just a subset of energy proposals thrown into the congressional hopper between 1945 and 1976, inclusively.[1]

Although my narrowed population allows me to reach confident conclusions about only those factors that account for the passage of atomic-energy and coal legislation, my research design is applicable to all other policy areas. Indeed, a central task in policy research is to ascertain whether policy processes really do differ across substantively different policy areas.

Agenda Formation versus Legislative Action

Scholars who study agenda formation might argue that my decision to only explain legislative action on proposals introduced in Congress, and not to estimate a model of agenda formation, will result in selection-bias problems

---

1. I stopped with 1976 because the 1977–78 *Congressional Record Index* had not yet been compiled when I designed the sample.

similar to those encountered by researchers who examine only those bills with roll call votes. By studying only the trivial set of proposals that come before Congress, it is possible to overlook the power that major corporations or other behind-the-scenes actors exercise in establishing the legislative agenda and thus to underestimate the overall influence of these actors (Bachrach and Baratz 1962).

While this argument has analytic merit, the severity of its empirical consequences varies across different policy areas. In education policy, where there appears to be a substantial discrepancy between the public discussion of ideas and their legislative introduction, a theory that explains only how influential various actors are in securing congressional enactment of education bills probably would significantly underestimate the overall power of certain groups.[2]

In the energy area, however, I have found an extraordinarily close correspondence between publicly suggested proposals and those ideas introduced into Congress. Except for a few notable exceptions, all the energy ideas I have read about have received congressional attention. In particular, those aspects of the status quo that distribute benefits to business interests and create costs for the general public, the policies most likely to remain off the agenda, have been subject to congressional scrutiny. In the 1950s, for example, a vigorous debate erupted on Capitol Hill over the petroleum depletion allowance.[3] And in the case of nuclear power subsidies, coal-state members of Congress frequently offered alternatives.[4]

That none of the latter proposals was enacted was immaterial to my selection; as long as a proposal was placed on the legislative agenda, it was included in my universe of cases. In the energy area, nondecisions do not appear to be a significant problem, and if corporate positions have large direct or indirect effects on the passage of proposals, the analysis I have conducted here should detect that fact.

Estimating the Probability of an Event

One can directly estimate the effect of factors on other phenomena only if the latter can be represented by continuous interval-level data. When the phenom-

---

2. For example, the proposal to end all direct funding of public institutions and give educational vouchers to individuals who then cash them in at their school of choice has not been introduced into Congress even though it has received prominent attention from Friedman (1962) and others.

3. Market methods for controlling production externalities and decentralized solutions to the energy supply problem (Lovins 1977) have received only partial legislative consideration. The 1950s debate can be found in *Congressional Quarterly Almanac* (1950, 577–79; 1951, 417, 418, 435; 1957, 614; 1958, 265).

4. *Congressional Quarterly Almanac* (1957, 583–86). Representative VanZandt (R–Pa.) was a frequent critic of government support for nuclear power.

ena to be modeled are discrete, such as the passage of policy proposals or the death of individuals, one can explain only the probability of the individual event or the change in the rate of the population event, both continuous functions, and not the event itself. Estimation of these probability functions, however, is not straightforward because one can gather data only for the occurrence of events and not their probability, which is, of course, unobserved. Estimation of event equations with normal ordinary-least-squares regression techniques would result in two errors. The generated function (a straight line) would represent the marginal effects of causes as constant for all values of probability from 0 to 100 percent (the slope of the estimated relationship would be constant).[5] Second, the estimated functional relationship would incorporate the passage and nonpassage data points as part of the function and thereby imply the existence of probabilities less than 0 and greater than 100 percent.

A more accurate view of the form of the probability function would incorporate the concept of pivotalness and limit the values to 0 and 100 percent (Shapley and Shubik 1954). A realistic event-probability function would have an S shape because the causes of approval have little effect near the 0 and 100 percent probability points and greater effect in between. For example, the effect of factors, such as the president's position, on the probability of proposal passage is probably larger if the likelihood of passage is 50 percent, than if it is either very probable or implausible that the proposal will be enacted. I use probit to estimate the model in this study instead of ordinary least squares because it fits the data on passage and failure to an unobserved probability function with just such characteristics.

Final Passage versus Other Stages

The enactment of policy proposals into law is a multistep process. In this study, however, I estimate an equation only for the last event in the sequence for the simple reason that the enactment of proposals into law is the most important phenomenon to explain. An understanding of committee and floor behavior would be intellectually interesting, but, ultimately, whether legislation becomes law is what matters.

In chapter 5, I noted that whenever one studies a set of events (such as legislative action) and then generalizes to phenomena in which the events examined are only one portion of a larger sequence (public policy), the estimates of factor effects may be biased. Because certain variables may influence only agenda formation, for example, a study limited to legislative action, a

---

5. Ordinary-least-squares coefficients are unbiased if the true marginal effects of factors are linear. The estimates, however, are inefficient because of nonconstant error variance.

subset of events in the policy process, will underestimate the effect of factors whose main consequence is to place ideas on the agenda.

Similar problems, though, will not be caused by my use of enactment, rather than prior legislative events, as my dependent variable. To be sure, many factors in the study (e.g., the position of the president) probably have much more influence at certain stages of the process (e.g., conference committee), but because of the way I measure actor beliefs, neither selection bias nor variable truncation results from my dependent variable being the last stage of the process. Case-selection problems do not occur because the differential effects that actor positions have on the separate stages of the legislative process do not determine whether a case is selected. Cases are not excluded, for example, because they fail to leave committee or pass the House.

A problem could occur, however, if the stage at which a variable effect takes place ends up determining whether I measure the factor correctly. If by not explicitly writing an equation for committee approval, for example, I miss the positions of those actors who only express themselves at that stage of the policy process, then my estimates of actor effects will be too large. I would overestimate the effect of actor beliefs because I might miss their preference expression in cases that did not advance far enough in the process. Even though my dependent variable is the last event in the policy sequence, however, I examine all stages to ascertain actor positions on proposals. Sometimes, of course, I am unable to determine actor positions on cases that do not leave committee, but I would have been no better off had I explicitly developed a theory of committee passage. The problem is that it is difficult to determine actor positions on proposals that are obscure and do not receive committee consideration.[6] Similarly, if important individuals such as the president do not express their beliefs until late in the legislative process, I will have difficulty in coding their beliefs about cases that do not make it past the first step. Explicit examination of each part of the policy-making process, however, would not solve the information problem.[7]

The Selection of Cases

As I explained in chapter 6, the procedures investigators use to choose their cases affect the accuracy and generalizability of their findings. To avoid problems, one must specify what constitutes a case, identify the universe of such cases, and then randomly select a sample of cases to study.

---

6. See app. 7A.

7. A more subtle problem could occur. If actor positions in later stages depend on outcomes of earlier stages, then the influence of those who contributed to the early outcomes would be underestimated. This is a simultaneity problem, however, and not a selection-bias problem. I examine specification problems in the last section of this chapter.

Case Specification

Specifying the unit of analysis usually is a straightforward task. For investigators studying the causes of voting behavior, the case is an individual voter. For those studying firms' behavior, it is a firm. And for those studying policy outcomes, it must be a policy proposal.[8] We know what voters and firms are, but what exactly is a policy proposal?

A *legislative policy proposal* is a group of words in a congressional bill or amendment that would have the government try to alter some aspect of citizen behavior or rearrange society's use of available resources. Since *bills* and *amendments* are aggregations of one or more proposals, one must develop a set of decision rules for consistently dividing legislative language into cases.[9] These rules must be able to glean the substantive calls for action from the routine administrative details, rhetoric, and general legalese found in legislation.[10]

In the energy-policy area, a *case* is a sentence or group of sentences in a bill or amendment that, in my judgment, would have altered the characteristics of energy markets. Three criteria are important in determining the boundaries of a case. The sentence or group of sentences must contain a reference to an explicit or implied governmental actor or agency engaged in an economic or regulatory action involving an energy commodity. Examples of governmental actors or agencies include the president, the Internal Revenue Service, and the Office of Management and Budget. Economic and regulatory actions include subsidies, loans, taxes, or direct regulation of consumer, firm, or worker behavior. Energy commodities include coal, oil, natural gas, uranium, nuclear power, solar power, and alternative energy sources.[11]

The following are some typical examples of proposals:

- Petroleum exports shall be taxed at the rate of one-half cent per gallon.
- The federal government shall determine the market demand for petroleum and allocate it among the producing states.
- Forty million dollars is authorized to be appropriated for nuclear fuel research and development.

---

8. For a similar discussion regarding bureaucratic policy-making, see Arnold 1979.

9. In my study, for example, the Coal Mine Health and Safety Act of 1969 (PL91–173) had 58 cases.

10. Furthermore, if the same proposal is thrown in the hopper many times during a single congressional session, then one should consider it to be only a single case; but if a proposal is introduced in eight different congresses, one should code it as eight different cases.

11. I do not include proposals dealing with non-nuclear–generated electricity (generally state-level issues); air pollution or transportation issues such as mass transit, van pools, and traffic management (issues only secondarily related to energy); specific mineral lease controversies (private bills); and studies of any kind or resolutions expressing the mood of the Senate or House of Representatives (rhetorical legislation).

The virtues of this case definition are twofold. First, actual behavior need not change as a result of the enacted legislation. If a tax placed on gasoline, for example, did not result in reduced consumption, it would still be an energy proposal because results are not necessary to the definition. Second, knowledge about the intentions of proposal sponsors is unnecessary. A tax on an energy product changes the characteristics of that market regardless of whether the sponsors intend to raise revenue or alter energy behavior. The five-cent increase in the federal gasoline tax enacted in the early 1980s clearly would be a case in my study. I would not have to determine whether Congress merely intended to raise revenue or also intended to discourage gasoline consumption.

Administrative Provisions

Since administrative and enforcement provisions constitute the bulk of most legislation, one must decide how to treat these types of provisions. Administrative provisions are not cases in my study, except when they are so severe that they alter the meaning of proposals in a bill.

This point can be illustrated by the following petroleum example. Suppose a senator introduced a bill to ban the interstate shipment of oil produced in excess of state quotas (i.e., "hot oil"). The law would be administered by the Bureau of Mines, and offenders could be fined up to $1,000. Also, suppose three amendments were offered on the Senate floor—the first to lower the fine to $5, a second to raise it to $2,000, and a third to raise it to $100,000. How many cases would the bill contain? The answer is three:

1. The interstate shipment of hot oil is banned.
2. The interstate shipment of hot oil is banned and punishable by a $5 fine.
3. The interstate shipment of hot oil is banned and punishable by a $100,000 fine.

The fact that the Bureau of Mines is to administer the law is substantively unimportant, and both the original $1,000 fine and the amendment to raise it to $2,000 serve only to support the first proposal—to make hot oil unprofitable. But changing the fine to be $5 essentially would nullify the ban, and increasing it to $100,000 would signify that the shipment of hot oil was no ordinary commercial crime.

In other instances, the issue of who administers a law is substantively important and enters into the case-decision process. For example, since the passage of the Coal Mine Health and Safety Act of 1969,[12] liberals have frequently introduced legislation to transfer jurisdiction over the law from the

---

12. PL91–173.

Department of Interior to the more pro-union Department of Labor. Proposals with such administrative characteristics are cases in my study.

Identifying the Population and Sample

The universe of cases for this study consists of all proposals introduced in Congress from 1945 to 1976, inclusively, that would have altered the economic characteristics of energy markets. The unit of analysis as far as congressional record keeping is concerned, however, is the bill and not what I call a proposal or case. I must choose cases from appropriately selected bills.

I identified energy bills and amendments by using the *Congressional Record Index*. The *Index* references most of the activities of the U.S. Congress in two ways: by the name of the member performing the action and by the affected policy area. By checking the *Index* subject headings where energy-related matters probably would be listed (see table 7–1), I should have found most of the bills and amendments that came before Congress. I then used the *Daily Digest of General Public Bills* and the decision rules discussed above to divide the bills into individual proposals. The *Daily Digest,* published by the Congressional Research Service (CRS), provides concise descriptions of all bills as they were introduced into Congress. I was able to find the full text or summaries of all the energy amendments by searching through committee reports, the *Congressional Record,* and the *Congressional Quarterly Reports*. Through these search procedures, I found a total of 3,971 different energy proposals, during the thirty-two-year time period.

I may have overlooked some energy proposals for two different reasons. First, energy provisions might be contained in bills whose titles led the CRS to classify them under index subject headings that I did not examine. Bills exempting farm vehicles from gasoline taxes, for example, were indexed under the "Farmers" category and not cross-listed under "Gasoline." While I caught these proposals, a bill that included a similar exemption for fishing boats would have gotten by me if it were categorized only under "Fishing." While a few bills that should have been included but were not undoubtedly slipped by me, I have no reason to believe the missing bills are of any particular type. Since random error does not bias the results but only makes them less certain, my lack of omniscience probably will not distort the analysis.

Second, in the course of dividing bills into proposals, I relied on the summaries in the *Daily Digest* and usually did not read the complete bills. However, on those occasions when I had access to full bills, I did not find any cause to change the way I had coded the proposals.[13] The *Digest* summaries

---

13. Yale's Government Documents Center failed to appreciate the benefit of spending $40,000 for a complete microfiche collection of congressional bills.

TABLE 7–1. Congressional Record Subject Headings

Agriculture	Gasoline	Petroleum
Anthracite	Imports	Price Controls
Atomic Energy	Internal Revenue	Public Lands
Atomic Energy Act	Mineral Leasing Law	Public Roads
Atomic Energy	Mines and Mining	Rivers and Harbors
Commission	Natural Gas	Reciprocal Trade
Biomass	Natural Resources	Synthetic Fuel
Coal	Naval Reserves	Tariff
Energy	Nuclear Regulatory	Taxation
Farmers	Commission	Tidelands
Foreign Trade	Oil and Gas	Trade Extension
Fuels	Oil Pollution	Uranium
Gas		

do not omit any substantive provisions of legislation for the sample of cases that I examined.

Sampling Strategies

Since gathering information on nearly 4,000 cases would have required an inordinate amount of time, I examined only a portion of them. But collecting data on even, say, 20 percent of these proposals still would have meant a great deal of work had I used ordinary random-sampling techniques because information on policy topics is organized by issue area and not by individual proposals. I modified the sampling procedure to create a list of cases that could be researched easily and yet would also possess the characteristics necessary for reliable, generalizable conclusions.

In the first step of this process, I divided my universe of cases into "political clusters" and then randomly eliminated half of them from my study (see table 7–2). Each cluster is a set of alternative proposals to a specific congressionally defined issue topic. Within the cluster "Coal—Black Lung," for example, are 76 policy ideas, such as extending the Black Lung program for 18 months, expanding the program's coverage to include surface mines, taxing coal at a rate of $1.25 per ton to pay for the program's benefits, and authorizing $10 million to build facilities for the treatment and research of pneumoconiosis.[14]

I grouped my cases into clusters because information in Congress—

14. If I had used simple cases as my sampling units, as most studies quite properly do, the sample I drew would have been distorted. Proposals such as that to repeal the oil depletion allowance were continually introduced into congresses without success and hence would have had a greater likelihood of being selected compared to proposals that passed the first time that they were introduced in Congress. To ensure that every proposal (popular as well as unpopular) had an equal chance of being picked, I combined all identically worded cases into "political ideas" for

TABLE 7–2.   Stratification and Cluster Categories

Atomic Energy	Coal
*Electricity sale	Anthracite subsidy
*Nuclear fuel enrichment	Bituminous allocation
Labor issues	General taxation
License allocation	Miner pensions
Uranium allocation	*Coal slurry pipelines
General nuclear plant regulation	*Power plant conversion
*Nuclear incident regulation	Transportation tax
Uranium mine tailings	Anthracite externalities
*Waste management	*Black Lung
Thermal pollution	General environmental problems
Health and safety information	*Coal mine safety and health
*Uranium reserves information	Surface mine regulation
*Electricity-sale market structure	*Foreign trade
*Plant entry	Market structure
Antitrust	Distribution of rent
Nuclear enrichment ownership	*Coal R&D
Distribution of rent	
General R&D	
*Co-op power	
Co-op power breeder	
Nuclear incident R&D	
*Waste management R&D	
General fusion R&D	
Breeder R&D	
*Radiation R&D	
Patent policy	

Note: An asterisk (*) indicates that the cluster was selected for the sample.

whether in the form of committee reports, interest-group testimony, or floor debates—tends to be organized by particular issues. And in the course of reading through all the documents, researchers will learn about actors' preferences on most of the different solutions, whether they are interested in all of them or just one. Furthermore, to become familiar with the substance of a proposal, researchers must read books and journal articles that tend to be issue rather than proposal specific. Since a simple 20 percent random sample probably would have included cases from all the clusters, the time savings that resulted from this first step should be obvious.

In the second step of this sampling procedure, I randomly chose 40 percent of the policy ideas from each of the selected clusters. For example, I

sampling purposes and then collected data on all of the cases comprising those ideas that were selected.

gathered information on 30 of the 76 Black Lung policy ideas. My final sample includes a total of 275 cases.[15] Table 7–3 provides summary statistics of ideas, cases, and proposals that became law in the universe, the clusters selected for the sample, and the actual sample.

One might wonder why I kept a full 50 percent of the clusters in my study and examined only 40 percent of the ideas within each cluster. The fastest way to gather information on 20 percent of the cases within my population would have been to eliminate 80 percent of the clusters from my study and collect data on all the ideas making up the remaining clusters. The danger of this strategy is that the values of certain variables probably would have varied only a small amount across the cases of the sample, and in such situations it is extremely difficult to determine how much influence variables have on policy outcomes. Specifically, the standard errors of the coefficients and overall estimate would be high, giving us less confidence in the results.

Suppose, for instance, that consumer groups expressed intense positions only on proposals dealing with nuclear insurance or coal mine safety. If I included only 20 percent of the clusters in my study, there is a high probability that neither of these clusters would have been selected, and the range of values on numerous variables could have been small.

Since the values of some variables may tend to differ mostly with the energy commodity under consideration, I "stratified" my population into nine commodity groups. Thus, in the first step of my sampling process, I actually divided my case population into political clusters, organized these clusters into fuel categories, and randomly eliminated half the clusters from each category.

But one still could argue that it would have been quicker to have kept only 20 percent of the clusters from each of the commodity groups. While stratification would go a long way toward ensuring a wide range of values in all the factors I planned to analyze, it wouldn't go far enough. In the above example, there is a strong probability that excluding 80 percent of the clusters from each strata would have meant excluding both the clusters that consumer groups, for example, were intensely interested in. By keeping half the political clusters in my study, I felt comfortably certain that I would observe a wide range of values in all the factors that I wanted to test. Of course, once I committed myself to including half the clusters, I was unable to collect data on all the political ideas within those clusters; hence, I randomly chose 40 percent of these ideas to study.

---

15. Only the 277 cases in the atomic-energy and coal categories were coded for data analysis because of time considerations. Two cases from 1945 were not used in estimating the model because economic contextual data for 1944 could not be found.

TABLE 7–3. Descriptive Characteristics of Universe and Sample

Fuel Category	Total Clusters	Total Ideas	Total Cases	Total Laws	Clusters Sampled	Ideas in Sampled Clusters	Cases in Sampled Clusters	Laws in Sampled Clusters	Sample Ideas	Sample Cases	Sample Laws
Atomic energy	26	456	591	322	10	145	205	108	75	100	62
Coal	16	580	745	115	6	320	370	108	160	177	53
Totals	52	1,036	1,336	437	16	465	575	216	235	277	115

Summary

In my study, a case is an energy-policy proposal—a group of legislative words that would alter the characteristics of the market for a particular energy commodity. I used a stratified cluster sampling procedure to randomly select 277 atomic energy and coal cases from among the universe of 3,971 energy proposals introduced into the U.S. Congress between 1945 and 1976.

Representation of the Theories

In chapter 5, I stated that the policy positions of the public, bureaucrats, the president, fellow members of Congress, and nongovernmental organizations may affect the positional behavior of members of Congress and indirectly affect policy outcomes. To represent these variables, I gathered data on the policy positions of those actors who plausibly might affect energy-policy outcomes (see table 7–4) for every atomic-energy and coal case in the sample, using congressional hearings, committee reports, floor debates, newspaper and trade journal accounts, and secondary sources.

An energy proposal becomes law not only because of the positions of actors toward the case itself, but also because of their positions on the bill that contains the proposal; hence, both types of data were collected for every case in the sample. In my coding procedures, actor positions on both the actual proposal and the bill that contained it could take any of nine values (see table 7–5) and were measured at three different stages of the policy process (House, Senate, and conference).

Members of Congress, then, had four positions for every case (chamber and conference stages for both the proposal and bill), whereas members of the administration and interest groups had six positions (House, Senate, and conference for both the proposal and bill).[16]

I coded the positions of these actors based on their own statements in the original and secondary sources I listed earlier or based on reasonable inferences when they did not make statements. To be coded as having intense support, actors had to use adverbs in their testimony. When people stated that they strongly opposed legislation or that a particular proposal was their num-

---

16. I did not gather public opinion data on the cases for several reasons. First, before 1973, pollsters asked very few energy questions. Second, the energy questions they did ask were not relevant to public policy. The typical question tapped people's anger toward energy events. Common examples were, Do you think energy prices are too high? Do you think the petroleum shortages are real? Are oil companies, Arabs, or politicians responsible for the current mess? From such questions, we learn that citizens are angry and that they do not enjoy losses in real income. We learn very little, however, about policy positions. Public opinion is better tapped by the economic and cost-benefit contextual data that drive politicians' anticipated reactions.

TABLE 7–4.   Actors Coded in the Study

Legislative
  House and Senate majority leaders
  House and Senate minority leaders
  House and Senate committee chairs
  House and Senate subcommittee chairs
  House and Senate committee ranking minority members
  House and Senate subcommittee ranking minority members

Executive	Oil jobbers
Energy Administrator	Auto manufacturers
Office of Management and Budget	American Gas Association
President	Independent gas producers
Secretary of Commerce	Integrated gas producers
Secretary of HEW	Gas pipeline owners
Secretary of the Interior	Gas distributors
Secretary of Labor	AFL-CIO
Secretary of the Treasury	United Mine Workers
Nongovernmental Organizations	Electrical workers
Nuclear producers	Oil, Chemical, and Atomic Workers
Private utilities	Nuclear construction workers
Public utilities	United Auto Workers
Rural co-ops	National Farmers Union
National Coal Association	National Association of Manufacturers
American Mining Congress	Chamber of Commerce
Bituminous Mine Operators Association	Sierra Club
National independent mine operators	Friends of the Earth
Surface mine operators	Americans for Democratic Action
American Petroleum Institute	Common Cause
Independent Petroleum Association	Nader groups
Small oil producers	Solar groups
Integrated refiners	Small refiners
Independent refiners	Seven Sisters
International Independent Oil	Service stations

ber one legislative priority, I coded their positions as one or eight, respectively. Testimony without adverbs was coded as a two or seven. Testimony that changed within any one of the legislative stages (House, Senate, or conference) presented difficulties. Genuine conversions in viewpoint were coded as changeable ending in support or opposition, while frequent or random changes in viewpoint were coded as divided or equivocal. Positions were coded as indifferent when the cases of interest to an actor were dropped from a larger bill, ending his interest in that legislation.[17]

---

17. Before estimating the model, I recoded these nine values into a true scale centered at 0.5 with 0 and 1 as endpoints. In the recoding, the original values of 0 (no preference/unknown), 4 (divided or equivocal), and 5 (indifferent) all became 0.5, the midpoint of the scale.

TABLE 7–5. **Actor Policy Positions**

Value	Position
0	No preference/unknown
1	Intensely against
2	Against
3	Changeable ending in opposition
4	Divided or equivocal
5	Indifferent
6	Changeable ending in support
7	Support
8	Intense support

Coding from Incomplete Information

The most problematic aspect of my coding procedures, of course, lies in inferences I made when information was incomplete. In the remainder of this section, I will discuss the general rules I developed to handle these difficulties. In appendix 7A, at the end of this chapter, I code actual cases in detail to illustrate the implementation of the general rules.

The availability of information on actor positions varies by type of actor and stage in the policy process. Interest-group and bureaucratic positions are the easiest to ascertain. The organization of the public records of the policy process (hearings, committee reports, etc.) allows easy discovery of these actors' sentiments. The president usually does not directly express a policy position; hence, formal congressional data keepers such as *Congressional Quarterly* are very conservative in their estimates of presidential positions. I am more willing to attribute a disposition.[18]

The positions of committee and floor leaders are more difficult to obtain than those of interest groups because interest groups give direct testimony in hearings, while congressional leaders speak largely to clarify the positions of those who testify. If legislation receives floor consideration, the majority and minority bill managers almost always give statements that illuminate the positions and struggles. In the absence of statements, I code committee and subcommittee chairs as favoring cases and bills that are approved by committee. If minority members issue a minority report, I use that as the basis for coding.

---

18. *Congressional Quarterly* does not attribute a position to the president in its roll call records in many cases in which I felt comfortable making an inference. For example, it did not attribute a position to the president on the passage of the Energy Policy and Conservation Act in the House (H.R. 7014 (September 23, 1975): *CQ* House vote #405). I coded the president as being opposed to the bill because it contained many provisions, including a rollback of domestic oil prices, that were contrary to proposals he had offered in his Presidential Energy Message.

Majority and minority leaders of the House and Senate rarely make statements. I seldom code them as having positions on proposals and code them as having positions on bills only when the original sources portray the policy struggle as a partisan one. A good example would be the struggle over public funding of nuclear reactors in the late 1950s and early 1960s, discussed in chapter 4. Democrats favored public ownership and expansion of nuclear power, while Republicans favored leaving decisions to private utilities.

Information availability also varies according to the stage of the legislative process under consideration. Proposals that are introduced into committee but receive no further consideration are often difficult to code. The most difficult are those proposals that are not part of any ongoing policy struggle. Cases of this type appear with just a sponsor's name and bill number and disappear without a trace of political attention. These proposals are not the subject of hearings, press releases, or floor testimony of any kind. I coded them on the basis of the context in which they were introduced. Examples are found in Appendix 7A.

Contextual Data

The economic conditions of energy firms, workers, and consumers may affect congressional energy-policy decisions in two ways. First, they may modify the credibility of statements made by actors regarding the economic necessity of their policy agenda. The pleas of firms for or against legislation, for example, may have more effect when the firms are in economic difficulty. Second, regardless of actor statements, members of Congress may respond directly to sectoral economic conditions by passing policies to augment incomes when declines occur and to redistribute incomes during boom times.

I collected annual data from 1945 to 1976 on numerous measures of the economic condition of producers, workers, and consumers of coal and nuclear power. Firms' conditions were represented by profit and production data; workers' conditions, by earnings and employment; and consumers' conditions, by price data (see table 7–6).

Simple annual percentage changes in these time series would not adequately represent the correct theory but instead would test whether the poor economic conditions of energy firms, workers, or consumers increase the likelihood that a proposal will become law, which, of course, is a nonsensical statement. The correct theory states that the worse the economic conditions, the greater the likelihood that a proposal will pass that benefits energy groups, and the smaller the likelihood that a proposal will become law that imposes costs on energy groups. Several changes, required to put the data in the correct form, are described in Appendix 7B.

TABLE 7–6. Sectoral Economic Conditions

Actor	Measure
Nuclear producers	Cost per kwh for installed nuclear plants > 300 mgW
	Cost per kwh for installed coal plants > 300 mgW
	Nuclear production capacity added
	Fossil production capacity added
	Nuclear production capacity ordered
	Fossil production capacity ordered
	Domestic uranium production
	Cost estimates for nuclear power ($/kwh in year ordered)
Nuclear workers	Employment in nuclear industry
Nuclear consumers	Production costs per kwh for nuclear plants
	Production costs per kwh for fossil plants
Coal producers	Coal production
	Small-mine production (< 10,000 tons annually)
	Medium-mine production (10,000–50,000 tons annually)
	Net income of coal industry
Coal workers	Weekly earnings of coal miners
	Coal employment
	Coal mine fatalities
Coal consumers	Coal price
Utilities	Net income of private utilities
	Electricity sales of private utilities
Utility workers	Weekly earnings of nonsupervisory electrical workers
	Employment of electrical workers
Utility consumers	Electricity price
Taxpayers	Real per capita disposable income
	Ratio of federal taxes to personal income

Note: All measures are annual averages.

Political Resources

Political resources are an essential component of any explanation of policy outcomes. In particular, they differentiate persuasion from influence relations. Data that represent political resources, however, are difficult to gather for several distinct reasons. First, records of campaign receipts and donations are not available for elections prior to the early 1970s. Second, time-series data on interest-group lobbying expenditures are impossible to obtain without the assistance of the groups themselves. Since most of these groups would not even discuss their positions with me, budget data were out of the question. A final, and more theoretical, obstacle involves finding a common metric for interest-group and intragovernmental-actor resources. The most likely units for interest-group resources would be dollars. Committee chairs and bureaucrats, however, do not spend dollars to enhance their policy positions.

I used intensity of position as a measure, albeit imperfect, of resources. The accuracy of this measure varies with the correlation between intensity and resource use. If position intensity and resource use are perfectly correlated, then the measures cannot be distinguished empirically. The opposite scenario would occur if an actor randomly used politically relevant resources when he had intense positions. If resources, in fact, are critical to enactment, then the simple position-intensity variable in this second situation would show no relationship with enactment. The more complicated interaction term (actor position intensity × political resources), on the other hand, would show a perfect relationship with enactment. If I used this second variable construction, the difference between intensity and resources would be found in the coefficients. I believe, however, that reality is closer to the first scenario than the second; therefore, my lack of an explicit measure of resources will not miss actors whose positions affect policy outcomes. It is unlikely that those who hold strong positions would randomly alternate their use of resources just to empirically test whether resources really are effective.

Allocation of Costs and Benefits

Many political scientists (Dunham and Marmor 1978; Wilson 1980; Arnold 1990) argue that the dispersion of costs and benefits from public policy actions is the key to their political acceptability. Ideally, one would measure the actual income changes per capita that would result from policy proposals, but that is not possible. As a proxy, I coded each case into one of twelve policy categories (table 7–7). These categories constitute a rough continuum ranging from concentrated-benefits–dispersed-costs policies (infrastructure expenditures) to concentrated-costs–dispersed-benefit policies (public participation in commodity production). In the actual analysis, I compressed the twelve categories into three: benefits (one through four), middle (five through nine), and harms (ten through twelve). I also had to control for whether the proposal was a new law, or an extension, increase, cutback, or repeal of an existing law. One would expect the repeal of policies that have concentrated benefits and dispersed costs to be as likely as the augmentation of policies that have concentrated costs and dispersed benefits. Table 7–8 illustrates the categories represented by the values of the final interactive cost-benefit variable.

TABLE 7–7. Cost-Benefit Policy Categories

1. Infrastructure expenditures
2. Research and development expenditures
3. Expenditures to remedy negative externalities
4. Indirect energy commodity subsidies (loans, price supports)
5. Allocation of energy commodities by regulation or price controls
6. Regulation of firms to remedy negative externalities
7. Direct energy commodity subsidy
8. Corporate taxation
9. Individual taxation
10. Regulation of consumers to remedy negative externalities
11. Use of market methods to remedy negative externalities
12. Public participation in commodity production

Summary

The policy positions of congressional, executive, and interest-group actors are the central factors in my model of policy outcomes. To determine which actors wanted which outcomes, I coded the coal and atomic-energy cases in my sample using primary and secondary historical materials. Whenever possible, I allowed these actors to speak for themselves regarding their positions on specific energy proposals and the bills the proposals were contained in. For obscure policy episodes, where actors left very few tracks, I made conservative, defensible inferences about their positions from my understanding of the context and from their views on similar cases.

The time series I used to represent the economic conditions of energy firms, workers, and consumers are quite straightforward. I had to modify them for use in the model, however, by creating interaction terms that combined economic conditions with the flow of costs and benefits.

TABLE 7–8. Cost-Benefit Variable Values

Value	Legislative Action
1.00	Repeal benefits and increase harms
0.75	Cut back benefits and maintain harms
0.50	All mixed proposals and new laws
0.25	Cut back harms and maintain benefits
0.00	Repeal harms and increase benefits

Design and Specification of the Model

Figure 7–1 graphically illustrates the relationships suggested by the theories of policy outcomes set forth in chapter 4. The classes of factors enclosed by circles are determined within the model. Intragovernmental actors—the House and Senate committee and party leaders, the heads of federal agencies, and the president—determine their positions with an eye toward each other and toward the probability of proposal passage. Interest-group positions, economic conditions, and the distribution of costs and benefits created by a policy proposal are determined outside the model and affect outcomes through two different mechanisms. Interest-group positions affect members of government through ordinary influence relations. Economic conditions and the distribution of costs and benefits affect outcomes through anticipated reactions and contextual effects. Those factors in the bottom bracket affect outcomes through the unobserved positions of rank-and-file members of Congress.

Figure 7–1 conveys only the generic structure of the model by illustrating the relationships between classes of variables. In order to actually specify the model, I had to test the positions of all the actors listed in table 7–4, the economic conditions listed in table 7–6, and the cost-benefit categories listed in table 7–7 for possible effects.

When political scientists and economists estimate empirical models of complicated phenomena, their specification choices are extremely crucial, yet the actual procedures used to arrive at the final specification are rarely reported. Authors merely state that indicators of plausible causes that do not appear in the final version of the model had coefficients that were indistinguishable from zero in preliminary versions of the model. For ordinary-least-squares single-equation estimation, this does not have severe consequences. In nonrecursive systems of equations, however, authors should be more specific about how exogenous variables were determined to be causes of some endogenous variables and not others and about how the reciprocal relationships among the endogenous variables were determined.

The main problems in specifying the model presented in figure 7–1 arise in determining which exogenous variables are causes of which congressional and bureaucratic positions, and which congressional and bureaucratic positions actually have effects on each other and on the probability of proposal passage. To reduce the number of equations I had to estimate, I first ran a simple probit equation for the likelihood of proposal passage.[19] Those variables whose estimated coefficients were less than their standard error were assumed to have no effect and were eliminated one at a time from the equa-

---

19. I assumed that any variable that did not have an effect in the simple probit model would not have an effect in the more elaborate two-stage probit specification.

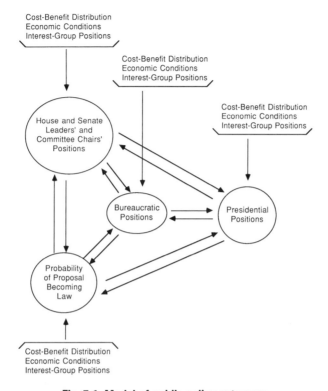

Cost-Benefit Distribution
Economic Conditions
Interest-Group Positions

Cost-Benefit Distribution
Economic Conditions
Interest-Group Positions

Cost-Benefit Distribution
Economic Conditions
Interest-Group Positions

House and Senate
Leaders' and
Committee Chairs'
Positions

Bureaucratic
Positions

Presidential
Positions

Probability
of Proposal
Becoming
Law

Cost-Benefit Distribution
Economic Conditions
Interest-Group Positions

Fig. 7-1. Model of public policy outcomes

tion. This rule, however, was not hard and fast. If a coefficient was substantively large, I kept it in the specification, regardless of the standard error, to ensure that it was not hastily eliminated.

If the coefficients of the other variables in the equation remained stable (did not change sign or change by more than one standard error) when a variable was dropped, then the variable was deemed to be superfluous and eliminated from consideration. If the coefficient of a variable did change dramatically when a variable was eliminated from the equation, I then checked for multivariate collinearity between the two variables. If one of the two variables had a strong and stable coefficient, it was retained. If neither of the two variables in question had a stable coefficient when alone, both variables were dropped.

For all those congressional and bureaucratic positions that remained in this simple probit specification (see table 7–9), I estimated separate ordinary-least-squares equations, with the exogenous interest-group and economic factors as explanatory variables. Technically, of course, variables that remain in

TABLE 7–9. Congressional and
Executive-Branch Policy Positions
Having Direct Effects on the Probability
of Passage in Simple Probit Model

House majority leader bill
House committee chair proposal
Senate ranking minority subcommittee proposal
Senate majority leader proposal
Office of Management and Budget proposal
Secretary of Labor proposal
House ranking minority subcommittee bill
President bill
Secretary of the Treasury bill
Secretary of Labor bill
Senate subcommittee chair bill

these equations may be indirect as well as direct causes of the congressional
and bureaucratic positions; however, I assumed that they were all direct
causes in order to create the first version of the fully specified model.[20] At this
point, I had specified a complete model with actor positions, economic conditions, and cost-benefit distributions. The interest-group, economic, and cost-
benefit variables in each of the equations for the congressional and bureaucratic positions were sufficiently different that identification was achieved and the
problem of reciprocal causation among the bureaucratic and congressional
positions could be tackled through two-stage estimation.

I estimated this preliminary model with two-stage probit. Those variables in table 7–9 with coefficients indistinguishable from zero were eliminated from the model. To recheck these results, I added all the exogenous and
predicted endogenous variables that were eliminated one at a time to the
probit equation to test for nonzero coefficients. In addition, all endogenous
congressional and bureaucratic positions that did not remain in the original
simple probit model (table 7–9) were added one at a time to determine once
again whether they had effects. Those variables that had t-statistics above 1.5
were then employed in a full two-stage probit estimation of the model. None
of these additional variables had coefficients larger than their standard errors,
and they were not included in the final model.

A significant drawback to the specification searches I have just described
is the possibility of overfitting, the attribution of a statistically significant
relationship where none really exists. If one uses standard (5 percent) signifi-

20. Indirect effects arise because an exogenous variable may actually be the cause of a
position held by a congressional or bureaucratic actor who, in turn, affects the dependent variable
that is actually in the ordinary-least-squares equations.

cance tests and estimates 100 different equations, 5 percent of the variables with significant coefficients will not really be causally related to the dependent variable. To test for this possibility, I took two random samples of the 275 cases (one 50 percent and the other 75 percent) and reestimated the model. None of the coefficients experienced sign changes or dramatic changes in value, although the standard errors did rise, of course. The final model clearly is not overfitted.

Conclusion

Cause and effect relationships that are inferred from natural data are extremely dependent on the research design and methodological techniques that are utilized. Problems may arise because of failure to adequately specify the events to be explained, the theories to be tested, the unit of analysis, and the population and sample of cases; failure to represent the causal factors with data; or failure to use appropriate statistical techniques. In this study, I explain the enactment into law of proposals introduced in Congress that would affect the characteristics of energy markets. I do not formally explain the formation of energy proposals, the enactment of policy proposals affecting other substantive areas, or the stages in the policy process prior to enactment. The restrictions I place on the scope of my explanatory activities, however, are not a source of bias.

The unit of analysis is a sentence or group of sentences in a bill or amendment that would alter the economic characteristics of the market for an energy commodity. From 1945 through 1976, 3,971 energy cases were introduced in Congress. Because of time constraints, I gathered data only on the cases in the atomic-energy and coal strata, a total of 277 cases. For each of these cases, I collected data on the positions of relevant political actors toward both the case and the bill it was a part of, as well as on relevant economic and cost-benefit conditions.

I specified the model in several steps. First, I assumed that interest-group positions and economic and cost-benefit conditions were determined outside the model, while congressional, bureaucratic, and presidential positions were reciprocally determined by each other and by the probability of proposal passage. To establish which congressional, bureaucratic, and presidential positions were really involved, I estimated a simple probit model of proposal passage and eliminated all the variables that did not have a significant effect. I then estimated simple ordinary-least-squares equations for those intragovernmental actors that remained, using interest-group positions and economic and cost-benefit conditions as independent variables. Using these equations, I then predicted congressional and bureaucratic positions, which were used to estimate a two-stage probit model, the results of which appear in the next chapter.

Appendix 7A: Coding Cases from Incomplete and Convoluted Information

Incomplete Information: Nuclear Regulation

After 1969, public-interest and environmental organizations began to attack the elite consensus that supported nuclear power. The Joint Committee on Atomic Energy, however, had an extremely stable pro-nuclear, nonpartisan membership (Green and Rosenthal 1963). Their outlook toward nuclear energy resembled congressional attitudes toward dams and flood-control projects. In addition to generating district support by conferring discrete local benefits, such commodities also command general political support because new technologies are often thought to offer an affluent, limitless future. Actual experience with nuclear costs and environmental failures, however, transformed legislators' image of nuclear power from a triumph of technology to an expensive, and possibly harmful, boondoggle. This change in perception, combined with politicians' aversion to risk, marked the end of general congressional support of nuclear power. The Joint Committee, however, remained adamantly pronuclear. Eventually, the committee became so unrepresentative of the divisions in the House that the Democratic caucus abolished it in 1977.[21]

The first legislative recognition of the lack of consensus was H.R. 9542 and H.R. 5111, introduced in 1971 and 1973, respectively. These bills would have allowed the Department of Interior, the Federal Power Commission, and the Environmental Protection Agency to share regulatory control over commercial nuclear power with the Atomic Energy Commission. The first clue about the nature of the bills was that their sponsor was Jonathan Bingham, a liberal Democrat from New York, who was not a member of the Joint Committee on Atomic Energy. These two cases represented attempts by Bingham to widen the circle of decision makers on nuclear issues. I coded majority and minority committee members, the administration, nuclear producers, and electric utilities as being opposed to these attempts to end the Atomic Energy Commission's monopoly, and coal groups (National Coal Association and United Mine Workers) and the Sierra Club as being in favor of them. The president and all other actors were coded as having no preference.

Incomplete Information: Coal Subsidies

The central feature of coal markets after World War II was the decline in production as commercial and private consumers switched to petroleum prod-

---

21. PL95–10.

ucts. Members of Congress from coal-producing states fought this decline with numerous policy proposals that never left committee, including:

- H.R. 6174, a bill to authorize the subsidy of coal-export rail transportation, introduced by Representative Bailey (D–W. Va.) in July, 1953;
- H.R. 6358, a bill to authorize research and development expenditures on the use of coal products as road-surface materials, introduced by Representative Dent (D–Pa.) in April, 1959; and
- S. 2720, a bill to establish a minimum price of 10 percent of market value for uranium services provided by the federal government, introduced by Senator Moss (D–Utah) and nine other liberal and coal-state senators in April, 1964.

The rail export subsidy and coal-as-road-material bills were obvious attempts to boost demand for a troubled commodity. I coded the coal operators and miners as being in favor of these items for obvious reasons, and I coded the Eisenhower administration as being opposed because of its general orientation toward markets and its attitude toward coal problems, in particular, as expressed in the legislative history of the 1954 Atomic Energy Act and the 1960 Coal Research and Development Act.[22] I also coded the private utilities as opposed because they would resist any legislation that raised the demand and, hence, the price of coal. In 1953, the chairman of the Interstate Commerce Committee, to which Bailey's bill was referred, was Charles Wolverton (R–N.J.), and the ranking Democrat was Robert Crosier of Ohio. Neither of them came from coal districts, and I had no specific information concerning their sentiments, so I coded them as having no position. The same was true for all remaining actors.

The road-material R&D bill was part of the larger 1959 struggle over coal research and development.[23] The language of the bill not only referred to road-material research in general, but to a specific firm in Pennsylvania that was to receive the contract. Representative Dent probably introduced this bill to provide evidence that he was fighting for his district and to send the bureaucracy a message that this firm in Pennsylvania should receive part of the action no matter what form of coal R&D was eventually adopted.

I coded the road-material R&D case the same as the rail export case because the context was largely the same. The coal operators and the miners favored the subsidy, while the Eisenhower administration opposed because it

---

22. See note 5 in chapter 4.

23. President Eisenhower resisted the creation of an independent coal research agency and vetoed a bill in 1959 creating one. In 1960, a bill creating an Office of Coal Research within the Department of Interior became law (PL86–599).

did not like legislative constraints on bureaucratic discretion. The House Interior Committee leaders were generally sympathetic to coal interests, but I coded them as having no preference because the bill was a message to the Appropriations Committee and Interior Department and not really a coal R&D policy bill per se.[24] I coded the utilities as having no preference because the proposal would have only minimal second-order effects on coal prices, their only concern.

The nature of the struggle underlying the bill to mandate minimum charges for nuclear fuel becomes clear once one realizes the sponsors were a coalition of liberal and coal-state Democrats and not members of the Joint Committee on Atomic Energy. The liberals did not like the subsidies to industry, and coal senators did not like the subsidy of a competitor. I coded members of the committee, nuclear industry representatives, electric utilities, and administration officials as opposed and the National Coal Association and United Mine Workers as in favor. I also coded the AFL-CIO as opposed because it supported nuclear power on every occasion from the late 1950s until the middle 1960s.[25] In the absence of any information, I coded the majority and minority leaders, the president, bureaucrats other than the Atomic Energy Commission chair, and all other interest groups as having no position.

Coding from Convoluted Information: Coal Conversion

The extension of coal-conversion authority from 1975 through 1977 illustrates how I coded cases in which a simple proposal was attached to a series of larger controversial bills. The Energy Supply and Environmental Coordination Act of 1974[26] gave the Federal Energy Administration the authority to order fossil-fuel boilers to use coal if they had the technical capability and if coal was available. In 1975, both coal-conversion and oil price-control authority was to expire. President Ford sent a variety of proposals to Congress to deal with energy markets, including Title IV of S. 594 (H.R. 2633), which would extend coal-conversion authority for two years, expiring in 1977.

The struggle over extension of coal-conversion authority did not attract much attention. The only alternative to President Ford's proposal was put forward by the coal industry and promoted by its perennial legislative spokesman, Senator Jennings Randolph (D–W. Va.). His bill, S. 1777, would have required that new electric plants be capable of burning coal by 1979; existing

---

24. The chairman was Wayne Aspinal (D–Colo.); the ranking minority member was John Saylor (R–Pa.). The chairman of the Subcommittee on Mines and Mining was Adam Clayton Powell (D–N.Y.), and the ranking minority on the subcommittee was Saylor.

25. See note 5 in chapter 4.

26. PL93–319.

electric plants, by 1980; and all industrial boilers, by 1985. This proposal differed from President Ford's because it mandated conversion for all existing plants, not just those that were already technically capable of utilizing coal, and it also removed FEA discretion over the process.

In contrast to the low-key struggle over coal conversion, oil pricing issues, always combined in the same bill as the coal provisions, were subject to open and prolonged conflict. The Senate passed four bills in 1975 in response to the president's energy program.[27] Neither the mandatory coal-conversion bill nor the administration proposal received formal committee approval, but Senator Randolph successfully offered an amendment during the floor debate of S. 622 to extend coal-conversion authority an additional six months until December, 1975. In addition, Senator Glenn successfully introduced an amendment to place a ceiling on the price of domestic crude oil produced in excess of May, 1972, levels (new oil).

In the House, the coal-conversion authority extension, as proposed by the administration, was approved by committee. However, as in the Senate, the bill that contained it, H.R. 7014, also contained oil-price rollback provisions that created Republican and oil opposition.

The conference committee retained the two-year coal-conversion extension sought by the administration and approved by the House and also retained the controversial oil price-control provisions.

I coded Thomas P. ("Tip") O'Neill and Mike Mansfield, the House and Senate majority leaders, respectively, as having no position on the coal-conversion proposal and as being in favor of the bill at both the House and conference stages because the struggle over oil price controls, the main feature of the bill, was partisan. Most Democrats favored retention of price controls, while most Republicans favored decontrol plus windfall taxes.[28] The House minority leader, John Rhodes (R–Ariz.), was coded as having no position on coal conversion and as being opposed to the bill at both the House and conference stages because of general Republican opposition to price controls and bureaucratic allocation. The Senate minority leader, Hugh Scott (R–Pa.), like many northeastern Republicans, consistently supported the use of allocation and price-control schemes and hence was coded as being in favor of the bill.

The Senate Interior Committee leaders were Henry Jackson (D–Wash.) and Paul Fannin (R–Ariz.). Both expressed support of coal conversion in

---

27. They were S. 349, the Energy Labeling and Disclosure Act; S. 622, the Standby Energy Authorities Act; S. 677, the Strategic Energy Reserve Act; and S. 1883, the Automobile Fuel Economy Act.

28. The chairman of the Ways and Means Committee, Al Ullman (D–Ore.), did propose a direct tax on gasoline and excessive auto fuel consumption, gradual decontrol of oil prices and a tax on the resulting rents, and creation of a federal oil-import monopsony and auction to counteract OPEC, but these proposals were defeated on the House floor by decisive margins.

1973,[29] so I coded them as favoring the extension. Jackson also supported the bill at both the Senate and conference stages, while Fannin opposed it because of the use of bureaucratic instead of price allocation.[30]

The House Interstate Commerce Committee leaders were Harley Staggers (D–W. Va.), chair, and John Dingell (D–Mich.), subcommittee chair. The ranking minority member was Samuel Devine (R–Ohio), and the subcommittee ranking minority member was Clarence Brown (R–Ohio). Staggers and Dingell were coded as in favor of both the case and the bill because they approved the committee report and led the floor fight. Both Brown and Devine signed the minority report to H.R. 7014, which attacked the oil-price rollback provisions, and were coded as opposing the bill.[31] No position could be found for Devine on coal conversion, but Brown remarked that he favored the coal position and was coded accordingly.[32]

President Ford and his administration clearly opposed using price controls and bureaucratic allocation to solve energy difficulties and just as clearly favored coal conversion, so I coded them as being in favor of the proposal and opposed to the bill at the Senate and Conference stages.[33]

Coal operators and mine workers enthusiastically endorsed the mandatory language in Senator Randolph's bill, so I coded them as favoring the proposal and bill, even though a mere extension was less than what they wanted.[34]

Petroleum interests had no position on the coal case itself but were extremely concerned with the oil pricing issue in the bills that contained the coal case. Producers and large integrated companies favored decontrol of prices plus windfall taxes with exemption if the excess profits were invested in petroleum supply-enhancement activities. Retailers, marketers, and small independent refiners favored continued allocation because the regulations assured them of supplies at controlled prices.[35]

29. *Congressional Record*, 93rd Cong., 1st sess., vol. 119, pt. 28: 37307 (Jackson), 37309 (Fannin).

30. *Congressional Record*, 94th Cong., 1st sess., vol. 121, pt. 32:41144.

31. House Committee Report 94–340.

32. *Congressional Record*, 94th Cong., 1st sess., vol. 121, pt. 23:2930.

33. U.S. Congress, House, *Energy Conservation and Oil Policy: Hearing before the Subcommittee on Energy and Power of the Committee on Interstate and Foreign Commerce*, 94th Cong., 1st sess., 1975, 178, 194, 1680.

34. U.S. Congress, Senate, *Greater Coal Utilization: Hearing before the Committees on Interior and Public Works*, 94th Cong., 1st sess., 140, 1673.

35. *Energy Conservation and Oil Policy*, 469 (independent refiners), 485 (small refiners), 557 (Independent Petroleum Association of America), 562, 575 (marketers), 594 (American Petroleum Institute), 1415 (retailers). Some small refiners did complain about the crude-oil entitlements program administered by the FEA. They wanted to retain crude-oil allocation, but also wanted the small-refiner bias of the entitlements program to be modified to eliminate any need for inland small refiners to send checks to the large multinational importers of expensive oil.

Public and private utilities opposed coal conversion but favored continued oil price controls to ease pressures on their costs.[36] Auto manufacturers favored decontrol, while the United Auto Workers favored continued controls.[37] Consumer groups had no position on coal conversion but did favor the retention of price controls. Environmentalists had opposed coal conversion in 1973–74, but now that it was in place, they preferred a simple extension as part of their strategy to force scrubbers on electric plants. In 1973, environmentalists opposed oil price controls as being a very inefficient way to ameliorate the difficulties suffered by low-income energy users. In 1975, their testimony was strictly concerned with pollution issues, so I coded them as favoring the bill because they were mainly concerned with a simple extension of the coal-conversion provisions, not with oil prices.[38]

Appendix 7B: Creation of the Economic Contextual Variables

First, the firms, workers, and consumers affected by policy outcomes in the coal and nuclear power cases that were coded for the empirical study were classified according to the income changes that would result from proposal enactment (gain, lose, or unaffected). In table 7–1A, I have illustrated these coding decisions for cases that I discussed in detail earlier in this chapter and in chapter 6.

The extension of coal conversion in 1975 created no direct gains or losses for the nuclear industry; created direct gains for coal producers and workers (because of increased demand for coal) and for the public (because of environmental gains); and created direct losses for coal consumers (higher coal prices), utilities and electrical workers (scrubber investments), and electricity consumers (higher prices).

The 1953 case to subsidize rail exports was identical in terms of income gains and losses to the coal-conversion case except that, in the former, coal consumers benefited from lower prices, while taxpayers had to pay the subsidy.

The 1956 proposal to construct prototype nuclear reactors, discussed in

---

36. U.S. Congress, House, *Presidential Energy Program: Hearing before the Subcommittee on Energy and Power of the Committee on Interstate and Foreign Commerce,* 94th Cong., 1st sess., 1975, 507 (Edison Electric Institute), 514 (American Public Power Association), 541 (rural co-ops).

37. *Presidential Energy Program,* 440 (General Motors), 484 (United Auto Workers).

38. *Energy Conservation and Oil Policy,* 614, 1514 (Nader), 1767 (environmentalists); U.S. Congress, Senate, *The Fuel Shortage and the Clean Air Act: Hearing before the Subcommittee on Air and Water Pollution of the Committee on Public Works,* 93d Cong., 1st sess., 1973, 66 (environmentalists).

TABLE 7–1A. Groups Affected by Costs and Benefits of Proposals

	Extend Coal Conversion	Pay Rail Exports	Construction Nuclear Prototype	FPC Veto Plants	Minimum Charge Nuclear Fuel
Uranium producers	Unaffected	Unaffected	Gain	Lose	Lose
Nuclear producers	Unaffected	Unaffected	Gain	Lose	Lose
Nuclear workers	Unaffected	Unaffected	Gain	Lose	Lose
Nuclear consumers	Unaffected	Unaffected	Gain	Gain	Gain
Coal producers	Gain	Gain	Lose	Gain	Gain
Independent coal producers	Gain	Gain	Lose	Gain	Gain
Coal workers	Gain	Gain	Lose	Gain	Gain
Coal consumers	Lose	Gain	Gain	Lose	Lose
Utilities	Lose	Lose	Lose	Lose	Lose
Utility workers	Lose	Lose	Lose	Lose	Lose
Utility consumers	Lose	Lose	Gain	Gain	Lose
Taxpayers	Gain	Lose	Lose	Gain	Gain

chapter 3, would have benefited both the builders and consumers of nuclear power and the consumers of coal and electricity (because of increased coal-market competition), but would have created losses for coal producers and workers (decreased utility demand for coal) and for private utilities and their workers (competition from public power).

The final two case examples, the FPC veto of nuclear policy decisions (1973) and the establishment of a minimum price for uranium fuel (1964), were coded as having similar (though not identical) income gains and losses. The FPC veto, as you may recall, was a liberal Democratic attempt to hurt commercial nuclear power; thus, all nuclear actors were coded as losing except for nuclear-electricity consumers, who would benefit from the prevention of unwise plant investments. Coal producers and workers would benefit from the increased demand for coal-fired electricity, but coal consumers and utilities would suffer from the increased market power of coal and the lower stream of earnings that results from a lower rate base (coal plants are less capital intensive than nuclear plants). Electricity customers would benefit from more cost-effective investments, and taxpayers gain from reductions in nuclear plant subsidies and externalities.

From this income-gain and -loss coding exercise, I created dummy (0 or 1) variables representing group winners and losers. I then multiplied the dummies by the percentage-change economic time series described in table 7–6 to create variables for economic condition winners and economic condition losers. The expected sign of the former is negative, and the expected sign of the latter is positive (the better the economic condition of those who gain benefits from a policy proposal, the less likely that the proposal will become law, while the better the economic condition of those who suffer losses from a policy proposal, the more likely that the proposal will pass). I have no reason to believe that the effect of economic conditions is different in magnitude for winners than for losers, so I multiplied the loser-condition variable by negative one and added it to the winner-condition variable.

CHAPTER 8

The Causes of Policy Decisions for Atomic
Energy and Coal

The central question in studying congressional action on energy policy proposals (and microeconomic policy proposals, more generally) is whether the
counterproductive outcomes described in chapters 3 and 4 are the only outcomes consistent with reelection constraints. If Congress chose microeconomic policies that both improved allocational efficiency and decreased in-
equalities in income and wealth distribution instead of its current tendency to
do the opposite, would members be more electorally vulnerable?

The answer to this question is crucial for those who wish to enact policy
reforms. If current policy outcomes are equilibrium solutions of the reelection
game, then those who want different outcomes face a situation analogous to
that facing consumers or workers who wish to change the practices of busi-
nesses. Firms may want to offer more safety precautions, higher wages, or
higher quality merchandise, but if they price their products out of the market
in doing so, these firms will not survive. Under this view, perverse aggregate
outcomes such as inferior merchandise or unsafe conditions are not necessarily the result of greed on the part of firm owners but instead may be the
unintended equilibrium results of attempts to sell products and earn wages.

Analogously, members of Congress may have private beliefs about
various policy proposals, but if they attempt to implement them and individual constituents or organized groups disagree, they run the risk of losing
future elections. Policy results may simply be the equilibrium outcome of the
reelection game.

In this chapter I demonstrate how one would implement the research
design described in chapter 7 to determine the relative importance of the
factors discussed in chapter 5. My results may disappoint the reader who
wants a simple explanation of congressional policy behavior because, in a
multivariate world, numerous factors have effects on outcomes. Some interest
groups have large effects, while others do not. Some congressional leaders
and bureaucrats also affect outcomes, although one reason they do is because
they support proposals that are likely to pass. The president has influence, but
only in certain contexts. Finally, proposals pass at some times and not others

simply because economic conditions change. In short, all of the theories examined in chapter 5 receive support from the data.

Some readers may conclude at this point that multivariate analysis isn't worth the trouble because the case-study literature already suggests that numerous factors contribute to outcomes. I urge you to read on, however, because multivariate evidence provides three insights that case-study evidence cannot. First, it tells us how much factors matter, not simply whether theories are true or not. Second, the simulations presented in this chapter illustrate that major policy changes often occur, not because of a change in any one factor (about which we could tell a dramatic story), but because of small changes in numerous factors (which don't make such great copy). Though the multivariate world is less colorful, it gives us a more realistic view of causation. Finally, I believe that the structure of and large variation in interest-group effects give us some insight into the important issue of congressional discretion.

The Model: Its Specification and Estimation

Figure 8–1 displays the model of policy outcomes for atomic-energy and coal that I estimated after the specification search described in the last chapter.[1] The signs in parentheses indicate whether a variable has a positive or negative effect on the factor that its arrow points to. Variables in circles are endogenous. Variables in brackets are exogenous. All exogenous actor positions are toward either a bill or proposal, as indicated by the endogenous variable they affect. The economic contextual variables are all annual percentage changes in the indicated measure interacted with dummy variables that represent whether the sector would gain, lose, or be unaffected by the proposal (see app. 7B).

The variable to be explained is the likelihood of a proposal becoming law. Some of the other variables, those in circles and in the bracket directly below the probability of proposal becoming law, have direct effects on the likelihood of passage, while the variables in the other brackets in figure 8–1 determine the positions of the endogenous actors and hence have only indirect effects on the probability of proposal enactment. I have estimated equations for both the direct and indirect effects. Because the variables in circles are determined within the system, I used two-stage estimation techniques—two-stage probit in the case of the outcome-probability equation and two-stage least squares for the actor-position equations.

---

1. The model and estimation results described in this chapter are based on the analysis of 275 atomic-energy and coal cases. The 275 cases constitute a random sample of atomic-energy and coal cases, but not of energy cases in general. The cases number 275 instead of 277 because the percentage-change economic variables could not be calculated for two cases from 1945.

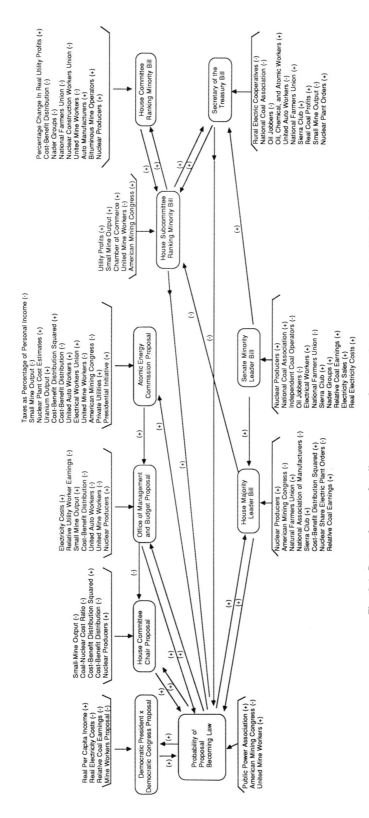

Fig. 8-1. Determinants of policy outcomes for atomic energy and coal, 1947–76

Table 8–1A, in the appendix to this chapter, provides the usual display of coefficients and their t-statistics for each equation.[2]

Interpretation of Results

Probit coefficients are difficult to interpret through simple inspection even in a single equation model, let alone in a multiple equation system such as I have utilized in this study.[3] To make the coefficients displayed in table 8–1A more meaningful, I have calculated the average change in probability of proposal passage that occurs when any single variable is allowed to vary from its minimum to maximum values and all the other variables in the model assume their natural values in each case.

Effects of Endogenous Variables

Table 8–1 lists the absolute increase or decrease in probability of passage that occurs when the value of each endogenous actor is varied from 0 (very opposed) to 1 (very favorable). For example, if the House committee chair (HCC) changes his position from strongly opposed (0) to strongly favorable (1) and the other endogenous actors' positions stay at their natural values across cases, the average increase in probability of proposal enactment is 84 absolute percentage points. The effects listed in table 8–1 include the multiple indirect effects shown by the arrows in figure 8–1 (as indicated by the numerous columns of endogenous actors that the effects can work through) but do not include the feedback effects that probability of passage has on some endogenous actor positions, which are listed separately at the bottom of table 8–1 and examined in the simulations presented later in this chapter.

Let me review the effects of the endogenous actors by first examining the five members of Congress who have effects. The positive effect of the House committee chair is not surprising: Almost half the cases involve nuclear power, and students of Congress have long believed that the Joint Committee on Atomic Energy enjoyed a unique ability to gain approval for proposals it favored. The positive effect of the House Committee Chair is modified consid-

---

2. Because the extensive specification search I utilized can lead to overfitting, that is, the inclusion of variables that capture what is really random noise, I estimated the model on both a 50 and a 75 percent sample of my 275-case sample. I eliminated any variable whose coefficients changed more than one standard error from those values estimated on the full sample. No variables changed that much, so I concluded that overfitting was not a problem.

3. A probit coefficient indicates the change in the standard normal cumulative density function that results from a unit change in a right-hand side ("independent") variable. To convert the change to changes in probability, one must integrate the standard normal between the two probit values.

TABLE 8–1. Effects of Endogenous Actor Positions on Probability of Proposal Passage in Order of Total Magnitude (in percentage)

Endogenous Actor Position	Direct Effects	Endogenous Actors along Causal Path														Total Effect
		HML	HML HRMSC	HML HRMSC Treasury	HCC	HRMSC	HRMSC Treasury	Treasury	Treasury HRMSC	HRMC HRMSC	HRMC HRMSC Treasury	Democratic President × Democratic Congress	OMB	OMB HCC	AEC OMB	AEC OMB HCC	
House committee chair proposal	+84																+84
Democratic president × Democratic Congress proposal	+73																+73
House subcommittee ranking minority bill	+65							−12	+4	+8	−2						+63
House majority leader bill	+68					−19	+3										+52
Office of Management and Budget proposal	+59				−26												+33
House committee ranking minority bill						+21	−4										+17
Senate minority leader bill		+32	−6	+1													+15
Atomic Energy Commission bill													+5	−10			+5
Secretary of the Treasury bill	−99					+57		−17	+5								−53
Probability of passage		+12	−2	+0.3	+59							+8	+7	−4	+2	−1	

Note: Abbreviations are as follows: HML (House majority leader), HRMSC (House subcommittee ranking minority), Treasury (Department of Treasury), HCC (House committee chair), HRMC (House committee ranking minority), OMB (Office of Management and Budget), AEC (Atomic Energy Commission). The probability of passage feedback effects cannot be totaled meaningfully, but these effects do illustrate the relative importance of strategic behavior in each actor's position.

erably, however, by the chair's own strategic behavior. As the probability of passage varies from negligible to virtual certainty, as determined by the other variables in the system, the House committee chair's position varies from almost neutral (0.4) to favorable (0.8), and this, in turn, has a 59 percent positive impact on the probability of passage.[4] The House committee chair has a large effect, in part, because he favors proposals that are likely to pass.

The House majority leader (HML) also has a large positive impact on outcomes, but, again, the effect is tempered by the legislator's own strategic behavior. As the effect of other variables in the system raises the probability of passage from 0 to 1, the House majority leader's position goes from almost neutral (0.6) to moderately favorable (0.7), and the probability of passage increases by 12 percentage points.

The positive effects of the three minority-party members are unexpected. Scholars generally do not view the Republican minority as having a large impact on policy, but my findings indicate that minority consent enhances the probability of passage, while strong minority opposition will doom enactment.[5] First, the cases in this study demonstrate successful Republican resistance to Democratic initiatives, such as the public funding of reactor construction and coal mine subsidy and safety laws. Second, as I will show in the next section, the House subcommittee ranking minority member (HRMSC) serves as the House leader of the energy-business coalition. The effect of the House subcommittee ranking minority member arises from this role and does not stem from his role as a leader in the minority party per se. Third, the positive effect of the Senate minority leader (SML) is lower than the combined effect of House counterparts because Everett Dirksen and Hugh Scott occupied the Senate role from 1959 to 1968 and 1969 to 1976, respectively. Both were from coal states and supported unsuccessfully many of the coal initiatives resisted by House Republicans.

The effects of administrative actors also operate largely as expected. The Atomic Energy Commission has a small positive indirect effect acting through the Office of Management and Budget, which has both a positive direct effect and negative indirect effect acting through the House committee chair. The Office of Management and Budget often resists spending that the House committee chair prefers, so there are no surprises here. The effects of the president and the Secretary of the Treasury, however, warrant some explanation.

---

4. Actor positions range from very unfavorable (0) to very favorable (1). The midpoint of the scale (0.5) represents no position.

5. During the time period discussed in this study, the Republicans were the majority party in the House on only two occasions, 1947–48 and 1953–54. Of the 275 cases used to estimate the model, one occurred in 1947–48 and seven occurred in 1953–54; thus, it is reasonable to refer to the House committee chair as a Democrat and the House subcommittee ranking minority member as a Republican.

In my initial two-stage specification of the model, the president's positions on neither the proposal nor bill had coefficients larger than their standard errors, suggesting that the president's position has no effect on outcomes. A colleague suggested that the president's influence would vary with the congressional party context, so I created interaction terms that had values only when the presidency and both houses of Congress were controlled by the same party.[6] This interaction term measures whether Eisenhower had effects in 1955–56 and whether Truman, Kennedy, and Johnson had effects in 1945–46, 1949–52, and 1961–68, respectively. The Democratic president × Democratic Congress term has a large positive effect (73 points), with modest feedback from strategic behavior (12 points). So the president has effects, but only if the party context in Congress is favorable.

The large negative effect of the Secretary of the Treasury does not imply that the department is an extremely inept player in energy politics but rather suggests that the interaction of the department's ideology and the nonrandom sample of proposals on which it chose to take a position precluded its success. The Treasury Department participated in only two energy-policy controversies (for a total of fourteen cases): mandatory coal utilization by power plants in 1975; and rapid amortization of coal-mine safety equipment, attached to various tax-reform bills, in 1969. On both occasions, the department opposed using the tax code to indirectly subsidize coal mining, and in both cases the opposite occurred. In short, when Treasury did participate, it did not get what it wanted—hence, the large negative coefficient.

Indirect Effects of Exogenous Variables

Table 8–2 lists the absolute increase or decrease in probability of passage that occurs when the indicated exogenous variable is varied from its minimum to maximum value and all the other variables assume their natural values in each case.[7] Because the number of variables and equations is so large, let me review several prominent patterns in the results. First, and most obvious, pronuclear producer groups have large positive effects on policy outcomes during the time period investigated (+51 on the proposal and +30 on the bill). Second, Congress is more attentive to public-power interests (+45) than private utilities (+2). Third, the United Mine Workers and United Auto Workers have large positive effects on the passage of bills (+35 and +33, respectively) but no ability whatsoever to enact specific proposals (−20 and −8, respectively).

---

6. Mark Hansen, assistant professor of political science at the University of Chicago, deserves credit for this suggestion.

7. For actor positions, the minimum value is zero and the maximum is one. The minimum and maximum values for the economic variables are the actual values experienced during the period 1945–76.

TABLE 8–2. Effects of Exogenous Factors on Probability of Proposal Passage in Order of Total Magnitude (in percentage)

Factor	Proposal Passage	Dem. Pres. × Dem. Congress	HCC	OMB	OMB HCC	AEC OMB	AEC OMB HCC	HML	HML HRMSC
Nuclear producers proposal			+54	+10	−13				
Public Power Association bill	+45								
United Mine Workers bill	+50								
United Auto Workers bill									
Nuclear producers bill								+21	− 4
Chamber of Commerce bill									
Oil jobbers bill									
Rural electric cooperatives bill									
Real per capita income		+13							
Auto manufacturers bill									
Sierra Club bill								+23	−4
Relative coal earnings		−9						+18	−3
National Coal Association bill									
Electrical workers bill									
Small-mine output			−17	+9	−6	−2	+1		
Private utility profits									
Bituminous Mine Operators bill									
Nader groups bill									
Electricity costs				+16	−11				
Real utility profits									
Electricity output									
Private utilities proposal						+7	−5		
Electrical workers proposal						+5	−3		
Uranium output						+6	−4		
Presidential initiative						+2	−1		
Nuclear plant cost estimates						+2	−1		
American Mining Congress proposal						−2	+1		
National Farmers Union bill								+71	−14
Taxes as a percent of income						−3	+2		
Independent Coal Operators bill									
Relative utility worker earnings				−13	+8				
Nuclear construction unions bill									
Real coal profits									
United Auto Workers proposal				−30	+20	+6	−4		
Nuclear plant orders									
Oil, Chemical, and Atomic Workers bill									
National Association of Manufacturers Bill								−21	+6
Nuclear share electric plant orders								−21	+4
Distribution of costs and benefits			−13	−9	+6		−9	+10	−2
United Mine Workers proposal		−14		−15	+10	−4	+3		
Real electricity costs		−29							
American Mining Congress bill	−45							−15	+3
Coal-nuclear cost ratio			−60						
Probability of passage		+8	+59	+7	−4	+2	−1	+12	−2

Note: Actor positions are toward either the specific proposal or the bill that contains the proposal. Economic variables are all annual percentage change for the indicated measure interacting with dummies that indicate whether the sector in question gains, loses, or is unaffected by the proposal. Column headings refer to endogenous variables in causal path. Abbreviations are as

HML HRMSC Treasury	SML HML	SML HML HRMSC	SML HML HRMSC Treasury	SML Treasury	SML Treasury HRMSC	HRMC HRMSC	HRMC HRMSC Treasury	HRMSC	HRMSC Treasury	Treasury	Treasury HRMSC	Total Effect
												+51
												+45
						−4	+1	−14	+2			+35
										+50	−17	+33
+1	+8	−1	+0.2	−4	+1	+10	−2					+30
								+26	−5			+21
	−12	+2	−0.4	+6	−2					+40	−13	+21
										+30	−10	+20
												+13
						+17	−3					+14
+1	+8	−1	+0.3	−4	+1					−20	+7	+11
+1	+4	−1	+0.1	−2	+1							+9
	+4	−1	+0.1	−2	+0.5					+8	−3	+7
	+15	−3	+0.4	−7	+2							+7
								+14	−3	+16	−5	+7
								+8	−1			+7
						+7	−1					+6
	+15	−3	+1	−7	+2	−4	+1					+5
												+5
						+5	−1					+4
	+5	−1	+0.2	−2	+1							+3
												+2
												+2
												+2
												+1
												+1
												−1
+3	−19	+3	−1	+9	−3	−12	+2			−57	+17	−1
												−1
	−6	+1	−0.2	+3	−1							−3
												−5
						−8	+1					−7
										−10	+3	−7
												−8
										−15	+5	−10
										−22	+7	−15
−1												−16
−1												−18
+0.3						−4	+0.7					−20
												−20
	+10	−2	+0.3	−5	+2							−24
−0.5									+17	−3		−44
+0.3												−60

follows: HCC (House committee chair), OMB (Office of Management and Budget), AEC (Atomic Energy Commission), HML (House majority leader), HRMSC (House subcommittee ranking minority), Treasury (Secretary of Treasury), SML (Senate minority leader), and HRMC (House committee ranking minority).

Fourth, as anecdotal evidence suggests, the coal industry has not been a potent lobbying force during congressional deliberations. Only the National Coal Association (+7) and Bituminous Mine Operators (+6) have positive effects on enactment. The Independent Coal Operators (−3) and American Mining Congress (−1 proposal; −44 bill) cause Congress to turn and run in the opposite direction. A priori, one would argue that an industry employing over 500,000 people in twenty states, as the coal industry did after World War II, should be able to obtain congressional action to resist market decline. The only event that arrested coal's decline, however, was the 1973 oil price shock, which increased the demand for domestic coal, an event that no one would argue was instigated by Congress in order to boost the coal industry.

The results of the model suggest that the inability of the coal industry to obtain political protection from decline is not unique, however. Of the nine economic sectors represented by terms in the model, only the nuclear industry and its utility workers really received benefits from Congress when they suffered economic misfortune.[8] The four measures of economic health in the nuclear industry registered improvements of 1 (nuclear plant cost estimates), 10 (nuclear plant orders), 18 (nuclear share electric plant orders) and 60 (coal-nuclear cost ratio) percentage points in passage probability as each measure declined from its maximum to minimum value. The economic condition of coal producers also had a modest inverse effect on the probability of proposal passage, but that was more than offset, however, by the negative effects of coal producer positions. The coal industry gets more out of Congress during hard times than good, but what it gets is a less negative response, not a positive one. In general, Congress does not appear to be sympathetic to economic losers.

Finally, the distribution of costs and benefits has effects on the probability of proposal passage even when the preferences of interest groups and economic conditions are held constant. Members of Congress actively anticipate voter preferences about the income flows that result from the enactment of proposals. Proposals that impose concentrated losses and create diffuse benefits are 20 percentage points less likely to be enacted (controlling for other exogenous variables) than proposals that create concentrated benefits and diffuse costs.

Structure of Exogenous Effects

The relationships between exogenous and endogenous variables in this model are very structured. The majority-party Democrats support the positions of

---

8. The six sectors that gain more benefits when they are better off are taxpayers, coal workers, independent small coal operators, private utilities, electricity consumers, and uranium producers.

farmers, environmentalists, and unions, while resisting those of business, except for nuclear producers. They favor proposals with concentrated benefits and diffuse costs, and unlike Congress as a whole, they favor proposals beneficial to the coal and nuclear industries more when those firms experience decline than when they prosper.[9]

The Republicans, the minority party in the House of Representatives, exhibit the opposite pattern. They look favorably on the positions of business and resist those held by farmers, unions, and consumer groups. They oppose pork-barrel proposals (those with concentrated benefits and diffuse costs) out of a mixture of conviction and their minority-party status, which allows them to take the high road and force the Democrats to take the heat for spending and waste. They also aid the coal and utility sectors more when those sectors prosper than when they decline. Finally, the House Republicans, unlike House Democrats, do not behave strategically. They do not support proposals just because they are likely to pass.

The Senate minority leader exhibits a mixture of both party traits, reflecting the tenure of Everett Dirksen, a traditional conservative, and Hugh Scott, with his coal, consumer, and environmental interests.[10]

Democrats versus Republicans

Eloquent examples of the important differences between the Democratic and Republican traditions can be found in policy histories on atomic energy and coal. From 1968 until the late 1970s, an intense debate occurred over federal compensation to miners for Black Lung disease. John Erlenborn (R–Ill.), ranking minority member of the Subcommittee on General Labor in the House Education and Labor Committee, typifies the Republican tendency to be suspicious of programs that hand out money to workers:

> I am just curious as to how different the problem of one with asbestosis, black lung disease, silicosis, the lung problems of talc miners, many other diseases that cause disability that are compensated under the social security disability laws, is really from that of the pneumoconiosis suf-

---

9. The effect of the distribution of costs and benefits on the House committee chair is curvilinear, a $-x + x^2$ relationship. New laws and those proposals with concentrated costs and benefits are each less likely to pass than proposals with concentrated costs and diffuse benefits (reforms) or proposals with concentrated benefits and diffuse costs (pork barrel). Three of the four economic contextual variables (coal-nuclear cost ratio, small-mine production, and nuclear share electric-plant orders) in the House committee chair and House majority leader equations denote that support for benefits increases during economic decline, while the fourth (relative coal earnings) indicates that support for benefits rises with prosperity.

10. In personal correspondence, Keith Poole has confirmed that Dirksen and Scott were placed in the conservative and liberal wings, respectively, of the Republican party in the Poole-Rosenthal spatial model of Senate roll call votes (Poole and Rosenthal 1985b).

ferer? . . . Do you think that the talc miner who spends his life in a talc mine has a different problem from the coal miner . . . or the one who has worked in the clothing business [or] the cotton and textile industries and [has] contract[ed] a lung disease?[11]

The Democratic response comes from John Dent (D–Pa.), the chairman of the General Labor Subcommittee. The thrust of his remarks is that we subsidize many groups in society, so why draw the line at coal miners?

One additional matter, and let me just read a statement from the Secretary of Agriculture, Secretary Clifford Hardin, when he said that the 1972 farm program would cost $2 billion, I voted for that and yet it comes out of the Treasury of the United States. It is paid for by coal miners and every taxpayer in the confines of this country through taxes because we think it is essential to the welfare of the farming communities of this great country. Therefore, can we do any less for the coal mining community?[12]

A crucial aspect of the Democrats' ideology is the belief that the benefits they favor primarily aid the little people. In the following exchange, Representative Dent reacts violently to the claim made by Stephen Kurzman, Assistant Secretary of HEW for legislation, that Black Lung payments subsidize the coal industry. Representative Dent espouses the widespread, but false, belief that expenditures aid only those who receive them. Incidence analysis and opportunity costs are not standard fare in Democratic populism.

Mr. Dent. I do not want the record to contain that statement. It is not a subsidy to the industry. The industry did not get a nickel out of this. I am not one to defend the industry very strongly, but this is not a subsidy to the industry paid by the Government. It is compensation to the workers under the law passed by the Congress. It was directly to the workers and not the industry.

Mr. Erlenborn. Mr. Chairman, if the industry had covered pneumoconiosis in the State workmen's compensation laws, it would have been financed over the years by the industry. So they can draw a legitimate conclusion that the industry was [subsidized].[13]

---

11. U.S. Congress, House, *Black Lung Benefits: Hearing before the Subcommittee on General Labor of the Committee on Education and Labor,* 92d Cong., 1st sess., 1971, 86.

12. U.S. Congress, *Congressional Record,* 92d Cong., 1st sess., vol. 117, pt. 31:40433.

13. U.S. Congress, House, *Black Lung Benefits Reform Act of 1975: Hearing before the Subcommittee on Labor Standards of the Committee on Education and Labor,* 94th Cong., 1st sess., 1975, 208–9.

Every now and then, however, Democratic members of Congress reveal that they understand that government underwrites much of what we call private enterprise. In the following discourse, Chet Hollifield, the House chairman of the Joint Committee on Atomic Energy, claims that subsidies to industry are ubiquitous in the American political economy. Republicans and Democrats, he argues, differ only on which groups receive subsidies, not on whether subsidies should exist at all. A neomarxist could not have said it better.

> I think the Senator has brought out a very important point. This criticism that has been made of the program ignores [some very important facts].

> For instance, the development of the airplane engine, the jet engine which we now have, was done at Government expense. The diesel was developed in the Navy at Navy expense. In the case of the railroads, in the beginning they were given every other section of land clear across the United States. . . . We have subsidized shipping. . . . We have subsidized trucking. We have practically subsidized every segment of our industry.

> If we want to go a little further, we can go into the rapid amortization of plant investment of our steel and auto companies during the war. Of course it was done under the guise of patriotism, but at the same time they accumulated their capital investment equities out of the rapid amortization from taxes that came from the American people.[14]

The Administration

The exogenous factors that affect the Atomic Energy Commission and the Office of Management and Budget also vary in a structured manner. The commission supports nuclear proposals, resists coal initiatives, and prefers new laws and pork-barrel proposals, just as the House committee chair does. The Office of Management and Budget resists unions and pork-barrel.

The role of the Secretary of the Treasury in the model is to defend the collective interest against the narrow demands of organized groups. This institutional perspective is exacerbated when the presidency is under Republican control and the Congress is Democratic. On these occasions, the tendency of the Treasury Department and Republican party to scrutinize transfers clashes severely with attempts by Democrats to aid their constituencies, such as public-power cooperatives and unionized coal miners.

---

14. U.S. Congress, *Cooperative Power Reactor Demonstration Program: Hearing before the Subcommittee on Legislation of the Joint Committee on Atomic Energy,* 88th Cong., 1st sess., 1963, 12.

Those variables with negative coefficients—the rural electric cooperatives, the National Coal Association, the oil jobbers, and the United Auto
Workers—all demand special privileges and subsidies. Variables with positive coefficients—the National Farmers Union and the Sierra Club—bring a
more comprehensive and, in the case of the Sierra Club, an almost welfare-
economics perspective to the policy process.[15]

Simulation of Indirect Effects

To illustrate the magnitude of the interest-group effects on the positions of
those actors that are determined within the model, I created two hypothetical
policy proposals. I then assigned reasonable positions toward the proposal and
the bill that contains it to those actors in each of the equations for the endogenous actors (see fig. 8–1). I then multiplied the position values by their
estimated coefficients and calculated a predicted position for each of the
endogenous actors. I used the endogenous values to estimate a predicted
probability of passage in the final probit equation, which I then entered into
equations where there were feedback effects. The results are dramatic. When
interest-group positions change, intragovernmental positions exhibit large
changes, resulting in large changes in the probability of passage.

The cases I used in the simulation exercise involve surface mining, a
cluster in the coal stratum that was not selected for the sample. The first
proposal would place severe restrictions on surface mining, while the second would repeal controls that were already in place. I chose these proposals because they would produce strong differences in interest-group positions, and I was comfortable coding them because of my familiarity with the
topic.

I assigned values to the policy positions of actors that appear in the House
committee ranking minority member equation, as indicated in table 8–3,
and allowed the remaining variables to assume their natural values in the data
set in order to calculate average effects across the 275 cases, as I did for tables
8–1 and 8–2.[16] The effects on the House committee ranking minority member's position are dramatic. The average predicted position is what would be
expected from a Republican. For the controls-repeal scenario the prediction is

---

15. The Sierra Club, for example, strongly opposed oil price controls because they gave
consumers a false signal about the true scarcity of a natural resource. U.S. Congress, Senate, *The
Fuel Shortage and the Clean Air Act: Hearing before the Subcommittee on Air and Water
Pollution of the Committee on Public Works*, 93rd Cong., 1st sess., 1973, 66.

16. The numerals in table 8–3 and all subsequent tables in this chapter are the actual
variable values used in the simulation equations. The cost-benefit and cost-benefit squared terms
are assigned 0.5 and 0.25 values in the simulations because the proposals are either new laws or
would create concentrated costs and benefits.

TABLE 8–3. Effects of Interest-Group Positions on Position of House Committee Ranking Minority toward Surface Mine Controls

Interest Groups	Position toward Passage		Position toward Repeal	
Nuclear producers	Strongly favor	(1)	Strongly oppose	(0)
Bituminous Mine Operators	Favor	(0.8)	oppose	(0.2)
Auto manufacturers	No position	(0.5)	No position	(0.5)
United Mine Workers	Strongly favor	(1)	Strongly oppose	(0)
Nuclear construction unions	Strongly favor	(1)	Strongly oppose	(0)
National Farmers Union	Strongly favor	(1)	Strongly oppose	(0)
Nader groups	Strongly favor	(1)	Strongly oppose	(0)
Predicted position of House subcommittee ranking minority				
Excluding feedback effects	.17		.84	
Including feedback effects	.13		.97	

.97 (extremely favorable), and for the controls-enactment case the prediction is .13 (extremely opposed).

Table 8–4 displays the same procedure for the House committee chair. In the case enacting surface mine controls, the House committee chair position is predicted to be .88 (extremely favorable); in the case repealing controls, the prediction is .045 (strongly opposed). Interest-group position changes have large and opposite effects on the House committee ranking minority and House committee chair positions, as might be expected in a structured party-conflict situation.[17]

Table 8–5 combines the estimated endogenous actor positions with the three groups that have direct effects on outcomes through the positions of rank-and-file members of Congress, which are not addressed in the model. As you can see, the predicted probability of passage of surface mine controls is 66 percent, while the probability of repeal is minuscule (less than 0.01 percent). The history of surface-mine legislation has followed the model's predictions fairly well. Surface-mine controls did become law in 1977, but only after much struggle. President Ford vetoed bills in 1974 and 1975. All attempts to modify the legislation since 1977 have failed, just as the model predicts.

If Coal Is So Ineffectual, Then Why Scrubbers?

I have argued quite strongly throughout this study that the conclusions of policy case studies should be treated with great caution because causation in

---

17. Tables illustrating the predictions of the other endogenous variables are located in the appendix to this chapter.

TABLE 8–4. Effects of Interest-Group Positions on Position of House Committee Chair toward Surface Mine Controls

Interest Groups	Position toward Passage		Position toward Repeal	
Nuclear producers	Strongly favor	(1)	Strongly oppose	(0)
Predicted position of House committee chair				
Excluding feedback effects	.78		.31	
Including feedback effects	.88		.045	

the world is multivariate and not bivariate, and because selection bias occurs in case studies. *Clean Coal/Dirty Air*, the Ackerman and Hassler case study I discussed in chapter 6, argues that a strong coal-environmental coalition forced Congress to mandate the use of scrubber technology in the smokestacks of new coal-fired electric plants.

In contrast, my findings (see table 8–2) indicate that two coal groups (the National Coal Association and Bituminous Mine Operators) have small posi-

TABLE 8–5. Effects of Congressional, Bureaucratic, and Interest-Group Positions on the Probability of Passage of Surface Mine Controls

Causal Actor	Position toward Passage		Position toward Repeal	
House committee chair	Favor	(0.88)	Strongly oppose	(0.045)
Democratic President × Democratic Congress	Strongly oppose	(0.03)	Oppose	(0.159)
Office of Management and Budget	Oppose	(0.24)	Moderately favor	(0.67)
House majority leader	Strongly favor	(1.34)	Strongly oppose	(−0.12)
House subcommittee ranking minority	Moderately oppose	(0.41)	Favor	(0.79)
Secretary of the Treasury	Favor	(0.70)	Oppose	(0.29)
Public Power Association	Strongly oppose	(0)	Strongly favor	(1)
American Mining Congress	Strongly oppose	(0)	Strongly favor	(1)
United Mine Workers	Strongly favor	(1)	Strongly oppose	(0)
House committee ranking minority	Oppose	(0.13)	Strongly favor	(0.97)
Senate minority leader	Favor	(0.70)	Neutral	(0.45)
Atomic Energy Commission	Oppose	(0.28)	Neutral	(0.55)
Predicted probability of passage				
Excluding feedback effects	.48		.0046	
Including feedback effects	.66		.00012	

TABLE 8–6.   Effects of Interest-Group Positions on Position of House Majority Leader toward Mandatory Scrubbers

Interest Group	Position toward Mandatory Scrubbers	
Nuclear producers	No position	(0.5)
American Mining Congress	Strongly oppose	(0)
National Farmers Union	No position	(0.5)
National Association of Manufacturers	No position	(0.5)
Sierra Club	Strongly favor	(1)
Predicted position of House majority leader		
Excluding feedback effects	.82	
Including feedback effects	.94	

tive effects, another (Independent Coal Operators) has a small negative effect, while a fourth (American Mining Congress) has a strong negative effect. To be sure, the United Mine Workers do have a strong positive effect at the bill level ($+35$) (offset by a strong negative effect [-20] at the proposal level), and the Sierra Club has an 11 percentage point positive effect over its value range, but, in general, my results do not suggest that a coalition of coal producers, mine workers, and environmentalists is the ideal group to lobby Congress successfully.

How can I reconcile the Ackerman and Hassler findings with my own? I assigned values to all the exogenous actor-position variables using Ackerman and Hassler's text as an authoritative source and calculated the predicted probability of enacting mandatory scrubber controls with and without feedback effects from strategic behavior. Table 8–6 displays the exogenous variable values used to predict the House majority leader's position.[18] As expected, the House majority leader is predicted to strongly favor (0.94) mandatory scrubbers. Table 8–7 combines the endogenous variable predictions of the House majority leader in table 8–6 with those variables displayed in the appendix to calculate the probability of mandatory scrubber enactment. As you can see, enactment is 86 percent probable when feedback effects are included, a result that confirms the Ackerman and Hassler results, but not their causal inferences. The coal coalition obtained its preferred policy position, not because its participants have large positive effects on policy outcomes, but because many important actors who do have large effects, such as

---

18. Actors in this equation and the other endogenous equations displayed in the appendix are coded as having no position if Ackerman and Hassler did not mention their involvement.

TABLE 8–7.   Effects of Congressional, Bureaucratic, and
Interest-Group Positions on the Probability of Passage of
Mandatory Coal Scrubbers

Causal Actor	Position toward Mandatory Scrubbers	
House committee chair	Favor	(0.70)
Democratic President × Democratic Congress	Strongly oppose	(0.045)
	Oppose	(0.31)
Office of Management and Budget	Strongly favor	(0.94)
House majority leader	Oppose	(0.25)
House subcommittee ranking minority	Neutral	(0.54)
Secretary of the Treasury	Neutral	(0.50)
Public Power Association	Strongly oppose	(0)
American Mining Congress	Strongly favor	(1)
United Mine Workers	Neutral	(0.44)
House committee ranking minority	Favor	(0.88)
Senate minority leader	Oppose	(0.18)
Atomic Energy Commission		
Predicted probability of passage		
Excluding feedback effects	.66	
Including feedback effects	.86	

the nuclear producer, public-power, and rural electric groups (see table 8–2) were not involved in this struggle and because the private utilities, the main opponent, were as lightweight as the coal coalition.

When public policy analysts confront cases whose results run counter to their theories, such as coal groups achieving a legislative success, they traditionally have reacted in one of two ways. They might argue endlessly about how to classify the case because, traditionally, the study of public policy has been arranged by subject—health policy, environmental policy, tax policy, and so on. Theories are preserved by classifying troublesome data in a different policy category. Coal scrubbing, for example, could be called an environmental rather than an energy issue, so environmental policy theories would be germane, rather than those concerned with energy politics.[19]

A second reaction would involve endless claims and counterclaims about what actor had caused the change. Some might say the United Mine Workers can win when they marshal their resources. Others might argue that coal-producer groups really have clout if they flex their muscles. In contrast, the

---

19. I can be accused of the same mischief. When I set the boundaries of the universe of cases for this study, I also excluded air pollution cases. I did so, however, not because I believe the politics of energy differ from the politics of pollution, but merely to simplify the research effort.

method of explanation I utilize encourages one to realize that small changes in numerous factors can cause dramatic aggregate differences. A change in policy outcomes probably does not occur because of a change in one actor's position. The policy outcome described in *Clean Coal/Dirty Air* should not be thought of as an exception to the generalization that coal interests are ineffectual but rather be understood simply as the result of numerous changes in the positions of those actors that affect coal-policy outcomes. Environmental and consumer support and neutrality from the nuclear and public-power interests were all necessary for coal groups to gain legislative approval of the proposals described by Ackerman and Hassler.

The Effects of Context

Does the effectiveness of actor positions on outcomes depend on the economic conditions within the relevant industrial sectors? The surface-mining and coal-scrubber scenarios presented in this chapter, up until this point, have allowed the economic contextual variables to assume their natural values in each of the 275 cases, so the effects I have described have been for average economic conditions. In this section, I will explicitly vary sectoral economic conditions in the surface-mining scenarios to determine their effects.

Tables 8–8 and 8–9 display the effect of varying economic context (specifically, average versus 1973 versus 1975 conditions) on the predicted positions of two endogenous actors, the House majority leader and the Atomic Energy Commission.[20]

Changes in economic context do not affect the positions of these two actors very much at all. Table 8–10 compares the effect of average, 1973, and 1975 economic contexts on the probability of enacting surface mine controls, combining the predictions of tables 8–8 and 8–9 with those of the other endogenous positions calculated in the chapter appendix. While no one actor's position is dramatically affected, the positions of all actors with positive effects on the outcome (except the House majority leader) were made more positive by the 1975 context and the position of the one actor with negative effects (the Secretary of the Treasury) was made slightly less positive. The net effect of

---

20. The economic contextual variables are interaction terms combining the actual annual percentage change of the indicated measure with dummy variables that indicate whether the sector in question would gain, lose, or be unaffected by passage of the policy proposal. See the appendix for average, 1973, and 1975 values for these variables and for an explanation of how I calculated them. The years 1973 and 1975 were chosen because energy economic conditions varied so much over that time period. Each surface mine case was coded as a new law with concentrated costs and benefits (0.5). See app. 7B for an explanation of the construction of the cost-benefit interaction terms. The nuclear industry and the public would benefit from controls, while the coal industry and utility sector would suffer losses.

TABLE 8–8. Effects of Economic Context on Position of House Majority Leader toward Surface Mine Controls

Variable	Average Context	1973 Context	1975 Context
Nuclear producers	1	1	1
American Mining Congress	0	0	0
National Farmers Union	1	1	1
National Association of Manufacturers	0.5	0.5	0.5
Sierra Club	1	1	1
Nuclear share electric plant orders	−5.70	0	0
Relative coal earnings	+1.85	−1.84	+14.81
Predicted position of house majority leader			
Excluding feedback effects	1.30	1.28	1.20
Including feedback effects	1.34	1.29	1.25

these small individual but reinforcing changes is a significant (21 percentage points) increase in the probability of passage. Context clearly can be the difference between passage and failure even though no large changes take place in any actor's position.

TABLE 8–9. Effects of Economic Context on Position of Atomic Energy Commission toward Surface Mine Controls

Variable	Average Context	1973 Context	1975 Context
Presidential initiative	1	1	1
Private utilities	0	0	0
American Mining Congress	0	0	0
United Mine Workers	1	1	1
Electrical Workers	0.3	0.3	0.3
United Auto Workers	1	1	1
Uranium production	+1.00	0	0
Nuclear plant cost estimates	+1.67	0	0
Small-mine output	+2.48	−22.50	+50.16
Taxes as percentage of personal income	+0.026	0	0
Predicted position of Atomic Energy Commission			
Excluding feedback effects	.265	.23	.20
Including feedback effects	.28	.25	.24

TABLE 8-10. Comparison of Effect of Average, 1973, and 1975 Economic Contexts on Probability of Passage of Surface Mine Controls

Variable	Position in Average Economic Conditions	Position in 1973 Economic Conditions	Position in 1975 Economic Conditions
House committee chair	0.88	0.865	0.889
Democratic president × Democratic Congress	0.027	0.065	0.099
Office of Management and Budget	0.24	0.193	0.331
House majority leader	1.34	1.29	1.25
House subcommittee ranking minority	0.41	0.37	0.48
Secretary of the Treasury	0.70	0.676	0.67
Public Power Association	0	0	0
American Mining Congress	0	0	0
United Mine Workers	1	1	1
House committee ranking minority	0.13	0.078	0.246
Atomic Energy Commission	0.28	0.247	0.243
Senate minority leader	0.70	0.630	0.673
Predicted probability of passage			
Excluding feedback effects	.48	.48	.696
Including feedback effects	.66	.667	.870

Do Legislators Have Discretion?

In a world where legislators maximize electoral outcomes, their own preferences can affect policy outcomes, and not adversely affect their probability of reelection, only when the behavior of challengers and voters is relatively unaffected by policy changes (when the slopes of the expected vote-gain and vote-loss functions are relatively low) or if members' views coincide with the views of voters. The slopes are low when challengers can't compete easily or when voter behavior is relatively inelastic with respect to policy changes.

The changes in the probability of proposal passage listed in table 8-2 are measures of the responsiveness of Congress to various actors' preferences. Members of Congress have discretion with respect to some groups (those with effects of 1 or 2 percent) and not others (those with effects of 20 to 50 percent). Discretion should not be viewed as a dichotomous concept, and scholars should not agonize over whether legislators have discretion or not. Instead, discretion should be viewed as a continuous concept that varies across groups and policy contexts.

Some may ask why interest groups have different effects on legislators' policy decisions. Why does congressional discretion vary? One possibility is that groups with low effects simply prefer policies that would create voter defections from incumbents to challengers. The expected value of vote gains from supporters is greatly exceeded by the expected vote losses because the policies preferred by the groups with low effects would impose losses on voters. Another possibility is that groups with low effects actually could have majority support from voters but have insufficient financial resources to fund challengers who would spread the message and defeat incumbents.

A final possibility is that members of Congress sever the link between their behavior and policy choices that are opposed by those groups with low effects. It has been argued that the Congress systematically manipulates parliamentary rules so that choices inimical to the interests of low-effect groups cannot be traced through roll call votes to individual members (Arnold 1990).

My data do not allow me to systematically test these hypotheses, but one could imagine such a test. The dependent variable would be the change in probability of passage created by a change in interest-group preferences from support to opposition (from the final column of table 8–2). The right-hand-side variables would be measures of the elasticity of voters' support with respect to policy choices favored by the groups, financial resources available to the group, and traceability. The equation would be very difficult to estimate. The latter two variables would be endogenous, while the first would be extremely hard to measure.

Conclusion

In chapter 5, several possible theories of congressional action on policy proposals were discussed—congressional discretion, interest-group or executive-branch dominance, and contextual interaction. The model I estimated and described in this chapter is consistent with all the explanations. Using two hypothetical, but nevertheless realistic, surface-mining policy proposals, I demonstrated that interest-group positions have large effects on congressional and executive-branch positions, which, in turn, have large direct effects on the likelihood of a proposal becoming law. Sectoral economic conditions had a significant but slightly smaller effect than actor positions.

I illustrated the usefulness of my multivariate explanatory approach by using the model to explain the events described by Ackerman and Hassler in *Clean Coal/Dirty Air*. The coal lobby was successful in obtaining enactment of provisions that mandate scrubbers and ensure demand for union-mined coal, not because the lobby suddenly had become powerful (an explanation contrary to the results of my model), but because it joined forces with environmentalists and neutralized the potential opposition through secrecy, and private utilities failed to mobilize the public-power cooperatives that do have effects on Democrats.

What role do legislators' own policy preferences play in the enactment of laws? In chapter 6 I described how the research designs and econometric models of existing studies were inadequate to answer the question. My own model also cannot provide definitive answers, but it does suggest that legislative discretion is best viewed as a characteristic that varies across groups and policies. A more difficult problem is to ascertain the relative contribution of voter preferences, financial resources, and traceability on congressional discretion.

Appendix 8

Table 8–1A displays the coefficients and absolute value of the *t*-statistics for the ten equations in the model.

Equation 1 is estimated by two stage probit (Maddala 1983, 244–45; Achen 1986, 49). Equations 2–10 are estimated by two-stage least squares. A blank cell in the table indicates that the variable had an estimated coefficient indistinguishable from 0 in that equation. Absolute value *t*-statistics are in parentheses. Standard errors in equations 2–10 were corrected according to Maddala's method (1977, 239). Standard errors in equation 1 were estimated with the bootstrap method (Peters and Friedman 1984). I estimated the final probit model 1,024 times using 1,024 different 275-case data sets. Each pseudosample was constructed randomly with replacement from my original data set; thus, in each of the 1,024 separate runs, numerous cases from the original sample were repeated, while other cases were not included. The standard deviation of the 1,024 coefficient estimates for each variable is the standard error of the coefficient.

Actor positions are toward either the actual proposal or the bill that contains the proposal. The construction of cost-benefit and economic contextual variables is described in chapter 7. Two hundred seventy-five cases were used to estimate the model. Two cases from 1945 could not be used because economic time-series data from 1944, which were necessary to calculate annual change values for 1945, could not be gathered. I tested the probit coefficients for stability across time by estimating the model twice, once as displayed in this table and another where every variable was multiplied by a dummy that split the sample into two approximately equal groups of cases, those before 1964 and those after. I then compared twice the difference in the log likelihood ratios against the chi-square critical values. The probability that the coefficients are stable across time is less than 1 percent.

Tables 8–2A through 8–8A display the interest-group positions used to

TABLE 8-1A. Determinants of Policy Outcomes for Atomic Energy and Coal, 1947–76, Estimated Equations

	Eq. (1) Probability of Proposal Passage		Eq. (2) House Committee Chair Proposal		Eq. (3) House Majority Leader Bill	
House committee chair proposal	3.71	(5.0)				
Democrat president × Democratic Congress proposal	2.35	(2.1)				
Office of Management and Budget proposal	1.89	(2.6)	−.34	(3.4)		
House majority leader bill	3.30	(2.7)				
House subcommittee ranking minority bill	2.07	(2.3)				
Secretary of the Treasury bill	−5.92	(2.4)				
Public Power Association bill	1.46	(2.0)				
American Mining Congress bill	−1.53	(2.0)			−.14	(3.1)
United Mine Workers bill	1.95	(3.0)				
Probability of proposal passage			.48	(11.1)	.11	(3.5)
Nuclear producers proposal			.48	(4.4)		
Cost-benefit distribution			−.59	(3.0)		
Cost-benefit distribution squared			.45	(3.0)	.09	(3.5)
Coal-nuclear cost ratio			−.0027	(2.4)		
Small-mine output			.0014	(2.3)		
Senate minority leader bill					.33	(4.8)
Nuclear producers bill					.20	(4.0)
National Farmers Union bill					.76	(5.3)
National Association Manufacturers bill					−.34	(4.8)
Sierra Club bill					.22	(2.8)
Nuclear share electric plant orders					−.0009	(4.3)
Relative coal earnings					.006	(4.2)
Constant	−5.31		.46		.01	
SEE	0.35		.26		.15	
N = 275						

TABLE 8-1A—*Continued*

	Eq. (4) House Committee Ranking Minority Bill		Eq. (5) House Sub-committee Ranking Minority Bill		Eq. (6) Senate Minority Leader Bill		Eq. (7) Democratic President × Democratic Congress Proposal	
House majority leader bill			−.27	(3.1)				
Secretary of the Treasury bill			.91	(4.1)				
American Mining Congress bill			.24	(3.6)				
United Mine Workers bill	−.20	(2.7)	−.19	(3.6)				
Probability of passage							.10	(2.9)
Cost-benefit distribution	−.17	(3.1)						
Small-mine output			.002	(4.3)				
Nuclear producers bill	.50	(7.0)			.22	(4.8)		
National Farmers Union bill	−.59	(2.7)			−.54	(3.8)		
Sierra Club bill					.23	(3.1)		
Relative coal earnings					.004	(3.2)	−.004	(2.0)
House committee ranking minority bill			.30	(4.4)				
House subcommittee ranking minority bill	−.40	(3.8)						
Bituminous Mine Operators bill	.34	(3.5)						
Auto manufacturers bill	.83	(3.1)						
Nuclear construction workers bill	−.38	(2.6)						
Nader groups bill	−.20	(2.7)			.44	(10.0)		
Real utility profits	.008	(3.3)						
Chamber of Commerce bill			.38	(4.5)				
Utility profits			.003	(3.1)				
National Coal Association bill					.01	(3.0)		
Independent Coal Operators bill					−.16	(3.5)		
Oil jobbers bill					−.35	(2.4)		
Electrical workers bill					.41	(5.2)		
Electricity production					.005	(3.5)		
Real electricity costs					.01	(6.0)	−.008	(3.0)
United Mine Workers proposal							−.18	(3.5)
Real per capita income							.01	(2.6)
Constant	.27		−.16		.37		.18	
SEE	.23		.19		.14		.20	
$N = 275$								

(*continued*)

TABLE 8-1A—*Continued*

	Eq. (8) Secretary of the Treasury Bill		Eq. (9) Atomic Energy Commission Proposal		Eq. (10) Office of Management and Budget Proposal	
Probability of proposal passage			.15	(4.5)	.11	(2.9)
Nuclear producers proposal					.32	(3.5)
Cost-benefit distribution			−.65	(4.2)	−.14	(3.1)
Cost-benefit distribution squared			.64	(5.2)		
Small-mine production	−.0008	(6.3)	−.001	(2.8)	.0014	(3.0)
Senate minority leader bill	.08	(4.0)				
National Farmers Union bill	.32	(5.4)				
Sierra Club bill	.10	(4.0)				
House subcommittee ranking minority bill	.06	(4.0)				
National Coal Association bill	−.04	(4.2)				
Oil jobbers bill	−.21	(5.1)				
United Mine Workers proposal			−.24	(5.5)	−.23	(4.8)
Rural electric cooperatives bill	−.16	(7.4)				
Oil, Chemical, and Atomic Workers bill	.11	(2.4)				
United Auto Workers bill	−.27	(7.8)				
Real coal profits	.00006	(2.8)				
Nuclear plant orders	.00015	(2.7)				
Presidential initiative			.13	(3.5)		
Private utilities proposal			.46	(8.2)		
American Mining Congress proposal			−.12	(2.2)		
Electrical workers proposal			.30	(2.2)		
United Auto Workers proposal			.37	(2.5)	−.49	(3.3)
Uranium production			.002	(3.5)		
Nuclear plant cost estimates			.002	(3.5)		

TABLE 8–1A—*Continued*

	Eq. (8) Secretary of the Treasury Bill	Eq. (9) Atomic Energy Committee Proposal	Eq. (10) Office of Management and Budget Proposal
Taxes as percentage of personal income		.009 (3.8)	
Atomic Energy Commission proposal			.24 (2.8)
Relative utility worker earnings			−.04 (2.8)
Electricity costs			.006 (3.6)
Constant	.49	.02	.58
SEE	.05	.19	.21
N = 275			

predict the endogenous actor positions toward surface mine controls and their repeal.

Tables 8–9A through 8–16A display the interest-group positions used to predict the endogenous actor positions toward mandatory coal scrubbers.

Tables 8–17A and 8–18A display the economic gain and loss assumptions and the resulting economic contextual variable values used to construct the endogenous actor positions in tables 8–19A through 8–25A.

TABLE 8–2A. Effects of Interest-Group Positions on Position of House Majority Leader toward Surface Mine Controls

Interest Group	Position toward Passage		Position toward Repeal	
Nuclear producers	Strongly favor	(1)	Strongly oppose	(0)
American Mining Congress	Strongly oppose	(0)	Strongly favor	(1)
National Farmers Union	Strongly favor	(1)	Strongly oppose	(0)
National Association of Manufacturers	No position	(0.5)	No position	(0.5)
Sierra Club	Strongly favor	(1)	Strongly oppose	(0)
Predicted position of House majority leader				
Excluding feedback effects	1.30		−.018	
Including feedback effects	1.34		−.117	

TABLE 8–3A. Effects of Interest-Group Positions on Position of House Subcommittee Ranking Minority toward Surface Mine Controls

Interest Group	Position toward Passage		Position toward Repeal	
American Mining Congress	Strongly oppose	(0)	Strongly favor	(1)
United Mine Workers	Strongly favor	(1)	Strongly oppose	(0)
Chamber of Commerce	No position	(0.5)	No position	(0.5)
Predicted position of House subcommittee minority				
Excluding feedback effects	.33		.76	
Including feedback effects	.41		.79	

TABLE 8–4A. Effects of Interest-Group Positions on Position of Senate Minority Leader toward Surface Mine Controls

Interest Group	Position toward Passage		Position toward Repeal	
Nuclear producers	Strongly favor	(1)	Strongly oppose	(0)
National Coal Association	Strongly oppose	(0)	Strongly favor	(1)
Independent Coal Operators	Strongly oppose	(0)	Strongly favor	(1)
Oil jobbers	No position	(0.5)	No position	(0.5)
Electrical workers	Moderately oppose	(0.3)	Moderately favor	(0.7)
National Farmers Union	Strongly favor	(1)	Strongly oppose	(0)
Sierra Club	Strongly favor	(1)	Strongly oppose	(0)
Nader groups	Strongly favor	(1)	Strongly oppose	(0)
Predicted position of Senate minority leader				
Excluding feedback effects	.70		.45	
Including feedback effects	.70		.45	

TABLE 8–5A. Effects of Interest-Group Positions on Position of Democratic President during Democratic Congress toward Surface Mine Controls

Interest Group	Position toward Passage		Position toward Repeal	
United Mine Workers	Strongly favor	(1)	Strongly oppose	(0)
Predicted position of Democratic president during Democratic Congress				
Excluding feedback effects	.017		.20	
Including feedback effects	.027		.16	

TABLE 8–6A. Effects of Interest-Group Positions on Position of Secretary of the Treasury toward Surface Mine Controls

Interest Group	Position toward Passage		Position toward Repeal	
Rural electric cooperatives	Strongly oppose	(0)	Strongly favor	(1)
National Coal Association	Strongly oppose	(0)	Strongly favor	(1)
Oil jobbers	No position	(0.5)	No position	(0.5)
Oil, Chemical, and Atomic Workers	Favor	(0.8)	Oppose	(0.2)
United Auto Workers	Strongly favor	(1)	Strongly oppose	(0)
National Farmers Union	Strongly favor	(1)	Strongly oppose	(0)
Sierra Club	Strongly favor	(1)	Strongly oppose	(0)
Predicted position of Secretary of the Treasury				
Excluding feedback effects	.70		.28	
Including feedback effects	.70		.29	

TABLE 8–7A. Effects of Interest-Group Positions on Position of Atomic Energy Commission toward Surface Mine Controls

Interest Group	Position toward Passage		Position toward Repeal	
Presidential initiative	No	(1)	No	(1)
Private utilities	Strongly oppose	(0)	Strongly favor	(1)
American Mining Workers	Strongly oppose	(0)	Strongly favor	(1)
United Mine Workers	Strongly favor	(1)	Strongly oppose	(0)
Electrical workers	Moderately oppose	(0.3)	Moderately favor	(0.7)
United Auto Workers	Strongly favor	(1)	Strongly oppose	(0)
Predicted position of Atomic Energy Commission				
Excluding feedback effects	.265		.60	
Including feedback effects	.28		.54	

TABLE 8–8A. Effects of Interest-Group Positions on Position of Office of Management and Budget toward Surface Mine Controls

Interest Group	Position toward Passage		Position toward Repeal	
Nuclear producers	Strongly favor	(1)	Strongly oppose	(0)
United Mine Workers	Strongly favor	(1)	Strongly oppose	(0)
United Auto Workers	Strongly favor	(1)	Strongly oppose	(0)
Predicted position of Office of Management and Budget				
Excluding feedback effects	.28		.68	
Including feedback effects	.24		.67	

TABLE 8-9A. Effects of Interest-Group Positions on Position of House Committee Chair toward Mandatory Scrubbers

Interest Group	Position toward Mandatory Scrubbers
Nuclear producers	No position (0.5)
Predicted position of House committee chair	
Excluding feedback effects	.54
Including feedback effects	.70

TABLE 8–10A. Effects of Interest-Group Positions on Position of House Committee Ranking Minority toward Mandatory Scrubbers

Interest Group	Position toward Mandatory Scrubbers	
Nuclear producers	No position	(0.5)
Bituminous Mine Operators	Strongly favor	(1)
Auto manufacturers	No position	(0.5)
United Mine Workers	Strongly favor	(1)
Nuclear construction unions	No position	(0.5)
National Farmers Union	No position	(0.5)
Nader groups	Strongly favor	(1)
Predicted position of House committee ranking minority		
Excluding feedback effects	.48	
Including feedback effects	.44	

TABLE 8–11A. Effects of Interest-Group Positions on Position of House Subcommittee Ranking Minority toward Mandatory Scrubbers

Interest Group	Position toward Mandatory Scrubbers
American Mining Congress	Strongly oppose (0)
United Mine Workers	Strongly favor (1)
Chamber of Commerce	No position (0.5)
Predicted position of House subcommittee ranking minority	
Excluding feedback effects	.33
Including feedback effects	.25

TABLE 8–12A. Effects of Interest-Group Positions on Position of Senate Minority Leader toward Mandatory Scrubbers

Interest Group	Position toward Mandatory Scrubbers
Nuclear producers	No position (0.5)
National Coal Association	Strongly favor (1)
Independent Coal Operators	Strongly favor (1)
Oil jobbers	No position (0.5)
Electrical workers	No position (0.5)
National Farmers Union	No position (0.5)
Sierra Club	Strongly favor (1)
Nader groups	Strongly favor (1)
Predicted position of Senate minority leader	
Excluding feedback effects	.88
Including feedback effects	.88

TABLE 8–13A. Effects of Interest-Group Positions on Position of Democratic President during Democratic Congress toward Mandatory Scrubbers

Interest Group	Position toward Mandatory Scrubbers	
United Mine Workers	Strongly favor	(1)
Predicted position of Democratic president during Democratic Congress		
Excluding feedback effects	.017	
Including feedback effects	.045	

TABLE 8–14A. Effects of Interest-Group Positions of Secretary of the Treasury toward Mandatory Scrubbers

Interest Group	Position toward Mandatory Scrubbers	
Rural electrical cooperatives	No position	(0.5)
National Coal Association	Strongly favor	(1)
Oil jobbers	No position	(0.5)
Oil, Chemical, and Atomic Workers	No position	(0.5)
United Auto Workers	No position	(0.5)
National Farmers Union	No position	(0.5)
Sierra Club	Strongly favor	(1)
Predicted position of Secretary of the Treasury		
Excluding feedback effects	.52	
Including feedback effects	.54	

160

TABLE 8–15A. **Effects of Interest-Group Positions on Position of Office of Management and Budget toward Mandatory Scrubbers**

Interest Group	Position toward Mandatory Scrubbers	
Nuclear producers	No position	(0.5)
United Mine Workers	Strongly favor	(1)
United Auto Workers	No position	(0.5)
Predicted position of Office of Management and Budget		
Excluding feedback effects	.37	
Including feedback effects	.31	

TABLE 8–16A. **Effects of Interest-Group Positions on Position of Atomic Energy Commission toward Mandatory Scrubbers**

Interest Group	Position toward Mandatory Scrubbers	
Presidential initiative	No position	(1)
Private utilities	Strongly opposed	(0)
American Mining Congress	Strongly opposed	(0)
United Mine Workers	Strongly favor	(1)
Electrical workers	No position	(0.5)
United Auto Workers	No position	(0.5)
Predicted position of Atomic Energy Commission		
Excluding feedback effects	.14	
Including feedback effects	.18	

TABLE 8–17A. Economic Gains and Losses Incurred by Various Energy-Policy Actors as a Result of Passage or Repeal of Surface Mine Controls

Interest Group	Controls	Repeal
Uranium producers	Unaffected	Unaffected
Nuclear plant producers	Unaffected	Unaffected
Nuclear plant workers	Unaffected	Unaffected
Nuclear electricity consumers	Unaffected	Unaffected
Coal producers	Lose	Gain
Independent Coal Operators	Lose	Gain
Coal workers	Gain	Lose
Coal consumers	Lose	Gain
Private utilities	Lose	Gain
Utility workers	Lose	Gain
Electricity consumers	Lose	Gain
Taxpayers	Unaffected	Unaffected

TABLE 8–18A. Measure of Economic Context, Average 1973, and 1975 Values

Percentage Change	Average Context	1973 Context	1975 Context
Real coal profits	−12.48	−71.160	−15.938
Small-mine output	+2.48	+22.498	+50.155
Coal worker earnings relative to all workers	+1.85	−1.840	+14.806
Utility profits	+1.13	−12.831	−17.010
Real utility profits	+0.43	−6.756	+7.094
Electricity sales	−0.27	−7.797	+1.577
Utility worker earnings relative to all workers	+0.15	+0.894	+1.428
Electricity costs	+1.75	−4.959	+13.226
Real electricity costs	+1.04	−0.692	+3.63
Nuclear share electric plant orders	−5.70	0	0
Coal-nuclear cost ratio	−1.47	0	0
Real per capita income	−0.42	0	0
Nuclear plant orders	−2.57	0	0
Uranium production	+1.00	0	0
Nuclear plant cost estimates	+1.67	0	0
Taxes as percentage of personal income	+.026	0	0

Note: All entries are actual annual percentage changes in indicated measures multiplied by dummy variables from table 8–17A, which indicate sector gains and losses. In the 1973 and 1975 scenarios, neither the nuclear sector nor taxpayers were affected by the proposals—hence, the values of 0.

TABLE 8–19A. Effects of Economic Context on Position of House Committee Chair toward Surface Mine Controls

Variable	Average Context	1973 Context	1975 Context
Nuclear producers	1	1	1
Coal-nuclear cost ratio	−1.47	0	0
Small-mine production	+2.48	−22.50	+50.16
Predicted position of House committee chair			
Excluding feedback effects	.78	.75	.71
Including feedback effects	.88	.87	.89

TABLE 8–20A. Effects of Economic Context on Position of House Committee Ranking Minority toward Surface Mine Controls

Variable	Average Context	1973 Context	1975 Context
Nuclear producers	1	1	1
Bituminous Mine Operators	0.8	0.8	0.8
Auto manufacturers	0.5	0.5	0.5
United Mine Workers	1	1	1
Nuclear construction unions	1	1	1
National Farmers Union	1	1	1
Nader groups	1	1	1
Real utility profits	+0.43	+6.76	+7.09
Predicted position of House committee ranking minority			
Excluding feedback effect	.17	.12	.22
Including feedback effects	.13	.08	.25

TABLE 8–21A. Effects of Economic Context on Position of House Subcommittee Ranking Minority toward Surface Mine Controls

Variable	Average Context	1973 Context	1975 Context
American Mining Congress	0	0	0
United Mine Workers	1	1	1
Chamber of Commerce	0.5	0.5	0.5
Small-mine output	+2.48	−22.50	+50.16
Utility profits	+1.13	+12.83	+17.01
Predicted position of House subcommittee ranking minority			
Excluding feedback effects	.33	.33	.49
Including feedback effects	.41	.37	.48

TABLE 8–22A. Effects of Economic Context on Position of Senate Minority Leader toward Surface Mine Controls

Variable	Average Context	1973 Context	1975 Context
Nuclear producers	1	1	1
National Coal Association	0	0	0
Independent Coal Operators	0	0	0
Oil jobbers	0.5	0.5	0.5
Electrical workers	0.3	0.3	0.3
National Farmers Union	1	1	1
Sierra Club	1	1	1
Nader groups	1	1	1
Relative coal earnings	+1.85	−1.84	+14.81
Electricity sales	−0.27	+7.80	+1.58
Real electricity costs	+1.04	+0.69	+3.63
Predicted position of Senate minority leader			
Excluding feedback effects	.70	.63	.67
Including feedback effects	.70	.63	.67

TABLE 8–23A.   Effects of Economic Context on Position of Democratic President during Democratic Congress toward Surface Mine Controls

Variable	Average Context	1973 Context	1975 Context
United Mine Workers	1	1	1
Relative coal earnings	+1.85	−1.84	+14.81
Real electricity costs	+1.04	+0.69	+3.63
Real per capita income	−0.42	0	0
Predicted position of Democratic president during Democratic Congress			
Excluding feedback effects	.017	.051	.068
Including feedback effects	.027	.065	.099

TABLE 8–24A.   Effects of Economic Context on Position of Secretary of the Treasury toward Surface Mine Controls

Variable	Average Context	1973 Context	1975 Context
Rural electric cooperatives	0	0	0
National Coal Association	0	0	0
Oil jobbers	0.5	0.5	0.5
Oil, Chemical, and Atomic Workers	0.8	0.8	0.8
United Auto Workers	1	1	1
National Farmers Union	1	1	1
Sierra Club	1	1	1
Real coal profits	−12.48	+71.16	−15.94
Small-mine output	+2.48	−22.50	+50.16
Nuclear plant orders	−2.57	0	0
Predicted position of Secretary of the Treasury			
Excluding feedback effects	.70	.68	.66
Including feedback effects	.70	.675	.67

TABLE 8–25A.   Effects of Economic Context on Position of Office of Management and Budget toward Surface Mine Controls

Variable	Average Context	1973 Context	1975 Context
Nuclear producers	1	1	1
United Mine Workers	1	1	1
United Auto Workers	1	1	1
Small-mine output	+2.48	−22.50	+50.16
Relative utility worker earnings	+0.15	−0.89	+1.43
Electricity costs	+1.75	+4.96	+13.23
Predicted position of Office of Management and Budget			
Excluding feedback effects	.28	.24	.37
Including feedback effects	.24	.19	.33

Part 3
Improving Congressional Performance

CHAPTER 9

What Can Be Done?

The U.S. Congress should provide goods that markets undersupply (because of positive market failures) and manage activities that markets oversupply (because of negative market failures). This view of congressional behavior raises four major issues. First, when should Congress alter market relationships? What principles should govern congressional management of the microeconomy? Second, what policies has Congress enacted to alter the behavior of markets in general (and energy markets in particular)? How do the policies Congress enacts compare with the policies that would improve energy-market performance? Third, how should we explain Congress's policy behavior? What are plausible theories of congressional decisions, and how should these theories be tested? Finally, once the determinants of congressional behavior have been ascertained, what can be done to align Congress's performance more closely with its goals?

In the seven previous chapters, I have attempted to answer the first three questions. Let me briefly review these answers, and then discuss the fourth.

When Should Congress Alter Market Relationships?

Policy choices about market activity involve questions either of allocational efficiency or of distributional equity. Congress should alter the characteristics of particular markets only when market failures exist, that is, on those occasions when markets do not effectively implement the Pareto rule. When transactions fail to occur that would increase all citizens' welfare (because of positive externalities) or when transactions occur that raise some citizens' welfare at the expense of others (because of negative externalities), Congress can provide public goods in the case of the former and create markets for harm in the case of the latter, thereby improving citizens' welfare.

When distributional issues are the source of voter concern, Congress cannot improve everyone's welfare simultaneously; it must tax some individuals to raise the welfare of others. However, certain redistributional methods offer more benefits and fewer costs than others. In particular, the legislature always should redistribute income and wealth through direct general taxation, rather than indirectly through the alteration of characteristics of particular markets. Deadweight loss, unintended benefits for the affluent, the capitalization of privileges in asset markets, and perverse allocational distortions all detract from the benefits of indirect microeconomic redistribution.

How Has Congress Altered
Energy-Market Relationships?

Petroleum-market policy disputes largely are conflicts over the proper distribution of excess profits and the fate of entrepreneurs whose incomes decline. Economies of scale in petroleum pipelines, the problems of capture in crude-oil reservoirs, and a poorly functioning market for long-term inventories are all market failures that could be alleviated by legislative action. But most petroleum-policy disputes arise, instead, from changes in prices or producer incomes that stem from the very low short-run elasticities found in crude-oil markets.

Congress has responded to these equity problems with petroleum pricing policies that indirectly augment either producer or consumer welfare, depending on whether prices are rising or falling. Firms and consumers, of course, react to the incentives created by these price changes, producing severe allocational distortions that undermine the original redistributive intent. Examples of this cycle are abundant. The tax privileges and prorationing schemes enacted to support producer incomes in the 1930s induced other producers to import oil to capture the excess profits created by the subsidies, which, in turn, led to domestic demands for import controls. When Congress attempted to help consumers during the 1973 and 1979 price shocks, the results were equally disastrous. The Emergency Petroleum Allocation Act and the accompanying entitlements scheme actually created incentives for owners of crude-oil inventories under long-term contracts to withhold the oil exactly when it should have been released. In addition, the entitlements program encouraged imports when our stated policy was to create energy independence.

While petroleum markets were as free from regulation in 1990 as they have been since the late 1920s, we still have no policy in place to deal with the next oil shock (which invariably will take place because of the underlying low elasticities for crude oil) except for that creating the three-month petroleum supply stored in Louisiana (for which no allocational scheme yet exists) and the tax on windfall profits, which, of course, will reduce prices exactly when they should rise.

Coal-policy disputes also largely involve equity issues between high-cost producers (northern unionized mines) and their lower-cost competitors (southern and western strip mines). Many coal disputes involve worker-safety and environmental concerns and thus have the appearance of market-failure struggles when, in fact, they are conflicts among producers and workers over income in a declining market.

Natural gas market operations are quite competitive and involve no market failures except for pipeline tariffs. The equity disputes that do arise occur when petroleum prices change rapidly and induce changes in the market for natural gas, its close substitute. Through an unfortunate error, the Supreme Court's 1954 decision in *Phillips v. Wisconsin*, price controls were imposed on natural gas. Once these controls existed, they were very difficult to remove, especially when oil price shocks in the 1970s induced similar rises in natural gas prices. By 1989, however, price-controlled natural gas had become such a small share of the market (6 percent) and prices were so stable that decontrol imposed no electoral consequences on members of Congress. When the next oil shock occurs, however, Congress will no doubt impose price constraints if no system is in place to ameliorate the inevitable equity problems that will occur.

Policy questions in nuclear power markets mainly involve questions of risk. The lower the cost of damage and the greater the incidence of harm, the better the market for risk will be (up to the point where risk can't profitably be shared). Nuclear power plants fail to meet both criteria. The harm they wreak is potentially extremely costly, and it doesn't occur often. Private entrepreneurs are generally unwilling to bear risks with these characteristics, and rightly so. From the late 1940s until the mid-1970s, however, Congress overrode the market's judgment and declared that the government would ensure nuclear power risks. Since the Three Mile Island disaster, the country and Congress have been less willing to bear nuclear power risks through policies suspending owner responsibility. The market for nuclear power has all but disappeared for now, but, as with natural gas and coal, these conflicts will all arise again when the next oil shock occurs.

Congress repeatedly alters the characteristics of energy markets, despite the absence of market failures, in order to augment the incomes of consumers and firms. Such attempts do not produce the equity effects Congress intends but instead create severe allocational distortions that exacerbate the original problem.

What Are the Causes of Congressional Energy-Policy Behavior?

A full explanation of congressional policy behavior would specify when market conditions are viewed as problems, why some ideas become legislative proposals, and why some policy proposals enjoy more legislative success than others. In this book I deal systematically only with the third question. Energy-market conditions are viewed as problems when price shocks impose stress on the incomes of consumers or firms or when disasters focus attention on environmental risks. When these events occur, the legislature faces greater pressure to enact proposals than at other times. I do not believe that I can explain why some ideas become actual legislative policy proposals while other ideas do not, but in the energy-policy area, at least, the consequences are minor. I find no systematic differences between the energy-policy solutions discussed in academia and those ideas actually introduced into Congress.

Policy proposals enjoy legislative success because they coincide with legislators' own preferences, because they coincide with the preferences of other actors (such as interest groups or bureaucrats) who can persuade or influence members of Congress to agree, or because members anticipate how the flows of costs and benefits that would result from the enactment of a proposal will affect voters' electoral behavior and act accordingly. Economic conditions may modify the effects of all these relationships in two ways. First, the effectiveness of pleas to alter market relationships to aid group x or group y may be determined by whether the requests are warranted by economic realities. Second, when employees, entrepreneurs, or consumers suffer economic difficulties, members of Congress may be more likely to support proposals that benefit the affected group.

To establish the validity of the various alternative explanations one must specify the events to be explained; define the unit of analysis; choose an appropriate population of cases and design a sample; gather data to represent the theories; and establish the marginal effect of factors, controlling for alternatives. Most of the existing policy studies fail to exhibit one or more of these research-design traits, casting doubt on the validity of their results. Conventional policy inquiries do not adequately compare alternative explanations or randomly select their cases. Even the more recent works using large data sets and econometric techniques have limitations. First, the explanation of the variation of policy positions across members does not explain aggregate policy decisions by Congress. Second, the isolation of the effect of members' ideology from the other causes of outcomes is very difficult because it is an unobserved endogenous variable. Finally, the largest problem with these quantitative studies is their use of roll call vote data to estimate their models. Members of Congress choose whether decisions are subject to a roll call, so parameter effects estimated from roll call votes will suffer from selection bias that cannot be corrected without a model of how decisions become subject to a roll call.

In studying energy-policy proposals introduced into Congress from 1945 to 1976, I attempt to sidestep some of the problems outlined above by clearly specifying my unit of analysis and the events to be explained, coding an appropriate sample of the cases, and estimating a model that allows all the alternative theories to be tested. My results, however, also have limitations because they are estimated only from coal and nuclear power cases.

The results of the estimation exercise support many of the theories suggested in chapter 5. Congress enacts policies because of the preferences of interest groups, the anticipation of interest-group influence, and the economic context. But substantial variance exists within these factor classes. Pronuclear producer groups have large effects on outcomes, while private utilities and the coal industry do not. The president has large effects if the congressional majority belongs to the same party, but bureaucratic agencies really don't have independent effects, except for the all-important Office of Management and Budget.

Legislators' anticipation of the effects of cost-benefit flows on voters was a more complicated process than expected. The relationship was curvilinear. Those proposals with concentrated costs and benefits were less likely to be enacted than were reforms (concentrated costs/diffuse benefits) and pork-barrel proposals (concentrated benefits/diffuse costs). Economic contexts also did not have the expected effect. Of the nine economic sectors represented by terms in the model, only the nuclear industry and its workers were more likely to receive benefits from Congress when they suffered economic decline. Taxpayers, coal workers, small coal producers, private utilities, electricity consumers, and uranium producers, on the other hand, were more likely to receive benefits on those occasions when they were better off economically. Even though the effects of economic context were individually small and contrary to my expectations, significant variations in economic context altered aggregate outcomes. For example, when I compared the effects of economic conditions in 1973 and 1975 with the average, the probability of passage of surface-mine controls was increased 21 percentage points (from 66 to 87 percent).

Although many readers may have given up trying to digest the meaning of all the numbers presented in chapter 8, I will have succeeded in this enterprise if I made two central points clear. First, empirical methods can be applied successfully to research problems in political science other than public opinion and voting behavior. Second, numerous factors have effects on policy outcomes; therefore, any given aggregate result that we wish to explain about Congress's behavior could be the product of any one of the millions of permutations and combinations of various factor values that yields the same probability of enactment. To answer any particular question about congressional behavior, one needs to estimate a model across a large number of cases and then confront the case that demands explanation. As I showed in the mandatory coal scrubber simulation, one does not have to invent new theory every time apparently aberrant outcomes occur (in this case, the enactment of policies favorable to coal interests). Small changes in the values of variables in the model produced the unexpected victory for coal groups, not a dramatic change in their power.

Congressional Reform?

The enactment of policies by a legislature to alter the microeconomy is a classic N-person collective-action dilemma. We all would be better off if legislators and their potential political opponents cooperated and did not grant particular groups or individuals market advantages through microeconomic policies in the absence of any compelling allocational reasons. Once political opponents defect from the cooperative solution, however, and support policy proposals that grant microeconomic benefits to certain groups in order to gain political advantage, despite the lack of any real market failure, the cooperative equilibrium quickly unravels. Once this defection becomes widespread, interest groups have extensive influence in the policy system.

The central dilemma faced by the founders of our country was the design of political institutions that were democratic and yet not overly responsive to the narrow interests of faction. Ironically, we face the same problem today. The structure of incentives created by district elections in a political economy where public activity occurs frequently has encouraged legislators to service organized interests in a series of separate games that have an outward positive-sum appearance because those who gain are quite aware of the benefits and those citizens at large who lose are unaware of their losses. Elections introduce a competitive element into political institutions that makes the enactment of policies to improve market outcomes very difficult. Political markets render Congress largely incapable of correcting market flaws for the same reasons that competitive private behavior creates the difficulties in the first place. Commentators as diverse as Lowi (1969), Stigler (1971), Mayhew (1974), Thurow (1980), Jackson and Leone (1981), Shepsle and Weingast (1984), and Niou and Ordeshook (1985) all have described this phenomenon using different frameworks and language but have not taken the next step and designed possible institutional remedies.

Possible Reform Proposals

For those who favor the enactment of policies that have a sound allocational and equity basis, my results offer both good and bad news. The good news is that interest-group influence is limited. Not all groups have large effects on policy outcomes. Unfortunately, those that do have large effects usually ask for microeconomic privilege. Three generic solutions are possible:

- Alter incentives so that the optimal self-interested behavior of Congress produces legislation whose allocational and equity characteristics are closer to the ideal.
- Use moral suasion to induce optimal behavior with or without the assistance of appropriate incentives.
- Encourage nonelected judges to overturn legislation on the basis of efficiency considerations.

I will discuss each in terms of analytic integrity and political feasibility.

Incentive Solutions

Congress produces bad public policies because its members face strong incentives to enact perverse legislation and because voters face strong incentives to reelect such members. One possible remedy for these difficulties would be the creation of institutions where members and voters found better policy outcomes to be in their self-interest. In this section, I will investigate three possible sources of reform—political parties, public-interest organizations, and constituency information.

Strengthen Parties

Under existing institutional conditions, if members of Congress take the high road and resist subsidy or regulation demands when no rationale exists for these policies, they increase their electoral vulnerability, particularly if the subsidy or regulation has obvious support in their individual district. The solution is not to eliminate democratic responsiveness or geographic districts (Shepsle and Weingast 1984), but to structure the incentives so that Congress, using Thurow's terminology (1975, 41), responds to "individual-societal preferences" instead of "private-personal preferences," that is, preferences about the rules of the game and not about ad hoc solutions to particular problems. Members, for example, should be responsive to the plight of workers whose incomes decline but not to requests to subsidize particular firms (Chrysler) or commodities (automobiles or steel).

Members' electoral fortunes must be tied to national aggregate outcomes and not to the survival of particular firms, people, or events. They should act as if Rawls' (1971) "Veil of Ignorance" had never been removed and carry on policy debate in terms of general solutions to the problems of market society. Parties can create such an incentive structure. Under strong political parties, members of the legislature are elected, not on the basis of their individual contribution to policy matters, but on the basis of their support of a particular set of structural solutions to market problems.

Analytically speaking, parties are a sound remedy for individual logrolling as long as the competing parties themselves don't defect and cater to private-personal preferences and as long as the government retains a reasonable ability to control the political economy. The problem with the strong-parties proposal is that it is completely incompatible with legislators' current interests. Mayhew (1974, 27, 177) states the argument succinctly.

> No theoretical treatment of the United States Congress that posits parties as analytic units will go very far. . . . Freedom to take positions is so firmly established among modern congressmen that something of a revolution would be required to upset it.

Reorganize Constituents
If political parties cannot be used to restrict legislators' ability to respond to demands for microeconomic privilege, then maybe the nature of demands made by constituents can be altered. Congress defers to the demands of the organized because those segments of society that suffer diffuse losses from both policy action and inaction are not adequately represented in the policy process (Olson 1965). Since 1970, the formation of groups such as Common Cause and Ralph Nader's Public Interest Research Groups has ameliorated the Olson problem, to some extent. My model, for example, suggests that the Nader groups and the Sierra Club have modest effects on the enactment of energy-policy proposals. Their effectiveness has had questionable benefits, however, because the policies they support, while done in the name of the public interest, have perverse effects on allocation and equity. Ackerman and Hassler (1981) and Frieden (1979) have documented how the pollution-control and land-use policies that these groups have advocated create privilege much as old interest-group policies did. The Sierra Club, for example, argued for the long-run marginal-cost pricing of oil in 1973, a sound position, but supported mandatory coal-stack scrubbing in 1977, a practice that requires enormous expenditures for questionable environmental benefits.

In theory, organizing points of view currently left out of the policy process is a viable solution. In practice, however, the analytic character of these groups' perspectives seems to decay over time as they form coalitions.

Augment Constituency Information
Principal-agent relationships exist whenever people utilize others to act on their behalf. The central problem in such relationships occurs whenever the agent can act in his own interests instead of the principal's because the information that would allow the principal to monitor the agent's behavior is unavailable, expensive, or distorted. The information difficulties arise because the only source of information about the agent's performance is often

the agent himself, who has strong incentives to distort and undersupply information that would allow the principal to adequately monitor performance.

The most examined principal-agent relationship is that between stockholders and managers of business firms. Market failures exist in the supply of information about firm performance because managers have a strong incentive to divert profits for their own use (shirking), but not to make shareholders aware of the diversion.

Rectification of shirking in the private sector has two components—the provision of adequate information and the existence of alternate manager teams willing to act on the information and buy the undervalued shares of a firm. Under laws administered by the Securities and Exchange Commission, corporations must report uniform, objective, and audited financial information to stockholders. Alternative management groups can use such information to develop a takeover offer that bribes shareholders into ousting the existing managers. These new managers can use their hierarchical authority to rearrange the firm to better reward the shareholders.

The relationship between constituents and members of Congress is analogous, though not identical, to that between owners of stock and managers of firms. Highlighting the differences, however, tells us what changes in institutional design would be necessary to solve congressional "shirking."

Owners of stock have one goal, the maximization of profits. Citizens, on the other hand, have more complicated contingent goals. Constituents have preferences about the rules of the game (collective outcomes) and preferences about behavior once the rules of the game already have been set (Thurow 1975, 41). Citizens have a strong interest in preferring rules of the game that prevent Congress from granting microeconomic privilege, for the reasons I outlined in chapter 2; however, if no such rules exist, then all citizens face equally strong incentives to lobby for their own microeconomic gains (Stigler 1971; Posner 1974; Niou and Ordeshook 1985). Members of Congress shirk their responsibility to carry out the first goal because the costs of group demands for microeconomic privilege are collective, obscure, and not obviously attributable to congressional activity. In short, the information that would causally link congressional activities with bad collective outcomes is undersupplied, allowing members to shirk their duty to act in constituents' collective interest.

A possible remedy for this situation is the congressional analogue to the regulation of corporate financial reporting practices. As Fenno (1978) has documented so carefully, members of Congress gain the confidence of their constituents through the creation of trust and other psychological means, not through the supply of objective, uniform information about policy outputs. What if congressional newsletters could no longer use statements that claimed that 5,000 jobs were created by a defense contract, but also had to say that procurement spending is capital intensive and creates far fewer jobs per dollar of expenditure than the forgone private spending? What if members could not just say that oil price controls kept the lid on prices, thereby implying that consumers benefited, but also had to add that most of the economic rents were redistributed to refiners and not to consumers, that consumers benefited in proportion to their income, and that oil imports increased as a side effect? In short, what if members' communications with their districts had to include, by law, the conclusions of policy analysis about costs as well as benefits? Members would be less likely to shun constituents' collective interests.

Some may argue that improvements in the supply of information about policies' effects will not improve congressional outcomes because members have no incentive to act on them. This view is only partially correct. Members of Congress, indeed, are punished electorally for poor aggregate outcomes (Kramer 1971), but they engage in district-centered games of privilege to shift voters' attention away from the diffuse aggregate losses that they, as individual members, can do little to control. As Mayhew (1974, 32) says,

> All in all, the rational way for marginal congressmen to deal with national trends is to ignore them, to treat them as acts of God over which they can exercise no control.

Improving the supply of policy-analytic information available to the public would not, by itself, solve the collective action problem that members of Congress face, but it would create increasing difficulties for those members who persist in exempting themselves from any responsibility for the actions of Congress as a whole.

The mandatory quarterly reporting of policy-analytic information to all constituents by such agencies as the GAO, CBO, and OTA would add to the list of aggregate outcomes that induce voters to exhibit the kind of electoral behavior Kramer describes. Such information might cause voters to include allocational efficiency as well as macroeconomic performance in the set of phenomena they utilize to judge a politician's performance.

A second major difference between shirking in Congress and the private sector is that nonofficeholders who use policy-outcome information to oust incumbents cannot pay voters the anticipated welfare gains created by policy improvement as managers pay shareholders the present value of anticipated profits during takeover attempts. The lack of a market for votes creates two risks for voters that reduce their incentive to act on negative microeconomic-outcome information. First, they must trust that their representative will actually implement policy change. Second, if he fails, they must hope that other members will not exclude the reform-minded district from benefits received under the current system. In short, under existing institutional rules, voters have few reasons to elect legislators who will not shirk their obligations to represent constituents' collective interest.

Some scholars suggest, however, that citizens may not have to act directly on negative-outcome information in order to alter elite behavior. Jacobson and Kernell (1983) and Jacobson (1989) argue that the effects of macroeconomic conditions on congressional elections observed by Kramer (1971) are caused by elite behavior and not by citizens actually throwing the rascals out because of negative national economic performance. If the provision of negative microeconomic information causes incumbents to retire or strong challengers to run, then the desired electoral turnover will occur even though citizens do not act directly on the information.

Moral Suasion

The inability of political entrepreneurs to pay voters the anticipated gains of institutional reforms implies that extremely nonoptimal political institutions can be very stable, whereas nonoptimal market institutions probably cannot persist for very long. The reform of political institutions through incentive changes is characterized by a utilitarian infinite regress. How can one improve policy outcomes? I have argued through incentive changes. Is it in anyone's interest to change incentives? No, not until the incentives change. In short, if people were strictly utilitarian, reform could not occur.

Political leaders understand these facts and use moral suasion to persuade people to alter both institutional incentives and their own behavior, even though neither action is compatible with their self-interest. Moral exhortation is both a very powerful and very fragile policy device. In the right context, such as a small town, norms and values can induce behavior that is not compatible with incentives because tastes do not diverge and deviations from the norms can be observed and punished. In a larger context, however, moral suasion is unlikely to work because tastes likely will diverge enough that some significant fraction of the population will not cooperate. Once the remaining citizens discover the lack of unanimity, they will become increasingly unwilling to sacrifice for the greater good.

Presidents, of course, frequently use normative argument to induce Congress and voters to behave contrary to their interests, but, as President Carter discovered, the ability of a political leader to alter citizen and congressional behavior through the use of moral exhortation is severely limited.

Courts

If Congress is extremely unlikely to constrain individual members' behavior through controls over nonparty resources or through the extensive supply of

policy-analytic knowledge, then more extensive use of the courts as omnis-
cient, unelected, welfare-economic actors is a final possible solution. The
New Jersey Supreme Court and Boston's federal district court, for example,
have ordered numerous changes in the last ten years in housing, sewage,
education, and mental health policies because the legislature in each state
failed to respond to genuine equity or allocational problems. Many commentators have deplored the increasingly policy-oriented activism of some of the
nation's courts, arguing that legal reasoning—with its yes or no emphasis on
facts and rights—cannot make the marginal and opportunity-cost decisions
that should be the basis of economic decisions (Horowitz 1977).

Horowitz's critique is sound, but instead of reducing their policy-making
role, as he advocates, perhaps the courts should increase their role but alter
their reasoning. For example, the courts could use legal reasoning to find that
the new source performance standards discussed by Ackerman and Hassler
(1981) are not based on sound welfare-economic criteria, a simple yes-no
question, and then employ competing teams of economists as masters to
design alternative plans, one of which the legislature would have to enact.

Richard Posner's appointment to the U.S. Court of Appeals and the
spread of the law-and-economics movement outside of its Chicago origins
suggest that the courts increasingly may use efficiency criteria in their decisions. A review of some famous decisions in the 1980s, however, suggests
that the courts are inconsistent in their use of economic reasoning. On July 2,
1980, the U.S. Supreme Court ruled 5 to 4 in *Industrial Union Department v.
American Petroleum Institute* that the benzene standard promulgated by the
Occupational Safety and Health Administration was illegal because it had no
reasonable basis. The Court, however, did not decide whether efficiency and
cost-benefit considerations should be the basis of OSHA's regulations. In *EPA
v. Natural Resources Defense Council* (1984), the Court ruled that EPA's use
of the bubble concept is legal. The bubble concept is an EPA innovation in air-
quality regulation that allows firms to trade off emissions in different parts of a
plant in order to minimize cost. In effect, EPA uses this concept to create an
air-rights market in which EPA monitors ambient air-quality outcomes and
allows point sources to trade pollution rights.

Three other cases, two national and one local, illustrate that the courts
also can be blind to efficiency criteria. In *National Association of Greeting
Card Publishers v. U.S. Postal Service* (1983), the Supreme Court ruled that
the U.S. Postal Service has wide latitude in its pricing authority and does not
have to price at marginal cost. On December 7, 1987, the New York State
Supreme Court ruled that density rights cannot be sold by New York City for
cash (Lueck 1987). In effect, developers cannot compensate localities for
scarce property rights. They, of course, are free to donate to campaigns and
secure majority-rule changes in zoning laws in which the public is not com-

pensated, but the court obviously does not realize that the cash solution actually makes the public better off.

Finally, on February 24, 1988, the Supreme Court ruled in *Pennell v. San Jose* that local rent control laws, particularly one in San Jose, California, do not constitute an unconstitutional taking of property without compensation. The two Reagan appointees, Justices Antonin Scalia and Sandra Day O'Connor, argued unsuccessfully that rent control established "a welfare program privately funded by those landlords who happen to have 'hardship' tenants."

I do not pretend to have presented a random sample of legal decisions, but I think that I can safely conclude that, although the law-and-economics movement certainly will continue to influence court decisions, the courts will not be the central actors in the effort to align congressional performance more closely with appropriate forms of collective action. In addition to the inconsistent acceptance of economic reasoning by the courts, the judicial solution to congressional policy failure also may not be viable because it reduces the legitimacy that courts require to implement their decisions. If courts become more active in making policy, the delicate balance between democracy and judicial review may tip too far in the direction of the courts.

Conclusion

Congressional policy decisions, on average, do not improve market performance. I used energy-market examples to support this argument, but examples from other markets could have been used to illustrate the same conclusion. Of the possible remedies I examine—stronger political parties, more public-interest groups, better constituency information, moral suasion, and more active courts—the augmentation of constituency information, combined with the increasing role of the law-and-economics movement, seems most promising. If voters were reminded frequently of the efficiency and equity effects of congressional decisions, they would be more likely to include microeconomic performance in the set of phenomena that cause them to throw incumbents out. Because a market for votes does not exist, however, voters cannot receive the benefits of collective action before they elect new officials, unlike shareholders in takeovers who do receive up-front benefits when they oust incumbent managers. On the other hand, if Jacobson and Kernell's (1983) views are even partially correct, poor microeconomic outcomes might produce better challengers and lead to the election of members of Congress more attuned to the importance of congressional microeconomic policy decisions in the overall performance of the American economy.

Bibliography

Aaron, Henry. 1972. *Shelter and Subsidies*. Washington, D.C.: Brookings Institution.

Achen, Christopher H. 1986. *The Statistical Analysis of Quasi-Experiments*. Berkeley: University of California Press.

Ackerman, Bruce, and William T. Hassler. 1981. *Clean Coal/Dirty Air*. New Haven: Yale University Press.

Adelman, Morris P. 1972. *The World Petroleum Market*. Baltimore: Johns Hopkins University Press.

Altshuler, Alan. 1979. *The Urban Transportation System*. Cambridge: MIT Press.

Arnold, R. Douglas. 1979. *Congress and the Bureaucracy*. New Haven: Yale University Press.

Arnold, R. Douglas. 1990. *The Logic of Congressional Action*. New Haven: Yale University Press.

Bachrach, Peter, and Morton Baratz. 1962. "Two Faces of Power." *American Political Science Review* 56:947–52.

Baker, Ralph Hillis. 1941. *The National Bituminous Coal Commission*. Johns Hopkins Studies in Historical and Political Science, series 59, no. 3. Baltimore: Johns Hopkins University Press.

Bauer, Raymond, Ithiel de Sola Pool, and Lewis Anthony Dexter. 1963. *American Business and Public Policy*. New York: Atherton.

Baumol, William. 1986. *Superfairness: Applications and Theory*. Cambridge: MIT Press.

Becker, Gary S. 1983. "A Theory of Competition Among Pressure Groups for Political Influence." *Quarterly Journal of Economics* 98:371–400.

Bernstein, Robert A., and Stephen R. Horn. 1981. "Explaining House Voting on Energy Policy: Ideology and the Conditional Effects of Party and District Economic Interests." *Western Political Quaterly* 34:235–45.

Blair, John. 1976. *The Control of Oil*. New York: Pantheon.

Buchanan, James M., and Gordon Tullock. 1962. *The Calculus of Consent*. Ann Arbor: University of Michigan Press.

Bupp, Irwin C., and Jean-Claude Derian. 1981. *The Failed Promise of Nuclear Power*. New York: Basic Books.

Carson, Richard, and Joe Oppenheimer. 1984. "A Method of Estimating the Personal Ideology of Political Representatives." *American Political Science Review* 78:163–78.

Chubb, John. 1983. *Interest Groups and the Bureaucracy*. Stanford: Stanford University Press.

Clarke, Edward H. 1971. "Multi-part Pricing of Public Goods." *Public Choice* 11:17–33.

Clausen, Aage R. 1973. *How Congressmen Decide*. New York: St. Martin's Press.

Clausen, Edward H., and Richard B. Cheney. 1970. "A Comparative Analysis of Senate-House Voting on Economic and Welfare Policy, 1953–1964." *American Political Science Review* 64:138–52.

Clausen, Edward H., and Carl E. Van Horn. 1977. "The Congressional Response to a Decade of Change, 1963–1972." *Journal of Politics* 39:624–66.

Coase, Ronald H. 1960. "The Problem of Social Cost." *Journal of Law and Economics* 3:1–44.

Cookenboo, Leslie, Jr. 1955. *Crude Oil Pipelines and Competition in the Oil Industry.* Cambridge: Harvard University Press.

Crandall, Robert W. 1983. *Controlling Industrial Pollution.* Washington, D.C.: Brookings Institution.

Dawson, Richard, and James Robinson. 1963. "Interparty Competition, Economic Variables, and Welfare Policies in the American States." *Journal of Politics* 25:265–89.

Diamond, Stuart. 1984. "OPEC Refineries Stir Two U. S. Studies." *New York Times*, November 14, sec. D.

Dorfman, Robert. 1981. "Transition Costs of Changing Regulations." In *Attacking Regulatory Problems*. ed. Allen R. Ferguson. Cambridge, Mass.: Ballinger.

Downs, Anthony. 1957. *An Economic Theory of Democracy.* New York: Harper and Brothers.

Duffie, Darrel, and Hugo Sonnenschein. 1989. "Arrow and General Equilibrium Theory." *Journal of Economic Literature* 27:565–98.

Dunham, Andrew, and Theodore Marmor. 1978. "Federal Policy and Health: Recent Trends and Different Perspectives." In *Nationalizing Government,* ed. Theodore Lowi and Alan Stone. Beverly Hills, Calif.: Sage.

Dye, Thomas. 1966. *Politics, Economics, and the Public: Policy Outcomes in the American States.* Chicago: Rand McNally.

Edelman, Murray. 1967. *The Symbolic Uses of Power.* Urbana: University of Illinois Press.

Elkin, Stephen L. 1974. "Political Science and the Analysis of Public Policy." *Public Policy* 22:399–422.

Faith, Roger, Donald Leavens, and Roger Tollison. 1982. "Antitrust Pork Barrel." *Journal of Law and Economics* 25:329–42.

Farquharson, Robin. 1969. *A Theory of Voting.* New Haven: Yale University Press.

Feldstein, Martin. 1983. *Inflation, Tax Rules, and Capital Formation.* Chicago: University of Chicago Press.

Fenno, Richard. 1978. *Home Style.* Boston: Little, Brown.

Fiorina, Morris P. 1981. *Retrospective Voting in American National Elections.* New Haven: Yale University Press.

Freedman, David A., and Stephen C. Peters. 1984. "Bootstrapping a Regression Equation: Some Empirical Results." *Journal of the American Statistical Association* 79:97–106.

Frieden, Bernard. 1979. *The Environmental Protection Hustle*. Cambridge: MIT Press.

Friedlaender, Ann F., 1969. *The Dilemma of Freight Transportation Regulation*. Washington, D.C.: Brookings Institution.

Friedlaender, Ann F., and Richard H. Spady. 1981. *Freight Transportation Regulation*. Cambridge: MIT Press.

Friedman, Milton. 1962. *Capitalism and Freedom*. Chicago: University of Chicago Press.

Friedman, Milton, and Anna Schwartz. 1963. *A Monetary History of the United States*. Princeton: Princeton University Press.

Gaventa, John. 1980. *Power and Powerlessness*. Urbana: University of Illinois Press.

Goldthorpe, John H., David Lockwood, Frank Bechhofer, and Jennifer Platt. 1969. *The Affluent Worker in the Class Structure*. New York: Cambridge University Press.

Green, Harold P., and Alan Rosenthal. 1963. *Government of the Atom*. New York: Atherton.

Gross, Bertram. 1953. *The Legislative Struggle*. New York: McGraw-Hill.

Groves, T., and J. Ledyard. 1977a. "Optimal Allocation of Public Goods: A Solution to the 'Free Rider' Problem." *Econometrica* 45 (May): 783–809.

Groves, T., and J. Ledyard. 1977b. "Some Limitations of Demand Revealing Processes." *Public Choice* 28:107–24.

Groves, Theodore, and Martin Loeb. 1975. "Incentives and Public Inputs." *Journal of Public Economics* 4:211–26.

Hager, George. 1989. "Natural-Gas Decontrol Package Bogs Down on Senate Floor." *Congressional Quarterly Weekly Report* 47 (June 10): 1396.

Hansen, John A. 1983. *United States Oil Pipeline Markets*. Cambridge: MIT Press.

Heclo, Hugh. 1972. "Review Article: Policy Analysis." *British Journal of Political Science* 2:83–108.

Heclo, Hugh. 1975. *Modern Social Politics in Britain and Sweden*. New Haven: Yale University Press.

Hershey, Robert D. 1985. "Refiners' Bid for Protection." *New York Times*, May 10, sec. D.

Hines, James R., Jr. 1988. "What Is Benefit Taxation?" Princeton University, Department of Economics. Typescript.

Hochschild, Jennifer. 1981. *What's Fair?* Cambridge: Harvard University Press.

Hofferbert, Richard. 1966. "The Relationship Between Public Policy and Some Structural and Environmental Variables in the American States." *American Political Science Review* 60:73–82.

Horowitz, Donald L. 1977. *The Courts and Social Policy*. Washington, D.C.: Brookings Institution.

Jackson, John E. 1974. *Constituencies and Leaders in Congress*. Cambridge: Harvard University Press.

Jackson, John E., and Robert A. Leone. 1981. "The Political Economy of Federal Regulatory Activity: The Case of Water-Pollution Controls." In *Studies in Public Regulation*, ed. Gary Fromm. Cambridge: MIT Press.

Jacobs, Jane. 1984. *Cities and the Wealth of Nations: Principles of Economic Life*. New York: Random House.

Jacobson, Gary C. 1989. "Strategic Politicians and the Dynamics of U.S. House Elections, 1946–86." *American Political Science Review* 83:773–93.

Jacobson, Gary C., and Samuel Kernell. 1983. *Strategy and Choice in Congressional Elections*. New Haven: Yale University Press.

Johnson, Arthur M. 1967. *Petroleum Pipelines and Public Policy*. Cambridge: Harvard University Press.

Johnson, James P. 1979. *The Politics of Soft Coal*. Urbana: University of Illinois Press.

Jones, Charles O. 1975. *Clean Air*. Pittsburgh: University of Pittsburgh Press.

Kahn, Alfred. 1971. *The Economics of Regulation*. Vols. 1 and 2. New York: Wiley.

Kalikow, Barnett. 1984. "Environmental Risk: Power to the People." *Technology Review* 87 (October): 55–61.

Kalt, Joseph. 1981. *The Economics and Politics of Oil Price Regulation*. Cambridge: MIT Press.

Kalt, Joseph, and Mark Zupan. 1984. "Capture and Ideology in the Economic Theory of Politics." *American Economic Review* 74:279–300.

Kau, James B., and Paul H. Rubin. 1978. "Voting on Minimum Wages: A Time Series Analysis." *Journal of Political Economy* 86:337–42.

Kau, James B., and Paul H. Rubin. 1979. "Self Interest, Ideology, and Logrolling in Congressional Voting." *Journal of Law and Economics* 22:365–84.

Kelman, Steven. 1981. *What Price Incentives?* Cambridge, Mass.: Auburn House Publishers.

Kiewiet, D. R., and D. R. Kinder. 1979a. "Sociotropic Politics: The American Case." *British Journal of Political Science* 11:129–61.

Kiewiet, D. R., and D. R. Kinder. 1979b. "Economic Discontent and Political Behavior: The Role of Personal Grievances and Collective Economic Judgments in Congressional Voting." *American Journal of Political Science* 23:495–527.

Kingdon, John. 1973. *Congressmen's Voting Decisions*. New York: Harper and Row.

Kingdon, John. 1984. *Agendas, Alternatives, and Public Policies*. Boston: Little, Brown.

Kneese, Allen, and Charles Schultze. 1975. *Pollution, Prices, and Public Policy*. Washington, D.C.: Brookings Institution.

Koford, Kenneth. 1989. "Dimensions in Congressional Voting." *American Political Science Review* 83:949–62.

Kramer, Gerald H. 1971. "Short-Term Fluctuations in U.S. Voting Behavior, 1896–1964." *American Political Science Review* 65:131–43.

Kramer, Gerald H. 1983. "The Ecological Fallacy Revisited: Aggregate versus Individual-Level Findings on Economics and Elections and Sociotropic Voting." *American Political Science Review* 77:92–111.

Kunreuther, Howard, Paul Kleindorfer, Peter Knez, and Rudy Yaksick. 1987. "A Compensation Mechanism for Siting Noxious Facilities: Theory and Experimental Design." *Journal of Environmental Economics and Management* 14:371–83.

Latham, Earl. 1952. *The Group Basis of Politics*. Ithaca: Cornell University Press.

Lewis-Beck, Michael, and John Alford. 1980. "Can Government Regulate Safety: The Coal Mine Example." *American Political Science Review* 74:745–56.

Lilla, Mark. 1984. "Why the Income Distribution Is So Misleading." *Public Interest* 77 (fall): 62–76.

Little, Ian Malcom David. 1957. *A Critique of Welfare Economics*. 2d ed. New York: Oxford University Press.

Lovejoy, Wallace F., and Paul Hoffman. 1967. *Economic Aspects of Oil Conservation Regulation*. Baltimore: Johns Hopkins University Press.

Lovins, Amory. 1977. *Soft Energy Paths*. Cambridge, Mass.: Ballinger.

Lowi, Theodore. 1969. *The End of Liberalism*. New York: Norton.

Lueck, Thomas J. 1987. "Judge in New York Strikes Down Sale of Coliseum's Site." *New York Times*, December 8, sec. A.

MacAvoy, Paul, and Robert Pindyck. 1975. *The Economics of the Natural Gas Shortage, 1960–1980*. New York: American Elsevier.

MacAvoy, Paul, and Robert Pindyck. 1983. *Energy Policy*. New York: Norton.

McDonald, Stephen. 1971. *Petroleum Conservation in the U.S.* Baltimore: Johns Hopkins University Press.

McLean, John G. 1954. *The Growth of Integrated Oil Companies*. Cambridge: Harvard University Press.

McRae, Duncan. 1958. *Dimensions of Congressional Voting*. University of California Publications in Sociology and Social Institutions, vol. 1, no. 3. Berkeley: University of California Press.

McRae, Duncan. 1970. *Issues and Parties in Legislative Voting*. New York: Harper and Row.

Maddala, G. S. 1977. *Econometrics*. New York: McGraw-Hill.

Maddala, G. S. 1983. *Limited-Dependent and Qualitative Variables in Econometrics*. New York: Cambridge University Press.

Mayhew, David R. 1974. *Congress: The Electoral Connection*. New Haven: Yale University Press.

Miller, Harlan B., and William H. Williams. 1982. *The Limits of Utilitarianism*. Minneapolis: University of Minnesota Press.

Mitchell, Edwin, ed. 1979. *Oil Pipelines and Public Policy*. Washington, D.C.: American Enterprise Institute.

Moyer, Reed. 1964. *Competition in the Midwestern Coal Industry*. Cambridge: Harvard University Press.

Mueller, Dennis C. 1989. *Public Choice*. New York: Cambridge University Press.

Nagel, Jack H. 1975. *The Descriptive Analysis of Power*. New Haven: Yale University Press.

Nash, Gerald D. 1968. *U.S. Oil Policy, 1890–1964*. Pittsburgh: University of Pittsburgh Press.

Neuman, George, and John P. Nelson. 1982. "Safety Regulation and Firm Size: Effects of the Coal Mine Health and Safety Act of 1969." *Journal of Law and Economics* 25:183–99.

Niou, Emerson, and Peter Ordeshook. 1985. "Universalism in Congress." *American Journal of Political Science* 29:246–58.

Nordlinger, Eric. 1981. *On the Autonomy of the Democratic State*. Cambridge: Harvard University Press.

Odell, Peter. 1970. *Oil and World Power*. New York: Taplinger.

Olson, Mancur. 1965. *The Logic of Collective Action*. Cambridge: Harvard University Press.

Olson, Mancur. 1982. *The Rise and Decline of Nations: Economic Growth, Stagflation, and Social Rigidities.* New Haven: Yale University Press.

Pashigian, B. Peter. 1984. "The Effect of Environmental Regulation on Optimal Plant Size and Factor Shares." *Journal of Law and Economics* 27:1–28.

Peltzman, Sam. 1976. "Toward a More General Theory of Regulation." *Journal of Law and Economics* 19:211–40.

Peltzman, Sam. 1984. "Constituent Interest and Congressional Voting." *Journal of Law and Economics* 27:181–210.

Peltzman, Sam. 1985. "An Economic Interpretation of the History of Congressional Voting in the Twentieth Century." *American Economic Review* 75:656–75.

Pettingill, Sam. 1936. *Hot Oil.* New York: Economic Forum.

Poole, Keith T., and Howard Rosenthal. 1985a. "The Political Economy of Roll-Call Voting in the Multi-party Congress of the United States." *European Journal of Political Economy* 1:45–58.

Poole, Keith T., and Howard Rosenthal. 1985b. "A Spatial Model for Legislative Roll-Call Analysis." *American Journal of Political Science* 29:357–84.

Posner, Richard. 1974. "Theories of Economic Regulation." *Bell Journal of Economics and Management Science* 5:335–58.

Posner, Richard. 1980. "The Ethical and Political Basis of the Efficiency Norm in Common Law Adjudication." *Hofstra Law Review* 8 (spring): 487–507.

Rae, Douglas W. 1969. "Decision Rules and Individual Values in Constitutional Choice." *American Political Science Review* 63:40–56.

Rae, Douglas W. 1975. "The Limits of Consensual Decision." *American Political Science Review* 69:1270–1294.

Rawls, John. 1971. *A Theory of Justice.* Cambridge: Harvard University Press.

Reich, Robert 1982. "Playing Tag with Japan." *New York Review of Books*, June 24, 37–40.

Reich, Robert. 1983. *The Next American Frontier.* New York: *New York Times* Review.

Rosenstone, Steven J., Roy L. Behr, and Edward H. Lazarus. 1984. *Third Parties in America.* Princeton: Princeton University Press.

Samuelson, Paul A. 1954. "The Pure Theory of Public Expenditure." *Review of Economics and Statistics* 36:386–89.

Sanders, Elizabeth. 1981. *The Regulation of Natural Gas.* Philadelphia: Temple University Press.

Schattschneider, Elmer E. 1960. *The Semi-Sovereign People.* Hinsdale, Ill.: Dryden Press.

Schneider, Steven A. 1983. *The Oil Price Revolution.* Baltimore: Johns Hopkins University Press.

Schultze, Charles. 1977. *The Public Use of Private Interest.* Washington, D.C.: Brookings Institution.

Schumpeter, Joseph A. 1950. *Capitalism, Socialism, and Democracy.* New York: Harper and Brothers.

Scitovsky, Tibor. 1941. "A Note on Welfare Propositions in Economics," *Review of Economic Studies* 9:77–88.

Sen, Amartya, and Bernard Williams. 1982. *Utilitarianism and Beyond.* New York: Cambridge University Press.

Shaffer, E. H. 1968. *The Oil Import Program.* New York: Praeger.

Shanahan, Eileen. 1986. "Deficit May Give Tax Lobbyists a Chance to Press Their Cases." *Congressional Quarterly Weekly Report* 44 (October 4): 2345.

Shapley, L. S., and Martin Shubik. 1954. "A Method for Evaluating the Distribution of Power in Committee Systems." *American Political Science Review* 48:787–92.

Sharkansky, Ira. 1968. *Spending in the American States.* Chicago: Rand McNally.

Shepsle, Kenneth. 1982. "A Review of the Politics of Regulation." *Journal of Political Economy* 92:216–21.

Shepsle, Kenneth, and Barry Weingast. 1984. "Political Solutions to Market Problems." *American Political Science Review* 78:417–34.

Silberman, Jonathan T., and Gary C. Durden. 1976. "Determining Legislative Preferences on Minimum Wages: An Economic Approach." *Journal of Political Economy* 84:317–29.

Simeon, Richard. 1976. "Studying Public Policy." *Canadian Journal of Political Science* 9:548–80.

Stigler, George. 1971. "The Theory of Economic Regulation." *Bell Journal of Economics and Management Science* 2:3–21.

Stobaugh, Robert, and Daniel Yergin. 1979. *Energy Future.* New York: Random House.

Surrey, Stanley. 1957. "How Special Tax Provisions Get Enacted." *Harvard Law Review* 70:1145–1182.

Taylor, Michael J. 1969. "Proof of a Theorem on Majority Rule." *Behaviorial Scientist* 14 (May): 228–31.

Teske, Paul. 1990. "The Political Demand for and Supply of Deregulation." State University of New York at Stony Brook, Department of Political Science. Typescript.

Thurow, Lester C. 1975. *Generating Inequality.* New York: Basic Books.

Thurow, Lester C. 1976. "Government Expenditures: Cash or In-Kind?" *Philosophy and Public Affairs* 5:361–81.

Thurow, Lester C. 1980. *The Zero-Sum Society.* New York: Basic Books.

Thurow, Lester C. 1983a. "From Infancy to Senility and Back." *New York Review of Books*, March 3, 9–11.

Thurow, Lester C. 1983b. "The Elephant and the Maharajah." *New York Review of Books*, December 22, 47–49.

Tideman, T. Nicolaus, and Gordon Tullock. 1976. "A New and Superior Process for Making Social Choices." *Journal of Political Economy* 84:1145–1159.

Truman, David. 1951. *The Governmental Process.* New York: Knopf.

Tufte, Edward. 1978. *Political Control of the Economy.* Princeton: Princeton University Press.

Tullock, Gordon. 1980. "The Transitional Gains Trap." In *Toward a Theory of the Rent-Seeking Society,* ed. James Buchanan, Robert Tollison, and Gordon Tullock. College Station: Texas A & M Press.

VanDoren, Peter. 1990. "Can We Learn the Causes of Congressional Decisions from Roll-Call Data?" *Legislative Studies Quarterly* 15:311–40.

Verleger, Phillip, Jr. 1982. *Oil Markets in Turmoil: An Economic Analysis.* Cambridge, Mass.: Ballinger.

Vietor, Richard. 1980. *Environmental Politics and the Coal Coalition.* College Station: Texas A & M Press.

Viscusi, W. Kip. 1983. *Risk by Choice.* Cambridge: Harvard University Press.

Vogel, David. 1983. "Cooperative Regulation: Environmental Protection in Great Britain." *Public Interest* 72 (summer): 88–106.

Watkins, Myron. 1937. *Oil: Stabilization or Conservation?* New York: Harper and Brothers.

Wildavsky, Aaron, and Ellen Tenenbaum. 1981. *The Politics of Mistrust: Estimating American Oil and Gas Reserves.* Beverly Hills, Calif.: Sage.

Williams, Stephen F. 1985. *The Natural Gas Revolution of 1985.* Washington, D.C.: American Enterprise Institute.

Williamson, Rene de Visme. 1936. *The Politics of Planning under the Code.* New York: Harper and Brothers.

Wilson, Graham. 1977. *Special Interests and Policymaking.* New York: Wiley.

Wilson, James Q. 1980. "The Politics of Regulation." In *The Politics of Regulation,* ed. James Q. Wilson. New York: Basic Books.

Wolf, Robert Paul. 1970. *In Defense of Anarchism.* New York: Harper and Row.

Index